THE
GOLDEN AGE
OF YACHTING

Origins, history, traditions and a detailed record

of great yachts, yacht races, yachtmen and designers

by a man who with his family was part of it . . .

Lady of 1900 handling a parasol in one hand.

THE GOLDEN AGE OF YACHTING

L. Francis Herreshoff

With a Foreword by PETER H. SPECTRE

Illustrated with one hundred forty-five
rare photographs and drawings

S

Sheridan House

Other Books by L. Francis Herreshoff published by
Sheridan House

Capt. Nat Herreshoff
    The Wizard of Bristol

The Compleat Cruiser
    The Art, Practice and Enjoyment of Boating

First paperback edition
published 2007 by
Sheridan House Inc.
145 Palisade Street
Dobbs Ferry, NY 10522
www.sheridanhouse.com

A CIP catalog record for this book is available from the
Library of Congress, Washington, DC

ISBN 13: 978-1-57409-251-6
ISBN 10: 1-57409-251-0

Printed in China

To the Memory of My Father

Contents

Illustrations

Foreword

Many years ago, at the beginning of an earlier career as a book editor, I was assigned a book to edit, *Sensible Cruising Designs* by L. Francis Herreshoff. It turned out to be a difficult assignment. In a matter of days after I began, the author died, leaving behind no cohesive manuscript, only a clip file of articles he had written for *The Rudder* magazine back in the 1940s and '50s. The articles were about various yachts L. Francis Herreshoff had designed and included detailed specifications on how to build several of them.

I was in a curious position. I knew virtually nothing about L. Francis Herreshoff. I didn't know how to spell his last name (Heresshoff . . . Hereshof . . . Herresshoff . . . Herresshof . . .). I didn't know how to pronounce it (Her-es-shoff . . . Hair-es-hoff . . . Here-es-hoff . . . Herre-soff . . . Herres-shoff . . .). I didn't know where he fit in among that great clan of Herreshoffs who had been racketing around the yachting biz for a hundred years or more: James B. Herreshoff, John B. Herreshoff, Nathanael G. Herreshoff, A. Sidney DeW. Herreshoff, L. Francis Herreshoff, Halsey Herreshoff—I couldn't tell one from the other, even though their names constantly popped up in the boating and yachting magazines I read when I was young. And I didn't know how to make sense of all those magazine clippings.

So I went on a reading jag. Herreshoff had published several books before then. I read them all:

The Common Sense of Yacht Design, a previous collection of articles that the author had published in *The Rudder* about the techniques and art of yacht design—a brilliant study and thorough explanation of what was right and what was wrong, and how to fix the latter once it had been identified by the author.

The Writings of L. Francis Herreshoff, yet another collection from *The Rudder*—the author's take on just about every subject that rattled around in his head, and not necessarily confined to the world of yachting.

Capt. Nat Herreshoff, the Wizard of Bristol, a biography, perilously close to hagiography, of the father by the son—a description and analysis of the accomplishments of the man who many believe was the greatest scientific practitioner of the art of yacht design of all time.

The Compleat Cruiser, a friendly lecture on how to cruise in small- and moderate-size boats in the proper—that is to say, in LFH's—manner, presented in the style of Isaak Walton's *Compleat Angler*.

What I gained from all that reading was that Herreshoff knew a lot about a lot, and that he was one smart cookie. He was also cantankerous, obstinate, opinionated in the extreme, and sometimes maddening. If, for example, he played shortstop for the Boston Red Sox, the play-by-play announcer on the radio would be polite and call him "colorful."

The colorful baseball player is an expert at his profession; so good, in fact, that he can say and do anything he pleases without fear of spending the remainder of his career in Dubuque, Iowa, as the batboy for a Class B farm team. The fans love a colorful player; umpires, managers, PR flacks, and sports columnists do not. When the colorful player pounds a homer over the left-field wall at Fenway and makes an obscene gesture at the opposing pitcher as he rounds the bases, the fans go wild in the centerfield bleachers and the coach pretends he didn't notice. The announcer, in the meantime, gets a little schizophrenic—on the one hand he can't help but rave about the superb bat handling; on the other he knows that baseball players are supposed to be models of decorum, representatives of The American Way of Life. He pauses for a second, gets a grip on his microphone, turns to his expert commentator, and says joyfully: "Gee, that Herreshoff sure is a colorful guy."

L. Francis Herreshoff was a colorful yacht designer. His designs were revolutionary in an evolutionary way, he was fearless in defending them, and many were a spit in the eye of then-conventional wisdom. He was colorful as a writer, too. Like Joseph Haydn in his "Surprise" Symphony, a passage by LFH will lull you to sleep with a long, technical description—how to lay a canvas-covered deck, for example—and then wake you up with a flash of wit, brilliance, and artistry: a succinct exposition, for example, on why beautiful boats last longer than ugly ones (because their owners love them and therefore care for them). How can anyone fail to appreciate a writer who jumps right out of the page, shakes his fist at you, and insults you, and then turns right around to become quiet and kindly, addressing you as "Gentle Reader?" His outrageousness is tempered by wisdom, so much so that for every time I have wished that he were still alive so I could stomp into his house and demand to know what in hell's bells he meant by THAT, there were several other times when I wished I could drop over, sit with him by the fire, and talk about yachts and boats and sailing and things.

The book that I found most valuable in understanding what L. Francis Herreshoff was all about is *An Introduction to Yachting*. (As that title is somewhat misleading, the book is reprinted here as *The Golden Age of Yachting*.) A large-format book with lots of pictures, at first blush it seems to be one of those shallow, simplistic guidebooks for the tyro with more money than brains who wants to be a yachtsman and goes out and buys white-duck trousers, a blue blazer with brass buttons, and a Breton fisherman's cap and then wonders what to do next. It isn't.

The Golden Age of Yachting is actually a history of yachting from its earliest days to the 1920s, when, the author believed, the Golden Age ended. It is not a standard-issue history, however; not one of those once-over-lightlys with a few words about Charles II's first yacht, the establishment of the New York Yacht Club, and Sir Thomas Lipton's several failed attempts to win the America's Cup, and a recitation, once (yawn) again, of J.P. Morgan's old saw about the cost of a fully found yacht: "If you have to ask, you can't afford one." Rather—while it has all the historical facts, the race results, and all the rest of what happened when, where, and how—it is effectively a dissertation by the author on what yachting means to him and what it can mean to you, the reader, when the grand sweep of the sport is not merely known, but understood. In other words, it is less about what history is and more about what it means.

L. Francis Herreshoff was an interesting combination of traditionalist and iconoclast. He saw yachting as a straight-line continuum, that what came would naturally follow what came before, even though that coming might have been revolutionary. He believed that the continuity of tradition maintained standards, and artistry, and sanity within the community of yachting, and that when those who didn't know any better—the arrivistes—started meddling with it, the beauty and pleasure of yachting was diminished. Like H.L. Mencken, he believed that he had been a boy at the end of the Golden Age and as an adult was living in the new, crass era of what Mencken called the "booboisie," and it was a damned shame that the continuity of tradition had been broken. (I suspect that is why this book ends in 1920.) He thought, to cite one of his niggling examples from another book, that the long-billed swordfisherman-style cap, popular in the 1950s, was fine for swordfishermen but was an affectation for yachtsmen. Why? Because a yachtsman is what he is, and what he is not is a swordfisherman. He believed, in another example from another book, that only a jughead would name a boat *Liquid Asset* or *Miss Behavin* or *Tootsy-Wootsie*, that true yachtsmen who understood the traditions of yachting would choose a euphonious name, such as *Andante* or *Gloriana* or *Persephone*. His iconoclasm emerged when he didn't like what the straight-line continuum of yachting produced and said so; for example, when he famously called fiberglass "frozen snot."

Of course, *The Golden Age of Yachting* is not about niggling. It is about understanding what yachting in the traditional sense is about and how gaining an appreciation of its history will help us in that understanding. Nothing illustrates this more than a passage L. Francis Herreshoff wrote in *The Common Sense of Yacht Design*. While it is not on the subject of history, rather the art of the yacht, it reveals much about the author and much about what he has in store for you in this book:

"One authority has said that good art depends principally upon persistent contemporaneousness, and things which are too old style or too modern are not compatible. While this may or may not be so in painting, it would seem that with the yacht the object should be to get the most pleasing effect without regard to à la mode. No doubt the best painters have been those who were entirely familiar with past techniques and could use them where necessary. So, too, with the designer. If he can borrow things from the eighteenth and nineteenth century and use them correctly, he has a great advantage over those who only know present day techniques. So, to me at least, the study of past art in yacht design seems the most fascinating part of the whole profession. In the study of old prints, pictures and models you can train the eye to recognize the beautiful. Of course any sensible art study will be helpful but, as the old Latin proverb says, ars longa, vita brevis."

PETER H. SPECTRE
February 2007

THE GOLDEN AGE OF YACHTING

1 *Yachting from 6000 B.C. to the Era of Great Steam Yachts*

It is a well known fact that the true lover of any sport is usually very fond of the antiquity of the particular kind of sport he is devoted to, so that an angler will quote Izaak Walton, the archer will boast of the effect archery had on Crecy and Agincourt and be proud of the fact that even in our changing times the yew bow of ancient times remained unchanged. So also the breeders of greyhounds will proudly trace their origin back to the Fourth Dynasty, 4000 to 3500 B.C., while the Saluki breeders think this breed can be traced back to the Sumerian Empire, 7000 to 6000 B.C., and that the Scottish staghounds are descended from the hounds of the Picts.

While I do not doubt the validity of these claims, still the fine models of pleasure craft found in Egyptian tombs prove that going on the water for pleasure is undoubtedly also very ancient. Some of these models (which were taken from the tomb of Mehenkwetre, Eleventh Dynasty, 2000 B.C.) are at the Metropolitan Museum of Art (see Figure 1). There is also good evidence that small paddle craft were used in Egypt in 6000 B.C.

Oldest Sport

Of course the sports of foot racing and hunting must be very ancient indeed, and probably the oldest sport of all was hunting for an attractive mate of the other sex. However, if sports are to be divided into two categories of those carried on with simple equipment and those performed with complicated and expensive gear, then yachting may be one of the oldest and noblest of the latter category, and I say noble because in ancient times none but kings and princes could have afforded such expensive accouterments to a sport.

Certainly in Greek and Roman times pleasure vessels were used, and Cleopatra's barge is often cited as an outstanding example, while it is well known that the Romans had large houseboats or floating villas, and the Chinese their flower boats for centuries untold. Due to the illiteracy prevalent in those centuries the history of yachting is obscure, still there is little doubt that the potentates who lived near the water used pleasure vessels of some kind or another. It is probable that in most cases they were rowing galleys propelled by slaves.

Silk Sails

Some of the races between the Greek galleys have been immortalized by Vergil, and a peculiarity of these early royal yachts was that they all seemed to carry purple silk sails. Some of the so-called Viking ships that were used as

Fig. 1. An Egyptian pleasure boat of the Eleventh Dynasty paddled by crew

burial vessels for queens and females of high rank have fittings and accouterments which in the opinion of experts indicate that these vessels have been built for pleasure. That brings us up to around the year 1000 A.D.

In England rowing has been looked upon as a manly sport ever since the Danish invasions, but during the time of the four and twenty barons they were so busy building castles and dividing the country among themselves that there was little time for anything else. Nevertheless the Normans were second only to the Danes in nautical matters, still going on water for pleasure was rare in early British times. One authority tells us that their pleasure was rather in heavy eating and drinking, a habit handed down by their Viking ancestors. Pleasure vessels received a bad name since their owners often were misconceived as privateers and pirates, and in fact it happened that one owner at least, who was brought before the authorities for plundering ships of his own nation, gave as an excuse the difficulty of telling friend from foe on the water.

First British Yacht

The first British pleasure vessel of which record exists was built in 1604 at the dockyard at Chatham and was designed or planned by no less a person than the great workmaster, Master Phineas Pett, gentleman, sometime master of arts at Emanuel College, Cambridge. This vessel was built for Prince Henry, the eldest son of King James I, and was intended to be used for teaching the young prince

about nautical matters. King James I was the son of Mary, Queen of Scots, and the one who finally arranged the union of England and Scotland although much of the preliminary work had been done during Queen Elizabeth's time. King James, in his time, was familiarly called Union Jack and when the crosses of St. George and St. Andrew were combined on the national flag it was called the Union Jack in honor of King James I. This little vessel for the prince was twenty-eight feet long on the keel and twelve feet wide, garnished both within board and without, according to the directions of the Lord High Admiral Howard. She was named *Disdain* and appeared in the naval list of 1618 and rated of thirty tons burden.

Pleasure boats were not called yachts in England until the time of Charles II. This came about as follows. During the long years when Cromwell was the self-appointed protector of the Commonwealth, Charles II resided mostly in Europe, much of the time in Holland, visiting the Prince of Orange who later was to become King of England as William III. Charles II became very fond of yachting while in Holland and when called back to his country at the restoration introduced the sport under that name. Yachting had been popular in Holland for several hundred years. The geography of that country, with its inland seas and canals, necessitated some sort of aquatic conveyance for those who had country seats separated by water from their places of business.

This conveyance was called a jaght, and the word derived from jagen, which originally meant a boat drawn by horses. These were swift light boats handsomely furnished and beautifully decorated and ran alongside the footpaths of canals. The English word yacht is derived from the Dutch jaght and before 1800 was sometimes spelled yatch and yatcht. In old Dutch the word jaght was by no means applied exclusively to vessels, for many other things connected with sport had this prefix, thus a jaght hond was a hunting dog, a jaght peered a hunting horse, and a jaght horen was a hunting horn.

Jaght Developed

By 1600, the Dutch had developed the jaght boat to a high state. Figure 2 shows a review of yachts in honor of Queen Mary of France in Amsterdam in 1638. On May 1, 1660, Parliament resolved to call Charles II back to the throne and he was escorted from Breda (where he was residing when the news arrived) to Rotterdam by a fleet of yachts. On this trip Charles hinted to some of the Dutch deputies who accompanied him that he intended to order a yacht for sailing on the Thames similar to the one on which they were sailing. The burgomaster of Amsterdam, in response to the hint, replied that there was a similar yacht on the building ways at Amsterdam and he took the liberty of presenting it to his majesty.

The king neither accepted nor refused it and in a few months this present arrived in England. We read in Pepys' diary of August 15, 1660, "To the office and after dinner to White Hall where I found the King gone this morning by five of the clock to see a Dutch pleasure-boat below the bridge where he dined and my Lord with him. The King do tire all his people that are about him with early rising since he came."

We who love yachts can well imagine the enthusiasm of the young king as he rose early in the morning to look at his new plaything. This yacht was named Mary after his mother. Her general dimensions were length of keel fifty-two feet, beam nineteen feet, draft ten feet, and one hundred tons burden. The Mary carried eight guns and a crew of thirty men, so we can guess that she was bulky and burdensome as most of all Dutch yachts have been. There seems to be no authentic picture or painting of the Mary, but Figure 3 shows a model of a yacht of that time, 1660, which is in a museum at Amsterdam. Figure 4 shows examples of yacht garnish or carvings in the same museum.

Forerunner

The Mary was to be the forerunner of about thirty yachts that King Charles had built during his reign of

Fig. 2. A review of yachts in honor of Queen Mary of France, 1638

Fig. 3. Model of a royal yacht about 1660

twenty-five years. Many other wealthy courtiers also had yachts built. Most of King Charles' yachts were English built and at least the first few were built by the brothers Christopher and Peter Pett who were at the head of navy yards and the sons of Master Phineas Pett of whom I have spoken. King Charles made naval architecture a court hobby and it was said he would stop to talk anywhere at any time with anyone about nautical subjects. One of his courtiers, Sir Anthony Dean, calculated a ship's displacement. Thus, by the use of mathematics and measurements taken from the model or design, Dean could tell how much water a ship would displace when launched, and if he knew the weight of the ship he could tell beforehand where she would float. This was done in 1666, a year easy to remember, for the plague of London was in 1665 and the fire of London in 1666.

Catamarans

King Charles also encouraged Sir William Petty in his experiments with catamarans between 1662 and 1664. Petty should not be confused with the one of the three Petts who were master shipwrights. Sir William Petty was a man of much learning who in 1652 was appointed physician general of the army of Ireland. He was one of the founders of the Royal Society, one of the earliest scientific societies in Europe. I believe Sir William invented the centerboard, or what he called the versatile keel. One of his proposed experiments for the Society was "to fix an engine with propelling power to a ship."

Several catamarans were built, and one of good size (about thirty tons burden) named *Experiment* was christened by King Charles. It is of special note that the first recorded ocean race was between the *Experiment* and a packet ship sailing between Dublin and Holyhead for a wager of fifty pounds sterling. This packet ship was supposed to be one of the fastest in the kingdom, but the catamaran beat it by several hours between Dublin and Holyhead in a gale of wind.

Merry Monarch

King Charles himself experimented with metal sheathing on yachts and with lead ballast. Of course it is well known that Charles II established the Greenwich Observatory and the Greenwich Hospital for sailors. He had the good sense to use Inigo Jones and Sir Christopher Wren in rebuilding London after the fire and although his court has been much criticized for its frivolity, still perhaps no other man could have better carried England through its most troubled times. When we consider the aftermath of the revolution, the Dutch war, the plague and the fire I think we should stress the importance of this sailor king who is often spoken of as the merry monarch and the grandfather of yachting.

At the death of Charles, his brother, the Duke of York, reigned for a few troubled years as James II and though he had no yachts built after becoming king, he was a yachtsman during Charles' time. The first recorded yacht race took place between the two brothers on October 1, 1661. The first recorded open sailing match was on January 12, 1663, under the auspices of the Royal Society. The yachtsmen must have been feeling pretty hot to race in January.

The Princess Mary

In 1689, William III and Mary II came over from Holland to reign in England. They both had claims to the throne and both were yachting people. They had a fine yacht named *Princess Mary* which is believed to have been built in Holland (which seems very likely for she lasted one hundred and thirty-nine years). *Princess Mary* was eighty feet long, with twenty-three foot beam and might well be thought of as the first of the large royal English yachts which have been sailing to the present time.

The first Atlantic crossing in a yacht was accomplished by the Quaker, George Fox, and a party in the yacht *Industry*. She left England in August, 1671, and after visiting Barbados and Jamaica arrived at Maryland where she remained several months, returning to Bristol, England, in June, 1673. This brings us nearly up to the time of Peter the Great of Russia who, it seems, had an English tutor when he was a boy. This tutor, Francis Timerman, who lived with him, told him about sailboats and Peter became most enthusiastic on the subject. He persuaded his august mother to have a house built for him on a lake that

Fig. 4. An example of yacht garnish

was suitable for sailing, together with a miniature ship-yard where he had two small frigates and three small yachts built under the supervision of Carsters Brand, a shipwright of Holland.

Naval architecture became a life hobby with Tsar Peter. After visiting Holland and England between 1697 and 1698, to study the art, he returned to Russia, took upon himself the title of master shipwright and made with his own hands models and drawings for the first vessels of the Russian navy. Perhaps Peter was second only to Charles II in his enthusiasm for naval architecture. It is a fact that Russia built a fine navy of sailing ships as the result of Peter's efforts.

The Onrust

We in this country were not much behind England in adopting the yacht, for New York had originally been settled by the Dutch and after the British occupied Manhattan in 1664 the customs of the old families persisted. When we realize that the second vessel built in this part of the country, and the first built in New York, was the *Onrust,* built by Adrian Block in 1614, we can see that these fifty intervening years could have had much Dutch influence. It is interesting to note that the *Half Moon* was a former Dutch yacht.

The first vessel built in this country is supposed to have been the *Virginia,* of thirty tons, built at the mouth of the Kennebec River in 1608. The early boats and yachts used around New York were of the periagua rig, a rig which persisted for some 250 years and was last used on the Block Island boats. The periagua (sometimes called pirogue) is often spoken of in early New York history and was similar to the yachts used in Holland around 1600. We can see from Figure 5 that the sloop was used as a yacht in the vicinity of New York as early as 1717. Sloop, or sloep, is a Dutch word and around New York they began building quite large ones for commercial purposes up and down the Hudson River and along the New England coast. The first American vessel to circumnavigate the globe was the sloop *Washington* of Boston, ninety tons, which left Boston in 1787 and returned in 1790.

First Yacht Club

In the meantime yachting had been nearly stopped in England, for that country was almost continually at war between 1739 and 1815. During this time strict naval laws were enacted to suppress smuggling since the smugglers carried information to the enemy and helped prisoners of war to escape. Ireland, however, was farther from the seat of war and therefore continued its yachting. That is one of the reasons why the Irish started the first yacht clubs. The first yacht club presumably has been the Cork Harbor Water Club, which was established in 1720. Its headquarters were in the castle on the picturesque island of Hawlbowline in the beautiful harbor of Cork.

The club seems to have been very aristocratic, as the upper stratum of Irish have always been. The membership was limited to twenty-five and each member was the owner of a yacht and was called captain. The club meetings were held every spring tide, which seems a very nautical arrangement in a time when calendars were not so plentiful as now. This club had a complete list of by-laws to control sailing and clubhouse life and I quote here order number four: "No captain to bring any stranger to the club unless they should lie at the captain's house the night before." Another rule was, "No admiral presume to bring more than two dozen of wines to his treat." The Water Club conducted its regattas much as the Dutch had. They consisted of miniature naval maneuvers regulated by flag signals hoisted from the admiral's flagship and it seems that they have had no races.

English Races

During all this time of wars England had many fine royal yachts for her kings and queens and as early as 1775 there were yacht races on rivers and inland waters. In this year the Duke of Cumberland, brother of George III, gave a twenty guinea silver cup for a yacht race on the Thames. This same year the Cumberland fleet was founded and is supposed to be the oldest yacht club in England. They raced rather small yachts in which the owner was called captain and was obliged to steer and handle his own vessel with the assistance of only two men. Hitherto yachting had been the sport of princes and no fixed type of yacht had been evolved though as a rule they were quite large. But now the smaller racing yacht was really coming into popularity. When the long peace after 1815 arrived, and it was again practical and legal to sail in the channel and the open sea, the many boats and vessels that had been used in the revenue service were about the only craft available. Because the boat builders for many years previous to this had specialized in building smugglers and revenue cutters it was natural that they turned to this type when peace allowed yachting again.

Smuggling Era

It is said that the first revenue cutters before 1700 were

Fig. 5. Sloops in New York about 1700. The boat in the center is the FANCY, owned by Colonel Lewis Morris

merely the large rowing boats called cutters that were used on large ships, and that early in the smuggling era these boats only hovered around ports and river entrances. However as smuggling became more profitable France and England developed fast sailing craft to intercept the smugglers at sea. Many of these boats were luggers, schooners and sloops. As the revenue service increased the speed of its vessels the smugglers in turn built more reckless sailing craft. Eventually a specialized type of sloop was evolved that could not only set a very large sail area, but could also shorten down to a small storm rig, for both the revenue craft and the smugglers were at sea, blow high or blow low.

The rig that was finally worked out was a specialized sloop that had a long housing topmast and a long running bowsprit that could easily and quickly be run all the way in. It is said that the details of this rig were worked out in France where the rig has continued to be called a sloop. When the English adopted this type of craft for their racing yachts they called them cutters after the revenue vessels, and continued to do so for the next hundred years. For many years the larger cutter yachts had painted gun ports in imitation of the revenue boats.

Cutter Supreme

Figure 6 shows some English racing yachts of 1846. You can see that one of them has a leg of mutton mainsail, but evidently that sail was not then the fastest because it is not as adaptable to quick changes in sail spread, which was important in those days of unlimited sail area. So the cutter rig reigned supreme for some years to come. At first the English cutter yachts had quite normal hull form, like the revenue craft and smugglers. Early in the game they were rated by length of keel, and this in time developed a model with a raking rudder post and greatly cutaway forefoot to get a short keel.

The Royal Yacht Squadron at Cowes on the Solent was started in 1815. At first it was simply called the Yacht Club, but one of its members was the prince regent and when he became King George IV in 1820 the club's name was changed to the Royal Yacht Club. In 1833, King William IV, as a mark of approval of the club, authorized the name to be altered to the Royal Yacht Squadron and allowed its members to display the naval ensign on their yachts. The Royal Yacht Squadron has often been referred to as the most exclusive club in the world. Undoubtedly its

Fig. 6. English racing yachts in the year 1846. The center boat is the CHAMPION owned by George Thornton

membership during the last hundred years has included more monarchs and titled men than any other club.

Time Allowance

Although yacht racing had been going on in restricted waters since the time of Charles II it is presumed that the races were generally match races of vessels of like size, for as I have mentioned, the early English yachts were rated by the length of keel. In 1829, the Royal Yacht Squadron attempted to classify various sized yachts for the purpose of time allowance. This was done in connection with the annual race for the Cowes Town Cup where the difference in size of the competitors was great. At first the yachts were simply grouped in four or five classes according to their tonnage and a separate cup was given for each class. It was not until 1838, when the first of the Queen Victoria Cups was raced for, that the yachts all raced in one class with an allowance of three minutes for each ten tons' difference in size. Although similar rules were tried during the next few years they were not satisfactory because of the difference in speed of rigs and types. So by 1843 the yachts were raced in two types—cutters and schooners. Cutters were classified as thirty, fifty, seventy-five and 105 tons, and schooners in two classes of over and under 140 tons. So we see that yachts in England were classified by tonnage alone for a long time and even today it is customary for a British yachtsman to describe the size of a yacht by her tonnage. However, as sail areas went free, the cutters carried an enormous amount of sail which they could safely do with housing topmasts and reefing bowsprits. Because there was no restriction as to waterline length the plumb bow came into use.

Narrow Beam

Another peculiarity of the cutter yacht was her narrow beam and great draft which came about as follows. The racing yachts were measured for tonnage the same way as merchant ships. Originally the customs offices multiplied the length by the beam by the depth of hold, then this figure was multiplied by a coefficient that changed the figure to tons. However, since it was often difficult to make the depth-of-hold measurement with cargo in the hold, and because it was found that the average depth of hold was about one-half the beam (on all vessels registered since Elizabeth's time), the rule was changed to length times the beam times half the beam. So as beam was measured twice and depth not at all, the English vessels, and particularly the racing cutters, became narrow and deep.

Eventually some of the racing cutters had a displacement of twice their registered tonnage and a beam of one-sixth their length while we in this country were racing sailboats that were only twice as long as they were wide. These were the early sandbaggers, the only measurement of which was the length on deck. This great difference in types of racing yachts made it very difficult for the English

when the schooner *America* went over to the Queen's Jubilee in 1851. If they had raced her measured under their tonnage rule she would have rated too high to have a chance so they gave a special race for her around the Isle of Wight without time allowance. There were cumbersome topsail schooners and brigs in this race, but because *America* was the largest racing type of yacht, in the latter part of the race she beat the others boat-to-boat which proved almost nothing, for they were to go on with their tonnage rules and we with our length rules for many years.

Era of Steam

This brings us up to the steam yacht era which might be said to coincide with the reign of Victoria when the upper classes in England enjoyed a prolonged prosperity. To be sure, there were a few steam yachts before and a great many after her reign, but after her time the large sailing yacht was again the leading lady. The first practical steamer was the *Charlotte Dundas,* propelled by a stern wheel and built in Scotland for the Clyde Canal in 1802.

During this year and the next Robert Fulton, an American, was carrying on experiments in France on the Seine with a steamboat propelled by paddles. In 1804, Fulton went to England and had the power plant for a steamer built for him by Bolton and Watt of Birmingham. He then returned to America and built the steamer *Clermont* which was propelled by this English engine. The *Clermont* came out in 1807 and was probably the first steamer to carry passengers on a scheduled run. However, as the pictures of the earliest European steamers appear to be experimental yachts, I for one consider that the steam yacht was started in Europe soon after 1800. Certainly both the passenger steamer and the steam yacht developed quickly, but when we consider that the English had steam passenger coaches with water tube boilers on the London roads soon after 1825, we can see that the steam engine was developing rapidly.

The Bridge

Of course the early steamers and steam yachts were all driven with paddle wheels. Many were steered from aft, as the sailing ships had been, but most of them had an elevated and railed-in platform running from the top of one paddle box to the other. This was called the bridge and it was the place where the man who conned the ship stood or walked back and forth and this explains the origin of our word bridge as used today.

Queen Victoria was an early patroness of steam yachts and perhaps had much to do with making this form of yachting stylish. Her first one was *Fairy,* 200 tons, built in 1844, and she subsequently had the steam yachts *Albert* and *Osborne,* and the two very large royal yachts *Victoria* and *Albert.* The *Osborne,* a side wheeler, came out in 1870, was 284 feet long, of 1,800 tons. She had a crew of 142 and speed of sixteen knots. She was used by Prince Albert around 1875 when he made official visits to different parts of the world. Many large and fine steam yachts were built in England and Scotland soon after this and by 1880 a steam yacht of 800 tons cost only about 25,000 pounds sterling, but it is said that it took the interest on a million dollars to run the large ones.

The Sunbeam

By this time many of the large yachts had made long voyages and circumnavigated the globe. Perhaps the most famous long distance cruiser was Lord Brassey's *Sunbeam* (Figure 7), which in 1876-1877 circled the globe on a 37,000 mile cruise. On another cruise she logged some 36,000 miles and in shorter cruises visited all parts of the world. I believe she crossed the Atlantic about ten times. Of course most of the steam yachts were auxiliaries and carried rather a full sail plan. The sails made them roll less and at times with fair winds the steam engine was slowed down to such a degree that it only developed a small amount of horsepower. Then the yachts used little fuel and had no drag from the propeller.

The earlier large yachts generally carried some square-sails or, as the sailor would say, crossed yards. Figure 8 shows the Earl of Crawford's ship-rigged *Valhalla*, 1,490 tons. The earlier steam yachts generally had captains who had learned seamanship on square rigged sailing vessels. As a general rule they were very professional men and rarely had any serious accidents. In those days it was not difficult to get good sailormen, but after about 1900 many of the large yachts removed their yards and seldom set sail. In saying that the sails of these auxiliaries made them steadier in a beam sea, I must mention that some of them were notable rollers with sail furled, and there were known instances of their rolling so deeply that the tips of the lower yards touched the water.

Fig. 7. SUNBEAM

Fig. 8. VALHALLA

Luxurious Interiors

Some of the steam yachts had very fancy and expensive interiors and while they might be much criticized today, still it should be taken into consideration that this was the time of rococo decorations. Figure 9 shows the drawing room of Sir Thomas Lipton's *Erin*.

The English yachts often stayed in commission most of the year, spending the winters in the Mediterranean and cruising the picturesque waters of Scotland and Norway in the summer. As a general rule the English steam yachts were strongly and heavily built. They were much of the same model as the iron Scottish clipper ships and not only were remarkably good sea boats, but some of them were probably the most beautiful vessels ever built. One of the things that added to their comfort and steadiness was their large displacement or weight, some of the weight coming

from the very heavy power plants used which generally consisted of a so-called Scotch boiler furnishing steam to a slow turning engine mostly made of castiron. A Scotch boiler consisted of a very large drum which encircled the firebox and many rather large tubes which carried the hot gases from the fire to the smokestack. Although these boilers were quite efficient for their time they were very heavy and not adaptable to quick changes in temperature, so that when once fired up they were usually kept going for months at a time.

Homes Afloat

Most of the English steam yachts were built in Scotland, some of the best of them being designed by St. Clare J. Byrne of England and G. L. Watson of Glasgow. On the whole the English steam yachts were the finest moving homes ever built or perhaps that ever will be built.

The American steam yacht was rather different. It was usually built of wood or of composite construction, generally with much less displacement for its length and with water tube boilers. While they were often faster than the English yachts they were as a rule very homely.

As for the size of steam yachts, around 1900 I would say there were several of over 1,500 tons and yachts in the past have been built up to over 4,000 tons. To give an idea of the larger steam yachts, compared to the modern small fry, I will quote a conversation I had last summer with a young man here in Marblehead.

It was during race week and that morning I had walked to Fort Sewall to have a look at the assembled boats in the harbor. The young man said to me, "Don't you think there are a lot of boats in?"

"Yes," I replied, "but their total tonnage is perhaps less than the tonnage of individual yachts I have seen in this harbor in the past."

"How could that be?" he asked.

I told him, "I have seen several yachts here in the past whose tonnage was well over a thousand tons, but about half of the boats that will race today weigh less than a ton and many of the open dinghies weigh about one-quarter of a ton. Now if we assume the average tonnage of yachts here as one ton, and there are less than a thousand of them, then you can see what I mean."

I went on to say, "I was here with the New York Yacht Club cruise some time around 1908 when there were two or three yachts of over a thousand tons, several of over 500 tons, and many of them of over 100 tons, when the total tonnage of yachts floating in this harbor may have been twenty-five times greater than it is today. That shows what high taxes have done to yachting."

Figure 10 shows a typical example of one of the later large yachts. She is the *Margarita* of 1,780 tons, owned by Anthony J. Drexel. Of the American owned steam yachts of over a thousand tons in those days I will cite the following:

Yacht	Owner	Gross Tons	Year
Aphrodite, Col. O. H. Payne		1,147.88	1898
Corsair, J. P. Morgan		1,136.00	1899
Margarita, A. J. Drexel		i,780.82	1900
Niagara, Howard Gould		1,443.87	1898

Fig. 9. Drawing room of Sir Thomas Lipton's ERIN

Yacht	Owner	Gross Tons	Year
Valiant, W. K. Vanderbilt		1,823.23	1893
Varuna, Eugene Higgins		1,573.65	1896
Lysistrata, J. Gordon Bennett		1,942.7	1900
Nahma, Mrs. Robert Goelet		1,739.83	1897
Warrior, F. W. Vanderbilt		1,097.80	1904

Delightful Odor

One of the things I remember about the large steam yachts was their characteristic and delightful odor. If you passed under the stern or close to leeward of one of them you smelled the combined odor of new varnish, linseed oil, brass polish, Havana cigars and champagne, all mingled with engine room smells and the slight odor of teak and other exotic woods, to say nothing of the burned gases of the naphtha launches. To a sailor this combination was delightful.

Unfortunately there have been handed down some strange stories about life in the larger American yachts, but I can assure you that these stories are not typical of the life that was actually led in these yachts when whole families were usually present. I believe life on the larger English yachts was the most refined of that of any class of society that has been known.

Their owners were often titled men and their ladies often descended from ancient earls. This perhaps was one of the reasons they were such good sailors. And it is well known that refined ladies enjoy cruising more than anyone, for they not only show a high appreciation of landscape, but actually have a temperament that gets the greatest thrill out of cruising in strange waters. It is a noteworthy fact that several of the large yachts of the past have been owned by ladies, so I will say something about the ladies in yachting.

Nordic Queens

Some of the Nordic queens of around the year 1000 were buried in their traveling boats or yachts and Cleopatra of the Nile has been much spoken of. Since the time of Charles II ladies have been almost indispensable in keeping yachting at a high standard. The champion of the long distance cruiser was the first Lady Brassey. She must have cruised something like 75,000 miles and died and was buried at sea from the Sunbeam in 1887. She wrote the book, *A Voyage in the* Sunbeam, which was published in many editions. This book was largely composed from letters Lady Brassey was writing to her father. This book is still about the best world cruise story for its description of places. Figure 11 shows Lady Brassey writing the journal aboard the *Sunbeam*.

Figure 12 shows Mrs. William Henn, who was perhaps the most popular yachtswoman as she and her husband are spoken of very fondly in the writings of their time. If her cruising mileage is less than Lady Brassey's it is because it was mostly done under sail. Mrs. Henn is the only woman who paid for a cup challenger, for she had *Galatea* built and sailed her for a couple of years after her husband died. She is the only woman who sailed over, and returned, on a cup challenger. She lived on yachts for about ten years and spent several winters in the Mediterranean, making her cruising mileage about 60,000 miles. Her racing mileage must have been very great.

Other Ladies

The other three ladies who have been in the afterguard of cup boats were Mrs. C. Oliver Iselin who raced on *Columbia* throughout the season of 1899 and proved very useful in taking down notes in pencil of actual events of the time, Lady Burton who read the stopwatch for Sir Robert Burton on *Shamrock IV* in 1920, and Mrs. Harold Vanderbilt who raced on *Ranger* in 1937. Also two daughters of Lord Dunraven should be mentioned for they generally sailed on *Valkyrie III*.

Around 1900 there were several famous helmswomen in England. A few of them owned and handled good sized racing yachts. Among them was Mrs. Henry Allen who raced successfully in the thirty-foot class on The *Solent* and won an aggregate of eighty-two firsts out of 118 starts in three years. Then there was Miss Cox who owned several successful small raters. Mrs. Turner-Farley of Falmouth owned and raced the fifty-two foot *Sonya* in what was the hottest class in England in 1905.

The French, English and American ladies who have owned large yachts are too numerous to be mentioned, and they contributed a great deal to the sport, first and last. The wealthy ones found the large steam yachts a most satisfactory way to entertain their friends. Women were allowed to join most of all the yacht clubs and were called flag members. Thus they had the privilege of carrying the club pennant, the use of club landings, et cetera, still they could not vote.

Fig. 10. MARGARITA, typical of a large steam yacht in 1900

Fig. 11. Lady Brassey writing her journal aboard the SUNBEAM   Fig. 12. Mrs. William Henn

2 Society and Traditions in the Steam Era

About seventy-five years after the clipper ship went out of use there was a great deal of interest manifested in these fine vessels. Several books were written about them, artists began making paintings of these romantic ships and model makers throughout the world spent much time making miniature clippers. But the clipper in its day, though a thing of beauty and always stirring to the sailor, was rather taken for granted by the general public who no doubt thought sail would always be with us. Steam yachts in their day also were rather taken for granted, but now that they are rare there are several people collecting information about yachts and pictures of them, and well they may, for if the clipper ship was thought to be romantic certainly the steam yacht was much more so. The clipper simply was a fast cargo carrier, manned by a tough crew. These ships had become refined through ages of experience with the sailing ship. It turned out that the steam yacht was to carry on the development that they had started with the clipper and eventually achieved far greater beauty of hull form and decoration, as I will later describe.

If the clipper ship was a commercial enterprise the steam yacht certainly was not, being instead entirely a thing of romance and the esthetic expression of the wealthier citizens of seagoing nations. While in this corrupt age some may refer to them as the playthings of the rich, I see them as something quite different, for the outstanding ones were a perfect combination of art and science and a moving home far grander and more satisfying than anything known before. This statement may

surprise some of the younger generation who have never seen a real steam yacht, but to cruise the Mediterranean in the winter and the northern waters in summer, and have the whole world as your cruising ground, with complete privacy, is something that would be difficult to arrange today.

The largest and handsomest of these yachts generally had an afterguard composed of the most aristocratic ladies and gentlemen in the world and often included royalty. As a rule these fine vessels were owned by landed proprietors who in the old days had secure positions in society. Many of them were lords, dukes, and princes, owning large tracts of land which in some cases had been granted to their ancestors in the times of and between the Conquest and Henry VIII. The ladies on the English steam yachts were often Anglo-Saxon beauties who could trace their ancestry back to the Doomsday Book and whose earlier ancestors had probably been Vikings, as their looks and love of the sea indicated.

Life on the large English yachts in particular was carried out with the strictest decorum, probably as luxuriously as these gentlemen and ladies had lived on shore for many generations. Of course there were exceptions to this rule, for there have always been scamps in all classes of society. Unfortunately the misdemeanors of these few have been exaggerated while little is remembered or recorded of the many long cruises that were arranged with refined ladies and gentlemen aboard. British gentlemen and ladies are quiet and retiring and as a rule love privacy.

The Captains

The captains of the larger steam yachts were often very capable men who had served their time under sail in the square riggers and so were accustomed to wind, weather and tide. They were masters at dead reckoning and capable navigators with the sextant. Most of them were familiar with the peculiarities of the seven seas and much at home in the principal harbors of the world. A great many of the large yachts made long cruises without any casualties whatsoever, and they had a long life. It seems remarkable that they did so well with the inadequate charts and meager aids to navigation that were then in use.

Many of these captains credited their success to the training they had received in the square riggers, which were certainly vessels that required an exact knowledge of seamanship and on which one had always to be ready for any eventuality. As a class these captains were both cautious and adroit. They were often large, handsome men who gave one a feeling of confidence. They were often received by the owner and his family as important family retainers and in many cases stayed with the same owner for the last forty years of their lives.

One of the reasons for their success was that they were strict disciplinarians and could train their crews in all of the various duties aboard ship. The larger yachts were managed better than the best trained naval vessels. They were run much more smoothly, were quieter and cleaner, particularly in regard to the crew's uniforms, for the usual navy jack tars only dress smartly when going ashore while the crew of the steam yachts was usually immaculate when the owner was aboard.

Although the captains of the large steam yachts hailed from several countries I should say though the best of them were Scotch and English. Most of them spoke in a refined manner and were affable and pleasant, perhaps having acquired these qualities from the gentlemen who employed them.

The Stewards

The stewards of the large yachts, both steam and sail, played an important role, contributing much to the general success of the cruise. Strange to say, they often received nearly the same pay as the captain. The best of them were usually English and had the training that only that country could then give to its servants. They certainly made life pleasant on board and were most helpful in the trying conditions of bad weather, at times on duty for long hours, particularly if there were children aboard. The larger yachts often had three or four messes at each meal hour and when under way a so called mug-up of coffee or tea could be had throughout the night. The first mess was for the owner and his party, and sometimes these were almost banquets when in port and entertaining guests from ashore. The second mess was for the captain and officers and the third was for the crew. Sometimes there was another mess when the stokers were too sooty to go into the forecastle.

The stewards generally did the purchasing for the culinary department and this, together with a well selected wine list for a long cruise, was a very important matter in which no doubt the captain had to be consulted, for in those days of few imperishable foods it was difficult to set a good table on a long trip in hot weather. However, some of the English stewards achieved a high reputation for serving good meals both in port and at sea, and in keeping the owner's quarters in fine condition for many years. When one considers the fancy interiors of those days, with their tapestries, carvings and bric-a-brac, this seems quite a feat. The stewards had to know almost as much about yacht etiquette as the captain himself so that they could give the proper answer to the ladies' questions as well as help with the children's training in that exact ritual.

The Chief Engineer

The chief engineer of the large steam yachts was usually a Scotsman and sometimes was quite a character. Many had served their time in the plant where the engine was built. If the engineer was not as strict a disciplinarian as the captain he nevertheless had such a love for the machinery under his care that it was fully as well kept as any of the deck gear. He usually kept the black gang (the stokers) under control with threats and persuasions. Some of these chiefs showed marked ingenuity in repairs at sea and in nursing sick machinery on long runs. As a rule they stayed aboard ship most of the time, for they hated to be separated from their engines. I can understand this since some of the older steam yachts had engines that were works of art and the designer strove for looks almost as much as the function of the piece.

The engines of those days had a great deal of hand work on them. Most of the working parts were planished or polished, there was much brass trim, and the cylinder lagging (or insulation) was often encased in polished teak sheathing. Perhaps another reason why some of these engineers did not often trust themselves ashore was that if they met another Scottish chief they might feel it their duty to destroy as much Highland Dew as possible, and it might be difficult to board the launch and ascend the gangway under the captain's eagle eye.

The mates, quartermasters, boatswains and sailormen of these yachts came from different nations, with Norwegians and Swedes perhaps predominating. They were a more transient lot than the senior officers and often spent the winter, or part of their time, in the merchant marine. Usually they were reliable hard workers. Up until sometime around 1910 they only got forty-five dollars a month, plus food and clothing on American yachts, much less on English boats, but they liked the life and always had a chance of promotion.

The reader may wonder why I have devoted so many words to the personnel of the steam yachts and so praised their aristocratic owners in these democratic times. The reason is that these men were the ones who, as a whole, built up the very high tradition that yachting enjoyed before World War I. They were almost wholly responsible for the decorum, prestige and respect that yachting had at that time. Much of our yachting etiquette was developed with the steam yacht.

As for the development of the steam yacht, they, like the merchant marine ships of 1860 and 1870, differed only from the clipper ships in having auxiliary steam engines to help them in light weather. Figure 13 shows a British steamer of that time which was in the China trade in competition with the clippers. Perhaps I should define a clipper ship more distinctly since many today confuse them with all square riggers. A ship, to be exact, is a vessel with three masts, having yards on all three masts, while the word clipper was a popular expression applied to the fine-lined sailing ships which usually carried rather light cargoes such as tea and opium, passengers and mail. It was said that they were called clipper ships because they often clipped a day or two off the record between ports, but I think it was a popular word of the day that was applied to fast moving things. "Going at a fast clip" is used today. It is a mistake though to refer to all square riggers as clippers as some of them, like the whalers, never moved at a fast clip.

Mail Steamers

Perhaps in referring to the early steamers that were modeled like the clipper ships I should speak of them as mail steamers. You will find little difference in their model except that the mail steamers had a smaller rig and a propeller aperture aft. The mail steamers soon gave up the aft position for steering (which was best under sail) for bridge amidships further forward which gave better visibility under all other conditions. The early steam yachts, which were smaller than the mail steamers, probably should be compared with the opium clippers that carried a light cargo, the opium itself weighing a few hundred pounds. These vessels usually had little parallel body amidships while the larger Scottish and English clippers were modeled narrow and slab-sided to reduce their measured tonnage under a rule then in use in Great Britain, rating them by multiplying the length between perpendiculars by the beam by half the beam. This rule did not apply to the American clipper ships which, though beamier, were slab-sided for some reason unknown to me. Figure 14 shows an unknown American clipper in drydock. She is not very slab-sided and is fine aft.

Figure 15 shows one of the opium clippers. No doubt they were the fastest sailing vessels of their size and era. After the time of the *Sunbeam* (about 1877) the steam yacht used sail less and less as boilers and engines were improved and became so economical that fairly long passages could be accomplished with steam alone. Even after yards were entirely abandoned the English and Scotch steam yachts used the clipper ship model to the end of their day. It is well known that George Watson, the greatest steam yacht designer of all time, patterned his handsome creations after the last of the Scottish clippers.

Fig. 13. British steamer of the 1860's in the China trade

Fig. 14. Unknown American clipper in dry-dock

Fig. 15. An opium clipper

Data on Steam Yachts

One of the men who has gone to great pains to collect data on the steam yacht is R. R. Moore who, I believe, served aboard an ex-steam yacht that was in the Coast Guard service between the last two wars. We will give the names and the outboard profiles of some of the yachts he has in his collection and if he completes the task it will be a remarkable feat.

What is published here is by no means his complete collection and in particular does not include many of the older yachts, but I selected some of them because my older readers will enjoy picking out the names of the steam yachts they have known, and younger readers will be impressed with the great number of large steam yachts the world once had. I do not want the younger readers to think this is a group of outboard motor boats. *Savarona,* owned by Mrs. Cadwalader, might equal in weight or tonnage more than 8,000 outboard motor boats. If *Savarona* were stretched out like a huge piece of elastic material, so that her draft and beam were equal to that of the average outboard motor boat, she would be something like fourteen miles long.

For those who are not used to looking at outboard plans of yachts I show here a few photographs of typical English type steam yachts of around 1900. Figure 16 is the *Erl King* designed by St. Clare Byrne, 200 feet long, of 443 tons, built in Leith, Scotland, in 1894.

Figure 17 shows *Wanderer,* designed by St. Clare Byrne, length 197 feet, tonnage 362. A Herreshoff steam launch is hoisted out on the davits.

Figure 18 shows *Tuscarora,* which was a great yacht and the first I saw with the deckhouse extended to the sides of the ship and the waist of the ship enclosed. She was first owned by the Scottish lady, Mrs. E. B. Laidlaw, and for several years afterward by Mrs. O. B. Jennings of New York. She was designed by G. L. Watson, was 204 feet long, of 540 tons, and came out in 1897. I think she cruised extensively and she probably was one of the last

to carry much sail. Here she has her main yard crossed, but she sometimes carried it up and down just forward of the foremast.

Neater and Modern

I can remember well the years between 1901 and 1905 when the larger steam yachts were leaving off their yards because of the difficulty in getting good crews to handle these complications and keep them free of soot. Strange to say, we boys at that time thought the yachts looked neater and more modern without the yards.

This photograph of *Tuscarora* illustrates well what these craft looked like under way. They burned soft coal and generally carried a large plume of smoke off to leeward which much increased the impressiveness of these remarkable creations. The English yachts as a rule were not very fast but due to their large displacement and deep forefoot they usually carried quite a bone in their teeth together with a quarter wave large enough to make small craft scamper for safety as they approached. They were about the best sea boats ever known and had a very easy motion, although some that crossed several yards have been known to roll deeply with no sail set if the sea corresponded to their period of roll. *Narada,* of 500 tons, rolled the tips of her yards under on one of her many Atlantic crossings. In speaking of *Narada* it is interesting to note that her owner, Henry Walters of Baltimore, Maryland, used her while cruising in European waters to gather his fine collection of paintings and art objects.

Fig. 16. The ERL KING, about 1894

Fig. 17. The WANDERER

Fig. 18. The TUSCARORA

3 Development of the Marine Steam Engine

The steam yachts of which I have spoken were generally of the English type, but we in this country had developed several types, most of which were not particularly handsome, generally much smaller and faster, but as a rule rather poor sea boats, and not intended for long voyages. The first that we will consider made a long, famous cruise —the *North Star* owned by the original Commodore Cornelius Vanderbilt who, I believe, did much of her designing. He was called Commodore Vanderbilt because he owned several lines of steamships which ran in many directions from New York, around 1840. He was one of our greatest American characters and a shining example of what could be accomplished in this country before the income tax, and though mostly self-taught he was a man of magnificent ability.

He started his fortune sailing a periagua out of Stapleton, Staten Island, in 1810, and though he helped his parents with his earnings he soon bought other boats for the traffic between there and Manhattan, and then turned to steam. This was at the beginning of the steamboat era, and Vanderbilt was one of the first to make a real success at running steamboat lines in America. Though he had real tough competition he quickly made a few million dollars and had some time to spare. This is in contrast to some of the English steam yacht owners we have spoken of whose fortunes may have taken five hundred years to build up, though they often had more time to spare.

However, Commodore Vanderbilt decided to have a fine large steam yacht so, with his extensive experience with steam ships and his own designing department he was

able to plan a very fine vessel. She was 270 feet long, 38 feet in beam, built principally of wood and apparently a very strong vessel for some of her components were 32,000 locust trunnels and a large quantity of one and one-half inch copper bolts. Her deck beams were 14 inches by 15 inches. She was a plumb-bowed, side-wheeler very much resembling the American steamships of the time but her interior was very finely and tastefully worked out in the style then in vogue, which included imitation marble walls and ceiling together with furniture in the saloon of rosewood carved after the style of Louis XV. There were ten staterooms connected to the main saloon, each decorated in a different color, some of which were green and gold, crimson and gold, orange, and so forth, with much of the upholstery and bedding in silk colored to match. The saloon and staterooms were steam heated, which was unusual at that time.

For captain and officers Commodore Vanderbilt could draw the most dependable men from his large fleet of steamers, but several of the hands who shipped for the cruise were young men of the best families in the country, who were attracted by the prospect of visiting so many places of interest in a short time.

The *North Star,* started on her famous cruise in May, 1853, with twenty-three guests aboard, one of whom was the Reverend Dr. Choules who, besides acting as chaplain, wrote a very interesting book about the cruise. She seems to have been able to maintain a very good speed for her time, though Commodore Vanderbilt stated he was more interested in safety than speed. Nevertheless, throughout the cruise, she averaged 259 miles a day. The various runs of the cruise were as follows:

	Miles
New York to Southampton	3,140
Trip round Isle of Wight	73
Southampton to Copenhagen	807
Copenhagen to Cronstadt	655
Cronstadt to Havre	1,461
Havre to Gibraltar	1,200
Gibraltar to Malaga	60
Malaga to Leghorn	807
Leghorn to Civita Vecchia	120
Civita Vecchia to Naples	155
Naples to Malta	340
Malta to Constantinople	838
Constantinople to Gibraltar	1,838
Gibraltar to Madeira	600
Madeira to New York	2,930
Total	15,024

On this cruise *North Star* consumed 2,200 tons of coal, averaging 28 tons a day. She was well received everywhere and Commodore Vanderbilt and his guests traveled by rail and carriage to the principal places of interest on shore. They returned to New York in September having visited many places in four months. And this was over a hundred years ago! Figure 19 is a photograph of Commodore Vanderbilt taken by Brady of Civil War fame.

More About Yacht Clubs

I have spoken of the early Irish and English yacht clubs, but throughout the world there were many rowing clubs dating from soon after 1800. Our first yacht club of importance was the New York Yacht Club which was organized in 1844 and incorporated in 1865.

I believe our next oldest yacht club is the Southern started in 1849, and the others follow about like this: Brooklyn, 1854; Atlantic, 1866; Columbia, 1867; Eastern, 1870; Seawanhaka-Corinthian, 1871; Larchmont, 1880, and, although the Boston Yacht Club was started in 1835, it folded up in about two years and was not again active until 1866. By 1890, yacht clubs had sprung up by the hundreds, but as the early activities of the first clubs were mostly in sail I will not dwell on them, now that I am speaking about steam yachts. Of course, during the Civil War and for a few years after, there was not much activity in this country with steam yachts, but it was during this period that the propeller was being adopted.

While it would be hard to say who, if not Archimedes, invented the screw propeller, it was Ericsson, designer of the *Monitor,* who made it practicable, and this development had much to do with the later development of the steam yacht. While the paddle wheel is actually much the most efficient means of propulsion (its surface does not have retarding friction), still the paddle wheel, while sometimes quite artistically arranged and well adapted to shallow water, had its glaring disadvantages. And yet several yacht owners stuck to the paddle wheel for years,

Fig. 19. Commodore Vanderbilt

and I can remember being on one or two New York Yacht Club cruises when there was more than one paddle wheel yacht along. Figure 20 shows a good sized one—*Clermont*—that was in commission up to nearly World War I. Figure 21 shows the *Turtle* which was running around Boston until about 1910.

Steamers Replace Sailboats

But to go back to the post Civil War days—by about 1870, more and more wealthy yachtsmen were selling their sloops and schooners and having luxurious steamers built to replace them. The American steam yacht, however, was of no fixed type and did not resemble the British ones. Instead, as I have said before, they were of much less displacement for the length, and as a rule were poor sea boats and strange looking. The principal purpose of the design seems to have been speed.

The early American steam yachts were designed or planned by untrained mechanical geniuses who had no feeling for beauty, or perhaps in some cases simply put together by the builder without a design, while in England and Scotland the engineer and architect had to have considerable training before he could practice his profession; hence the British steam yacht was usually engineered throughout in a very safe and conservative way following well proved systems of construction.

Fig. 20. The CLERMONT

Fig. 21. The TURTLE

This was particularly so in regard to the boiler and engine, which in the early days were usually designed and built by one of the large British manufacturers, who at that time were far ahead with heavy machine tools, and who sometimes built locomotives and naval armament. Thus, with their conservatism, the power plants were strong, heavy and long lasting. Perhaps the power plant alone weighed a hundred pounds per horsepower, while the total weight of the yacht per horsepower may have been as great as four thousand pounds; but today a racing motorboat or some highly developed automobiles weigh only about eleven pounds per horsepower. I think the Scottish engineers of those days used the pulling power of a full grown Clydesdale as their standard, for we find records of thousand ton yachts going twelve knots with five hundred horsepower.

Engines Differed Greatly

However, the greatest difference between the English and American yachts generally was in the quality and type of boilers or steam producers. The British, in almost all of their yachts except the small fast ones, stuck to the very heavy fire tube boilers; that is a boiler where the hot gases from the fire flow through large tubes which are surrounded by water, and the water in turn was surrounded by a very heavy shell. Now there are a great many types of

fire tube boilers including the locomotive boiler, but with years of experience, a type for marine use called a Scotch boiler was developed.

This famous type of boiler at one time was used throughout the world in the merchant marine, and used almost exclusively on the large British yachts. It did have fairly good economy for the simple reason that the fire is practically surrounded by water, but is subject to internal strains if different parts change their temperature, so with this type it is necessary to get up steam very gradually.

The Water Tube Boiler

The water tube boiler was the type most often used on American yachts, and these were made in more varieties than the fire tube. In general, a water tube boiler is one that carries its water in a great many small tubes that run to drums or receivers. Fig. 22 shows a Scotch boiler. These boilers are lighter and not at all subject to strains from changes in temperature, particularly if the tubes are slightly bent. With a well designed water tube boiler, steam can be gotten up as rapidly as desired without any serious strain.

There is little doubt that the English were the first to make water tube boilers, for they used this type of boiler in the steam carriages and omnibuses in use around London in 1830. These boilers used pressures up to two hundred pounds, had feed water heaters and jets in the stack. It is too bad that self-propelled vehicles were legislated off the roads of England for the next fifty years or so, for it allowed the French and Germans to get ahead of the British with the automobile.

Of course the first marine steam engines were for paddle steamers, so they turned over very slowly. They often had large cylinders with the stroke considerably more than the bore. They ran on very low pressures as the boilers were often of copper and had flat places in them, so these early steam engines, both ashore and afloat, depended on vacuum for nearly half of their power. Fig. 23 shows a steam engine of about 1875.

Although there may have been thirty pounds pressure in the boiler, it is doubtful if there were ten pounds mean effective pressure on the piston, but on the vacuum side perhaps twenty inches vacuum. So, during the side wheel days a great deal was worked out about valve gear to gain economy, such as valve timing, and reversing mechanisms. Then when the propeller came in there was quite a little engineering data to work from.

The Table Engine

While it is true that the first screw propellers were very large, evidently in an effort to reduce slip, they soon found that smaller screws turning over faster were better, but the first slow speed propeller engines were often of the type called a table engine. They were called table engines because the cylinder was supported by a stout table. The theory of course was to reduce the height of the engine and

I can remember when an engine of this type was in daily use in a small steamer in Narragansett Bay. It must have been a very old engine and perhaps had been in one or two previous hulls.

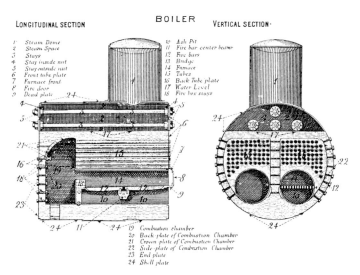

Fig. 22. A Scotch boiler

As engines were speeded up and used higher pressure, they could be much reduced in size so that by 1875 one might look as shown in Figure 26. This picture shows quite clearly the so-called Stevenson link valve gear which is used to reverse the engine by sliding the link one way or the other to bring the forward or reverse eccentric into use. In the picture the link is in neutral position, but when shifted one way or the other would work the valve stem up and down at a proper timing for going ahead or reverse.

The Popular Slide Valve

The most popular valve for many years throughout the world was the slide valve as shown in Figure 24. The principal advantage of the slide valve was that it stayed tight almost indefinitely, because the pressure of the steam in the valve chest kept it firmly pressed against the valve seat, and steam at low temperature is somewhat of a lubricant. But the slide valve was superseded by the piston valve on most advanced engines after 1890, because it allowed a much greater flow of steam and the valve did not have to stay open so long, which is an advantage. A single cylinder engine has a great deal of vibration from its heavy reciprocating parts and cannot be speeded up much, so two-cylinder engines were used to reduce the vibration and improve starting and reversing.

Figure 25 shows a two-cylinder simple engine. That means one where the cylinders are of the same size and the steam is expanded or used in each cylinder separately. This is the type of engine that the locomotives still are using because the exhaust is ejected up the stack to increase the draft of air through the fire. Although tugboats for many years were also noncondensing for simplicity's

sake, still, as I have said, with the early engines the vacuum of the condensing engine increased the power so that two-cylinder compound engines became customary after about 1870, for marine use.

The Compound Engine

The compound engine differs from the simple engine by using the steam in one cylinder after the other, and the high pressure cylinder was often about half the bore of the low pressure cylinder. The compound engine with its large low pressure cylinder not only gave greater volume for the vacuum to work in, but it had a thermal advantage of importance, for the high pressure cylinder could stay at a much higher temperature when the steam was only partly expanded or cooled off in it. Therefore, the incoming steam from the boiler was not cooled off so much and shrunken before it started to do its work. Although a compound engine is larger and heavier than a two-cylinder simple engine of the same horsepower, still its economy is so much better that the boiler and coal bunkers could be smaller giving quite an overall saving in weight, space and cost of fuel.

On shore it never was very customary to expand the steam in more than two cylinders, but marine engineers

Fig. 23. A steam engine of about 1875

soon began to design triple and quadruple engines. Some of the triple expansion engines had four cylinders instead of three, then the last expansion of the steam took place in two instead of one very large cylinder. Thus

the engine was easier to balance, and I will say one of the troubles in running of these engines with different sized pistons was the difficulty of balancing them so there would not be too serious vibrations at their ends.

Five Cylinders

Some of the quadruple engines had five cylinders for the same reasons, and in that case the third, fourth and fifth cylinders were of the same bore. Figure 26 shows an engine of that class designed by my father in 1887. These engines had piston valves, and because the five cylinders made the engine so long, he arranged the valves at the sides instead of between the cylinders as had been customary, and drove the valve gear by a separate crank shaft which could be advanced or retarded in relation to the main crank shaft. Thus the two eccentrics and the complicated Stevenson link valve gear for each cylinder were done away with.

This was one of the first large, light engines in the world and you will see most of the parts below the cylinders are light steel forgings which have been machined all over. Other engines throughout the world were mounted on heavy cast iron frames. Five of these engines were built: two went in the torpedo boat *Cushing*, and one each in the following yachts: *Say When*, *Ballymena*, and *Vamoose*. Figure 27 shows *Vamoose* running. She came out in 1891 and was owned by William Randolph Hearst who was

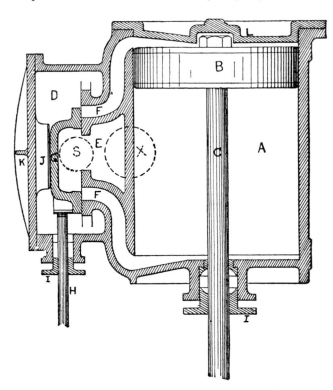

Fig. 24. Section of cylinder and valve chest

A. Cylinder.	H. Valve stem.
B. Piston.	I. Glands.
C. Piston rod.	J. Guide to relieve valve of pres-
D. Valve chest.	sure.
E. Exhaust port.	K. Ribs on steam chest cover.
F. Steam ports.	S. Position of steam pipes.
G. Slide valve.	X. Position of exhaust pipe.

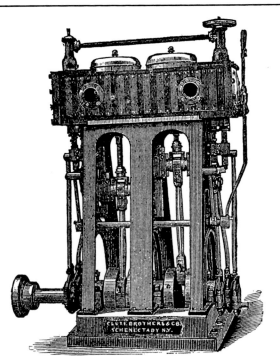

Fig. 25. A two-cylinder simple engine

Fig. 26. A quadruple expansion engine

quite a young man then. I think she went about 28 miles an hour and was credited with being the fastest yacht in the United States that was capable of running in a seaway. However, Captain Nat Herreshoff, as well as most other marine engineers, gave up quadruple engines in favor of the triple expansion engines after about 1890.

You may wonder why I have given the development of the steam engine so much space, but it is a fact that there is no book that tells about these things in simple words without confusing the reader with a lot of doubtful mathematics that have long since been proved wrong. I believe though there are many young men today who take an interest in steam and would like to know the whys and wherefores without tiring study.

Fig. 27. The VAMOOSE running

4 *Hey-Days*
of the Steam Yacht

Propellers

I have said that propellers were very large when they first came into popular use right after the Civil War, and had little slip, but as time went on it turned out that by reducing the surface, by improving the shape and reducing the size, much increase in speed and efficiency could be gained, so that by about 1900, the size of propellers was half what it had been originally, and it was obvious that the best result could be obtained with a slip of approximately thirty per cent, for if the propeller has enough surface to make the slip less, then too much of the power is absorbed in surface resistance.

Propellers of every conceivable shape have been tried in many countries during the last hundred years; four-bladed ones it seems were originally the most common, but later on three-bladed wheels became popular because they had less vibration. The reason for this is that with the four-bladed wheel, two blades at a time, or the wake they make, swung by the rudder post simultaneously, so the four-blader was no better than the two-blader in this respect. However, the two-bladed propeller is the most efficient if you have room for its diameter, so during the last few years five- and six-bladed wheels have come into use where it is desirable to reduce the diameter, as is necessary on shallow draft river towboats that use a reduction gear of high ratio.

While the ordinary three-bladed wheel would theoretically be better with narrower blades and less surface, still in practice the wide blade types that are sometimes called

42

turbine propellers have become almost standard. They were called turbine propellers because the English developed this type to use with turbine-propelled craft before the reduction gear came into use, and the propeller's revolutions per minute were very high. Also some English craft had two or three propellers on one shaft so that their diameters could be less.

Most propellers today are what are called true screws—that is the pitch of the blades is such that any part of the blades will push water backward at the same rate as a corkscrew goes through a cork. This shape is the best if the blade surfaces are to be machined or checked for pitch. But while a true screw is undoubtedly best on a very high-speed hydroplane which has no slip after she gets up to speeds of over sixty or so miles an hour, nevertheless on slow-speed vessels with much slip, a wheel with less pitch near the hub and more pitch at the tips than a true screw is said to be the best.

There are two reasons for this: The first is that near the hub there is a following wake, and at the tips some of the water is escaping on an angle so that more pitch deals with it better. The second reason is that when the pitch of the blades is either too coarse or too fine there is a loss in efficiency and the true screw wheel is apt to be too coarse at the hub and too fine at the tips.

Some people believe that the parts of the blades which are at about 45 degrees do the most driving, and I must say that what is called a square propeller—one where the diameter and the pitch are alike—is the most efficient, but you must have the speed of your craft and the revolu-

Fig. 28. ELECTRA

tions per minute of the propeller in certain proportions to get this combination, and that is where the reduction gear comes in. In the early days, many yacht builders had to design and make the patterns for their propellers, and the improved propellers of today are mostly derived from the early experiments on yachts and torpedo boats both here and abroad.

Fig. 29. NOURMAHAL

Although we have gone up to about 1890 with steam engines we will go back to the year 1848, for in that year the Congress enacted a law which gave yachts a certain status with the several privileges as we know them today, and required them to be registered. The principal privilege was that they could sail in and out of all ports of the United States without entering or clearing at a custom house. In 1849, the New York Yacht Club, the only club of consequence then, was requested to submit a design for a yachting ensign which was accepted and approved and has since been carried on all registered yachts.

Navy Interest in Steam Yachts

One of the reasons for this new status for yachts was that the government, or the Navy Department, thought yachts might be a useful auxiliary to the Navy in the emergency of war, and believed that experiments and trials with them would be of use. Of course they had the steam yacht in mind and steam yachts and power boats certainly have been of great use during the wars, for training purposes in particular, but the Navy has made few exhaustive tests of their usefulness in this respect. How-ever, one was the test of the small fast steam yacht *Leila* in 1881, and a seventy-seven page report of these trials was written up and printed in pamphlet form by three chief engineers of the Navy Department, one of whom later became Admiral B. F. Isherwood who is credited with putting steam on a firm foundation in our Navy.

Leila was 100 feet long; 15 feet 4 inches beam on deck; 11 feet 9 inches beam on waterline; displacement 37 tons. She had a very light coil boiler and a compound engine that developed 150 indicated horsepower at 188 revolutions per minute. Her consumption of anthracite coal was 2.2 pounds per horsepower hour; her best speed was 15.5 statute miles per hour, or 13.45 knots. Her propeller was a true screw of four blades, 4 feet 7 inches diameter, and 8 feet pitch. Her boiler was seven feet in diameter and composed of three separate coils as follows: the first at the top acted as a feed water heater; the next section, which was quite long, was the steam producer and made up of a tapered tube that was rather difficult to make, and it is interesting to note that the water entered at the top and circulated downward so that the hottest part of the coil was near the fire, quite the reverse position of the water in the usual boiler.

After the water and steam had traveled through this

Fig. 30. ATLANTA

Fig. 31. ALVA

section it was conducted to a so-called separator which separated the dry steam from the water. This was necessary in that type of boiler, for more water was fed into these boilers than was evaporated so that the lower tubes were not burnt. After the steam left the separator it went through the third coil that was at the outside and away from the fire. The coil acted as a superheater and produced very dry steam that was capable of much expansion. The engine was a compound with the cyclinders mounted on cast iron columns which acted as guides for the crossheads, and made a beautifully simple arrangement. I am stressing the fact that some of the engines with this type of frame by the same builders lasted well over thirty years of intermittent use.

This particular model of engine, however, had an ingenious double slide valve that allowed an adjustment of the valve timing while the engine was running, and quite a little space in the government report was devoted to the performance of the engine with different valve settings or cut offs. There was a tank called the hot well in the pipe line between the condenser and the feed water pump which contained enough water to make up for the variations in the used feed water. *Leila* was three years old when these trials were made and she was considered a fast craft, but in the next few years speeds were very much increased.

I will not show you pictures of the early American steam yachts simply because they were very homely and their most conspicuous feature was a lot of scalloped and often striped awnings, yet with the large yachts by 1885 more fixed types were being built, and several of the large ones were designed by Gustav Hillman of City Point, N. Y. He seemed to favor a clipper bow that was carried out into a

sort of a beak instead of the usual bowsprit of the sailing ship. His yachts usually had rather full, round sterns, and while usually narrow on deck they had rounding and slightly tumble-home sides amidships, and to my youthful eyes looked like gigantic iron pots. We will show some of these yachts and a few other earlier ones with notes.

Figure 28, *Electra,* designed by G. Hillman for the famous Elbridge T. Gerry. She came out in 1884, was 174 feet long, of 316 tons. *Electra* came out at the beginning of the electric era and she was completely illuminated with incandescent lights, and had a searchlight of 15,000 candle power, and a powerful refrigerating machinery. *Electra* was the flagship of the New York Yacht Club from 1886 to 1892, and was a familiar sight on New York Yacht Club cruises for some twenty-five years.

Figure 29, *Nourmahal,* designed by Hillman for J. J. Astor. She came out in 1884, was 250 feet long, of 768 tons, and was probably our finest large yacht of the time and well kept up. I cannot tell you whether this was the first Astor yacht of this name for the Astor family were steam yacht owners almost from the start, and I think there have been at least four yachts of that name.

Figure 30, *Atlanta,* designed and built by William Cramp and Sons of Philadelphia for Jay Gould in 1883. She was 249 feet long, of 568 tons, had a 1,000 horsepower engine, and was said to cost $250,000. Today she would cost several millions. She was very fast for a large yacht of her time, and when new is said to have made runs of over 17 nautical miles an hour. She had a crew of 52 good men and true.

Figure 31, *Alva,* certainly a fine vessel as might be expected as she was designed by St. Clare J. Byrne of Eng-

Fig. 32. ALVINA

Fig. 33. CARMINA

Fig. 34. VIKING

Fig. 35. KISMET

land though built in this country by Harlan and Hollingsworth of Wilmington, Delaware. She was 285 feet long, of 1,151 tons. *Alva* was built for W. K. Vanderbilt in 1886 and, as you can see, was of pure clipper ship model in the best tradition. She proved to be a very excellent sea boat and could maintain a speed of 14.5 nautical miles an hour. Unfortunately she did not have a very long life as she was sunk by collision in the shallow waters of Cape Cod without loss of life because she took bottom before her superstructure was submerged. This was partly because she normally drew about 17 feet of water, which was a considerable draft for a steam yacht of those days.

By 1900, there were several capable steam yacht designers in this country, and one of the offices which turned out good looking successful steam yachts was Tams, Lemoine and Crane who designed the handsome steam yachts *Dreamer, Rheclair, Noma,* and *Vanadis,* besides the fine auxiliaries *Aloha I, Aloha II, Ariadne,* and the famous schooner *Endymion* which once held the record for an Atlantic crossing under sail. Probably the reason this firm designed handsome vessels was that Clinton Crane had attended the school of Naval Architecture in Glasgow. Mr. Crane was still with us when I wrote the manuscript of this book and certainly is the dean of all American yacht designers, and perhaps the only one we have had who designed successful yachts of the largest and smallest types, as well as high-speed motorboats. We are sorry not to be able to show you pictures of Mr. Crane's yachts, but there is a picture of *Noma* as she looked in her race with *Kanawha.* Another designer of the time who developed good looking yachts was Albert S. Chesebrough, of Bristol, R. I., a cousin of mine from whom I learned much about the history of steam yachting.

Figure 32, *Alvina,* 214 feet long, designed by Mr. Chesebrough in 1901, Figure 33, *Carmina,* 168 feet long, also designed by Mr. Chesebrough in 1903. Perhaps a more typically American steam yacht is Figure 34, *Viking,* designed by Theodore D. Wells for Mr. George F. Baker in 1909. She was 155 feet long, 301 tons.

Figure 35, *Kismet,* is what the medium-size American steam yacht was apt to resemble. She was 140 feet long, and although she was steel the smaller ones down to 100 feet were often composite, that is they had steel frames and wooden planking, while those still smaller were all wood.

Valuable Trophies

Some of my younger readers may wonder whether the larger steam yachts raced much, and I will say that for a great many years there were valuable trophies offered for them but very few races were held, the reason probably being that after a steam yacht had run her trials it was pretty well known how fast she was so there was little point in racing. Nevertheless, two of the important races were between the steam yachts *Kanawha,* 227 feet long, and *Noma,* 252 feet long. I saw part of this race from the deck of my father's steam yacht *Roamer* and was much impressed. The race was for what was called the Lysistrata Cup given by James Gordon Bennett, and it was held off Newport in August, 1903, over a triangular course of 60 nautical miles. *Kanawha* won by nearly four minutes running at about 20 knots.

Noma would have done better if she had not had a very heavy and complicated interior. In this race *Kanawha* burned anthracite coal and *Noma* bituminous. This was a great year in yachting and the race was held on the last day of the New York Yacht Club cruise in which the 90-footers *Reliance, Constitution,* and *Columbia* were competing for the honor of defending the America's Cup. Yes, 1903 was indeed a great year in American yachting.

The other steam yacht race was held the next year in June off Sandy Hook competing for the same cup. This time *Kanawha* raced *Hauoli,* 147 feet long, and the race was a little closer with *Kanawha* winning by about three minutes with both yachts making about 20 knots over the 60 nautical mile course. Comparisons of the two yachts are given below.

A Large Spectator Fleet

Quite a fleet of the large yachts was out to see this race, including *Delaware, Lysistrata* (for which the cup was named), *Virginia, Laurita, Viking, American* and others. *Kanawha* received great fame for winning these two races, and, as the deed of gift of the cup stated that if a yacht won it twice in succession her owner would have permanent possession of the cup, this second victory of the *Kanawha* retired the cup and I presume that is one reason that no more races with large yachts were held. However, there was another cup called the Niagara IV Cup that was given by Howard Gould for steam yachts between 75 feet and 160 feet in length and for which several of the smaller and faster steam yachts competed in Long Island Sound. Then there had been for a long time the large trophy called the American Yacht Club's International Challenge Cup for Steam Yachts.

	L.o.a.	Tons	Boiler pressure	Engine revolutions	Amount of coal burned on course
Kanawha	227 feet	475	250	300	15 tons
Hauoli	211 feet	299	250	298	12 tons

Fig. 35A. MAYFLOWER

(see page 90)

5 *The Decline of the Great Steam Yachts*

People have asked me why my father did not build some of these larger yachts, and the answer is that he preferred to build many small ones rather than a few large ones, and that the financial risk and worry was much less that way. From what one hears of other builders he certainly was right for some of them lost their shirts, or had them pretty well torn.

Many wonder why the large steam yachts went out of use so quickly and they think the diesel engine had something to do with it, but I believe the diesel had little effect for the most recent theory in engineering is that with modern materials a steam plant might be built as compact as the diesel and still have as good an overall economy. The reason for it is that the first cost of the large diesel is very great and they seem to require very costly repairs. The pressures and temperatures in a large diesel are so great that frames and beds crack in a few years while the inner vital parts, like pistons and valves, warp, crack and burn. Of course the small diesel, say under 500 horsepower, is very satisfactory and reliable with wonderful overall economy, and it is a fact that some firms gear three or four of their satisfactory small models together when large horsepower is required, but this is not a compact arrangement.

A steam boiler could now be made which would be safe with four times the pressure that was usually carried before World War I, and if the steam were well superheated it might have eight times as much expansion as was customary in those days. Now if the engine were made very small so as not to absorb or radiate heat, it would be a very

economical power plant. Of course the small engine would have to be run at high speed and use a reduction gear as the turbine does. But more of this later.

The three events that forced the large steam yacht almost out of existence are 1. The income tax; 2. World Wars I and II; 3. What is spoken of as the Roosevelt era. I will say a few words about each one.

If I remember correctly, the income tax started about 1913 and was not very severe at first. But as the years went by it is no secret to any of my readers that the income tax increased, it seems almost year by year. Between this accelerating income tax and the continuously mounting death dues on estates and inheritances, today it is next to impossible for a young man to build up an honest business and accumulate the kind of savings that will support a steam yacht later.

During both of the world wars practically all of the larger yachts were either turned over to the Navy by their owners, or taken over for the duration. At the first part of World War I, I was a member of one of the inspection sections of the Navy who had the job of inspecting the yachts and vessels taken over, valuing them and making recommendations for alterations to fit them for naval use. After the war, I served for a while evaluating and returning some of these vessels to their owners. In the meantime, I was in command of a small 92-foot steam yacht for about nine months, so altogether had a good first-hand opportunity to see what happened.

Well, the principal function of the ex-yacht was to train crews so they would be capable of more serious service, and perhaps in many cases this was accomplished quickly. The first year much of the personnel was made up of yachtsmen and college boys of good quality, but after the draft for the Army started a number of the crews were composed of what then were called slackers or draft dodgers who were lazy, ignorant and irresponsible, who took no interest or pride whatever in keeping up their ship but instead often tried to put her out of commission so that when she was laid up at the repair dock they could sleep all day and chase women at night, both of which occupations they never seemed to tire of.

Many of the ex-yachts were in the Scout Patrol section of the Navy and had the large letters S P painted on their bows so that many of the civilians on shore referred to this as the Slackers' Paradise Service. On a yacht in the old days an owner or the captain not only had the opportunity of picking out a good crew, but if they were found to be unsatisfactory they could be paid off and put on the beach at once. Not so in the Naval service, for there you had to take what was issued and could only have them transferred if found incapable, and this required a lot of red tape and sometimes a courtmartial. This is why some of the yachts in Naval service were not kept up even one half as well as a private yacht and that is why they depreciated so rapidly. Some of them, like the steam yacht *May*, also left their bones where they were cast ashore. A few of us who were around at that time thought there would never be many large yachts again but we were wrong in this assumption.

I do not like to digress from the subject of yachts but I feel that something should be said of the politics of that time which had a powerful effect on our economy and later was to give us Roosevelt. This was prohibition, the law that was slipped over on the nation when many of our able-bodied men and women were away from home, either in the various services or working on munitions. This was before the days of absentee voting.

However, the country swung Republican after the war and not only was our recovery astonishingly rapid but during the economical administration of Coolidge we were rapidly paying off the national debt so that a great many capable men thought that we had an era of prosperity before us in spite of the income tax which was then not so exorbitant. Our wealthy citizens did not see the writing on the wall and still had confidence, so that between about 1925 and 1928 large steam and diesel yachts were being built more rapidly than at any time in history. *Nourmahal, Alder,* and *Alva,* Figures 36-37-38, all came out in this period.

Downfall of the Large Yacht

Before this, stocks and bonds had been unnaturally high and when they started to fall they went so low that the year 1929 is called a panic year, and little recovery was made before the election of 1932 when, although both Hoover and Roosevelt had complicated platforms which most of the voters could not understand, Roosevelt was

Fig. 36. NOURMAHAL. Commodore Vincent Astor's 260-foot yacht, built in 1928, typifies the kind of private vessel the great depression killed

Fig. 37. ALDER. Mrs. William Boyce Thompson's ship, 280 feet of seagoing luxury, was built before the era of the runaway income tax

Fig. 38. ALVA. Mrs. W. K. Vanderbilt's 259 ft. waterline vessel; another vote of confidence in the late 20's continuing prosperity

for repeal of prohibition while Hoover was against it. This was something the average person could understand, and Roosevelt and the Democrats won quite easily.

Roosevelt created the New Deal and put into effect many administrative changes that resulted in deficit financing to an unheard-of degree, so that the national debt grew from 22½ billion at the beginning of his first term to about 258½ billion at his death. All these measures, including the government financed organizations started by Hoover, made necessary a pyramidal increase in the income tax and started a rat race that is still going on today.

Under these conditions, of course, the steam yacht, and for that matter almost all large types of yachts, have gone out of existence while the New York Yacht Club has been practically brought down to the status of a public lunchroom.

I am sorry to have taken up so much space to describe the decline of the large yacht and perhaps should have stuck to such technical things as the pressure on one side and the vacuum on the other side of a piston, but not to make you think that I have written the above from the point of view of a well-to-do man I must tell you that I had a vacuum in my pocketbook for several long years after I was disenrolled from the Navy and was starting a small profession from scratch without help.

But we will return now to the steamers for, while we have covered the larger and older ones, we must take up the smaller yachts which on the whole, excepting for romance, are perhaps the most interesting to think about today.

The Development of Steam Launches

The word "launch" was the name given to the longest of a ship's boats in old times. Also in the Mediterranean the long open boats used for both oar and sail were called "launches," so I suppose that when a steam plant was put in one of the ship's launches it was called a "steam launch," and certainly the English stuck to this model for a long while. Figure 39 shows several at Yarrow's yard soon after it started, or perhaps around the year 1870. But I must mention that some of the early steam launches used on the Thames were miniature clipper ships as far as model was concerned, and sometimes retained the bowsprit though no masts were carried.

Their most conspicuous feature was fancily-fringed awnings from bow to stern. Perhaps these craft usually ran at less than six or eight miles an hour, however they were undoubtedly quiet and steady so that a run in one on the upper Thames or other smooth water must have been very pleasant. The early English launches were heavy and low-sided with little flare forward, so they must have been very wet in a seaway.

By about 1880 in this country we had developed launches and small steamers like Figure 40, some of which had comparatively light power plants, so that they went partly over the water instead of through it. But the steam launches of the time of my youth were pretty wet craft, nevertheless, though there were usually some sheltered warm places back of the boiler. I recall that my pleasantest

Fig. 40. A small American steam launch, typical of the 1880's. Length, 33 feet overall

Fig. 39. Small steam launches of the early 1870's at Yarrow's Yard, Isle of Dogs

trips on the water were in small steam yachts and launches in which perhaps I steamed two thousand miles or more, and have run in, or watched the construction of perhaps a hundred. As far as the lines of the large steamers are concerned, they were inspired by the sailing clippers as shown in Figure 41. I list here some of the small steam yachts built by the Herreshoff Manufacturing Company between 1875 and 1885; the list is interesting since it gives the speed of these vessels.

Speedwell, 1876, for Walter Langdon.
  Length, 45'; breadth, 6'9"; depth, 3'3"; draft, 2'8"; speed, 12 m/h.
Kelpie, 1878, for William H. Graham, Baltimore.
  Engine 3½" and 6" by 7"; boiler, 42" diameter; Herreshoff coil; speed, 12 m/h.
Leila, 1878, for William H. Graham, Baltimore.
  100' x 15'; engine 9" and 16" by 18"; Herreshoff coil boiler 6½' diameter; speed, 16 m/h.
Dolphin, 1879, for Robert Lenox Kennedy.
  Length, 42'; breadth, 8'6"; depth, 4'; draft, 3'; speed, 10 m/h.
Idle Hour, 1879, for B. F. Carver.
  Length, 60'; breadth, 9'; depth, 4'7"; draft, 3'5"; speed, 15 m/h.
Sinbad, 1879, for F. S. deHauteville, New York.
  Length, 42'; breadth, 8'8"; depth, 3'9", draft, 3'2"; speed, 10 m/h.
Edith, 1880, for William Woodward, Jr., New York.
  Length, 60'; breadth, 9'2"; depth, 4'7"; draft, 3'5"; speed, 15 m/h.
Gleam, 1880, for William H. Graham, Baltimore.
  Length, 120'; breadth, 16'; depth, 6'5"; draft, 5'8"; speed 17 m/h.
Sport, 1880, for Joseph P. Earl, New York.
  Length, 45'; breadth, 8'2"; depth, 3'2"; draft, 1'2"; speed, 10 m/h.
Camilla, 1881, for Dr. J. G. Holland.
  Length, 60'; breadth, 9'; depth, 4'7"; draft 3'5"; speed, 15 m/h.
Juliet, 1881, for Morris and Jones, Bartom-on-the-Sound.
  Length, 45'; breadth 9'; depth, 4'3"; draft, 3'; speed, 11 m/h.
Lucy, built for F. S. Birch, New York.
  Length, 42'; breadth, 8'6"; depth, 4'; draft, 4'7"; speed, 10 m/h.
Aida, 1882, for Mark Hopkins, St. Clair, Mich.
  Length, 95'; breadth, 12'6"; depth, 6'3"; draft, 4'6"; speed, 16 m/h.
Augusta, 1882, for Charles Kellogg of Athens, Pa.
  55' x 6½'; engine, 6" x 24"; boiler, Herreshoff coil, 42" diam.; speed, 14 m/h.
Nereid, 1882, for Jay C. Smith, Utica, N. Y.
  Length, 76'; breadth, 12'6"; depth, 6'3"; draft, 4'6"; speed, 14 m/h.
Orienta, 1882, for J. A. Bostwick, New York.
  Length, 125'; breadth, 17'; depth, 8'6"; draft, 6'6"; speed, 17 m/h.

Siesta, 1882, for H. H. Warner, Rochester.
  Length, 98'; breadth, 17'; depth, 8'6"; draft, 5'6"; speed, 13½ m/h.
Magnolia, 1883, for Fairman Rogers, Philadelphia.
  Length, 99'; breadth, 17'6"; depth, 8'6"; draft, 4'; speed, 11½ m/h. At the time this vessel had twin screws and was the only yacht of its kind in the United States.
Ossabaw, 1883, for Archibald Rogers, New York.
  Length, 69'; breadth, 9'; depth, 5'; draft, 3'6"; speed, 16 m/h.
Permelia, 1883, for Mark Hopkins, St. Clair, Mich.
  Length, 100'; breadth, 12'6"; depth, 6'6"; draft, 4'6"; speed, 19½ m/h.
Marina, 1884, for G. A. Bech, Poughkeepsie, New York.
  Length, 87'; breadth, 12'6"; depth, 7'3"; draft, 5'; speed, 14 m/h.
Lucille, 1884, for Charles Kellogg, Athens, Pa.
  Length, 69'; breadth, 9'; engine 6" and 10½" by 10"; boiler, Herreshoff patent safety 56" square; speed, 19 m/h.
Ladoga, 1885, for George Gordon King of Newport, R. I.
  Length, 97'; breadth, 13'; engine, 8" and 14" x 14"; boiler, Herreshoff safety, 67" square.
Lucille, 1885, for Charles Kellogg, Athens, Pa.
  Length 90' x 11½'; engine 8" and 14" by 14"; boiler, Herreshoff safety, 67" square; speed, 17 m/h.
Polly, 1885, for C. A. Whittier of Boston, Mass.
  Duplicate of *Lucille* (1884) above, except speed, which was 17 miles.
Stiletto, 1885, for Herreshoff Company.
  94' x 11'; engine, 12 x 21" by 12"; boiler, Herreshoff patent safety, 7' square; speed, 25 m/h.
Now Then, with a speed of over 24 miles an hour. Screw steamer built in 1887 by the Herreshoff Manufacturing Company for Norman L. Munro.

Figure 43 shows *Stiletto* designed, power plant and all, by my father in 1885. She was owned by my father and uncles and was sold to the United States Navy for a torpedo boat in 1887 and ran in this use some twenty years.

Fig. 41. The lines of large steam yachts of the 1880's were inspired by the sailing clippers

6 *The Fast Steam Launch and Small Steam Yacht*

The *Now Then* was built by the Herreshoff Company in 1887 for Norman L. Munro. She was 85 feet long and when new ran from Newport to 24th Street, New York City, a distance of 170 miles, at the rate of 24 miles an hour. She was the first steamer of any size I know of that had a flat stern to prevent her from changing her trim when at speed. It is unfortunate that pictures of fast moving vessels could not be taken in those days and I believe there are actually no good pictures of these fast steamers.

I must say something about the fast steam yachts of that time for they certainly were the sportiest things a private individual could own. Before 1890 there was nothing but the steam cars on rails which could maintain a speed of over 20 miles an hour for any great distance, and while many steam trains were running at around 60 miles an hour, still they could only run, of course, in the direction the rails were laid.

At that time several men had ridden a hundred miles on a bicycle in one day, but it is very doubtful if a horse could draw any useful rig a hundred miles in a day without hurting himself. But, although some men on a bicycle or on horseback could go over twenty miles an hour for a mile or two, nothing but the steam yacht could maintain a speed of over twenty with comfort. On a yacht, the owner could have a guest or two along with him, all with their separate berths, with just as good meals as on shore, while protection from the weather was nearly perfect as many of the steamers had steam heat. Although the fast steam yacht was always more dangerous than the slow one, the speed that was then achieved was thrilling. In speaking of speed

and danger I would say the fast steam yacht was much safer than fast travel on shore before 1900, and while there probably are no statistics about horse-drawn vehicles it would be my guess that there were more serious accidents with this means of transportation per miles run than with the modern automobile which travels about eight times as fast. The frequency of automobile accidents today is mostly due to the great numbers there are on the road; for instance, it might be said that there are over fifty times as many people on our highways as there were before 1900. So you see the fast steam yacht that could make twenty miles an hour with safety and comfort was quite *the* thing.

As for the sailing yachts, when used for commuting purposes they were very poor. Although the sailing yacht might have even more comfort and accommodation than the steamer, with some tide and weather conditions she would be unable to maintain a schedule. The small fast steam yacht was an ideal commuter for the wealthy men who had estates up the Hudson or along Long Island Sound.

By 1900, the small American steam yacht had developed into something like *Scout,* Figure 44. She was built for August Belmont, was 81 feet long and when new capable of making 21 miles an hour. There were eight of this design of small steamers built and they set the style for a great many others so that some of their characteristics were retained in the design of similar craft for the next thirty years. In the old days, many would call *Scout* a steam launch, but today we would think of an 80-footer as

Fig. 42. NOW THEN. With a speed of over 24 miles an hour. Screw steamer built in 1887 by the Herreshoff Manufacturing Company for Norman L. Munro.

a large and expensive yacht. Although I do not know the proper designation or classification of the different sizes and types of steam yachts, I should say a launch was a craft only slightly decked over at the ends. The length was quite varied, for one at least, *Javelin,* was 90 feet long.

The next class, of which there were many, was called cabin launch. They may have ranged in length between 40 and 100 feet, and the larger steam yachts perhaps were called flush-decked yachts, which again were subdivided into types such as auxiliary, cruising, and fast yachts.

In 1897, an extremely fast steamer was built in England named *Turbinia,* Figure 45. She was one of the first vessels to use turbines instead of reciprocating engines. *Turbinia* was 100 feet long, 9 feet beam, weighed 44½ tons, had 2000 horsepower. She had three turbines, with three

propellers on each of her shafts, making a total of nine propellers. At first she made less than 20 knots, but after very expensive changes were carried out she finally reached a speed of 35 knots, and so became the fastest boat in the world. But she could hardly be classed as a yacht, for her machinery took up so much space there was little room left for accommodations.

This naturally made an American want to acquire even greater speed, so Mr. Charles R. Flint, who was a very adventurous man in many ways, thought he would make a try at a world record. Thus he had the famous *Arrow* built with very great care and expense. Her hull and steam plant were designed by Charles D. Mosher who made a specialty of fast steam launches and light boilers. *Arrow* was very much the same shape or model as the torpedo boats de-

Fig. 43. STILETTO. Herreshoff-designed and built, became U.S. Navy torpedo boat in 1887, and continued in that service for twenty years

Fig. 44. SCOUT was built for August Belmont as a tender to the MINEOLA

signed for the French Navy by Normand, and ran with her forefoot in the water. Her hull was built by S. Ayers and Sons of Nyack, New York, and was a fine job. She was of light construction; her frames were steel below water and aluminum above. She was double-planked mahogany; her power plant consisted of two water tube boilers and two quadruple expansion engines of 2,000 horsepower each, so she compared with *Turbinia* as follows:

	LOA	Beam	HP	Weight	Claimed Speed	Weight Per HP	Year
Turbinia	100′	9′	2,000	44.5 tons	35 knots	49 lbs.	1897
Arrow	130′	12.5′	4,000	66 tons	39 knots	36 lbs.	1902

The weight per horsepower of these vessels was much less than any before. For instance, the weight per horsepower of the best torpedo boats was in the neighborhood of 120 pounds, and the best racing motorboats did not get down to a weight of less than these figures until around 1905. Hence, in spite of their rather queer model they were undoubtedly fast, and I do not doubt that *Arrow* went very fast for a few minutes one day. Right after her record run one of her boilers was removed and she never was seen going very fast thereafter. *Arrow* had quite good accommodations in her large stern and was used as a yacht for several years.

Perhaps some of my readers would like to hear how Mr. Flint made some of the money to build *Arrow*, but as this tale was told to me about fifty-six years ago I cannot vouch for its truth or the accuracy of my memory. However, it

Fig. 45. TURBINIA, built in England, was one of the first turbine-driven vessels, had nine propellers, 2000 hp, speed of 35 knots

seems that Mr. Flint was interested in a type of ship's gun called a dynamite gun. This weapon was developed about the time of the Spanish War and consisted of a long tube built into a ship that fired or propelled its projectile by compressed air. The projectile was filled with a powerful charge of gun cotton. Our Navy had one or two of these vessels, one named *Vesuvius* was a very well-designed ship but the dynamite gun proved entirely impractical because of its short range and because the guns could not be trained or elevated, so it was next to impossible to hit the target.

But Mr. Flint heard of a revolution in one of the Central American countries where the rebels had captured the Navy and were trying to compel the land forces (which were loyal) to come to their terms. Mr. Flint had nerve enough to take a contract to suppress the naval forces, so, hiring some sort of a seagoing tugboat, he had a dynamite gun built in her and acquired an expert crew to handle this tricky machine. I believe they were the same men who had been demonstrating it to our government. As I was told the story, they only took two shells or bombs along on this adventurous trip.

Swiftsure, Figure 46, was designed and owned by my father. She was a long, narrow double-ender that went very fast for her small horsepower. She was 52 feet long and 6 feet beam, and I believe she could get up to something like 27 knots, or 31 miles, for short bursts of speed, but never averaged over about 25.5 knots on long race courses that had sharp turns. *Swiftsure* was built in 1904 and her speed was remarkable for a coal-fired boiler without forced draft. She probably was the last fast American steam launch to run on salt water.

Figure 47 shows what was probably the last English fast steam launch. Her name was *Rose En Soleil* and she was built by Simson Strickland & Co. Ltd., who made a specialty of steam launches. She was built for Lord Howard DeWalden and was 40 feet long, 5 feet wide. She had a water tube boiler fired with four burners using some kind of refined kerosene for fuel. She had a pair of very compact quadruple expansion engines and is said to have made 27.29 knots over an Admiralty measured nautical mile, and won some open races for high speed power boats in 1905.

But I don't want the reader to think that steam launches

Fig. 46. SWIFTSURE, 1904, another Herreshoff-designed and built yacht, had coal-fired boiler without forced draft, yet could make 26 knots

When they arrived off the port that was being besieged by the rebel navy they could see this flotilla or fleet lined up as if ready to shell the city. There was a bellbuoy at the mouth of the harbor so, taking very careful aim, Mr. Flint and his crew succeeded in firing one of his so-called dynamite shells so that it landed very close to the buoy. When the shell exploded the bellbuoy, chain and all, went up in the air while almost at the same time the flags on the rebel fleet came down. Mr. Flint collected the fee for this contract and, it is said, lived happily ever after. *Arrow* for many years was spoken of as the "forty-mile-an-hour" yacht, for the equivalent of 39 knots is 45 statute miles. Figure 57 shows *Arrow* at full speed in 1902. She was the last out-and-out attempt at speed in a steam yacht that I know of.

were ever very common, for the high grade ones were certainly rarae aves thus quite worth anyone's time to examine carefully. They probably were built as nicely as anything of their size and time. Perhaps there are one thousand times as many outboard motor boats at present as there were steam launches any year in the past. The principal reason there were so few steam launches in this country was that the law prohibited them from being run without a licensed steam engineer, and in order to get this license the applicant had to have operated a steam boiler for two years.

A Licensed Female Steam Engineer

This reminds me that the only female steam engineer I have heard of was the late Mrs. Rosamund Tudor Burgess,

Fig. 47. ROSE EN SOLEIL, probably the last English fast steam launch, using refined kerosene for fuel, she made 27 knots over Admiralty mile

and if I remember rightly she served her time firing the furnace in their house so she could be licensed to run the steam plant in Starling Burgess' small steam tug *Ox*. The law now has been changed so that anyone in this country at least can run a steam launch. But while the law was in force, quite naturally everyone turned to the internal combustion engine, so that the last of the steam launches were the tenders or so-called "starboard launches" on steam yachts which had a licensed engineer or two aboard. So

the internal combustion engine started to become popular by 1905, although a few steam launches were built up until about 1915.

Steam has become unpopular for propelling automobiles for another reason, namely that steamers were barred from almost all automobile races, and until about 1905 almost everyone admitted the steam auto was the best hill climber, fastest accelerator, and actually the fastest on the straightaway up to 1906, when a Stanley made 127.5 miles per

Fig. 48. CIGARETTE, built in 1905, was a typical fast commuter. Despite her 122 foot length she had limited accommodations for passengers

hour. However, by this time the several automobile build-ers who had been making steam carriages shifted to the gasoline engine, but some recent engineers are of the opin-ion that if one-tenth the man hours had been devoted to developing steam that went into the perfection of the gasoline engine, an automobile of greater performance and less cost than our present cars might have been the result.

The reason for this is, of course, the great expense and complications that have been found necessary to acquire a transmission which will let the gasoline engine perform well. Some of the modern transmissions are nearly as com-plicated and expensive as the engine which drives them, but the steam engine need not have any transmission or clutch, for it will pull almost equally well at any speed. As for economy, with the steam boiler much of the heat or power went up the stack or was radiated off in the engine, but as the moving parts of the internal combustion engine are dealing with hot flame they have to be cooled either by liquid or air. So it is said more than 25% of the power in these engines escapes through the cylinder walls, head, valves, etc. Much of the advance in the design of the gaso-line engine has occurred during the last fifty years and been helped by modern materials and lubrication, but prac-tically no effort has been made in that time to improve the small, light steam plant.

New Interest in Steam Today

However, I speak of this now only because there is some interest at present in steam engines, perhaps caused by the possibility that some sort of a reactor or steam generator will be developed to produce steam more economically than the boiler, with some new sort of fuel. At any rate, an oil-burning steam plant could be made at the present time that would be about one-quarter the size of the steam plants of around 1900, and have a far greater fuel econ-omy than the gasoline engine. With very high boiler pres-sure and superheated steam the engine could be surpris-ingly small, particularly if run at as high revolutions per minute as the internal combustion engine. Thus a power plant could be made that would be quiet, reliable, and of better all-around economy than the diesel, for the diesel, except in the smaller sizes, has proved to be expensive to run because of its expensive repairs, and because in many cases the diesel fuel has risen in price more than the burn-ing fuels.

Before finishing about steam yachts I must not forget to mention a type that was generally called a commuter. It was a rather fast, moderate size boat and did not have much accommodation. Figure 48 shows *Cigarette*, 122' long, designed by Swasey, Raymond and Page in 1905, and Figure 49 shows the steam yacht *Viking*.

Fig. 49. VIKING, built for George F. Baker, Jr. in 1929, was 272' overall. Burnell Poole's dramatic aquatint captures the spirit of the steam yacht at sea

7 Origin of the America's Cup

If Queen Victoria had been the great patroness of steam yachts, her son Prince Edward, both as prince and king, was certainly the principal figure who stimulated an interest in the larger racing sailing yachts. For this reason we will devote some lines to his life, for few Americans have a very clear idea of his yachting activities.

In Prince Edward's youth the royal family often spent the summer at Osborn House, a very pleasant location on the Isle of Wight just to the east of Cowes Roads where the Royal Yacht Club had its ancient clubhouse. Osborn House was on slightly elevated land and thus had a magnificent view over The Solent which is the sheet of water that has seen more important yacht racing than any place in the world. I do not say The Solent is the best place in the world for yacht racing, for it contains numerous shoals and usually has considerable flow of tide together with amazingly steep little seas, but the British yachtsmen apparently look upon these hazards as part of the game which make a test of piloting and seamanship as much a part of racing as the comparative speed of the yachts.

A good view of The Solent is shown in the painting by A. W. Fowles of the schooner *Cambria* (Figure 50) as she appeared in a practice race before sailing over in 1870 to become the first challenger for the America's Cup. If the reader has sharp eyes he can see in the distance near the left border of the picture not only one of Victoria's early Royal yachts, but on top of the hill beyond he can see Osborne House. This painting gives a good impression of Cowes Roads with the river Medina beyond, while the town of Cowes and the castle of the Royal Yacht Squadron

are somewhere back of the principal yachts. The painter of this picture not only has made accurate portraits of the individual yachts but has shown exactly the way the seas appear off Cowes Roads. Fowles lived at Ryde, only a few miles eastward of this scene, and was perhaps the best yachting painter between 1850 and 1870. This painting was formerly owned by Arthur Hamilton Clark, author of those two great source books—"The Clipper Ship Era," and "The History of Yachting"—now in the author's possession. It gives a fine impression of what was often before young Prince Edward's eyes in his youth.

At quite a young age the prince was allowed to accompany Lord Alfred Paget on his 37-ton *Dagmar*. Lord Paget, I believe, lived in the neighborhood of Osborne House and was of a family of the best yachting tradition. Thus the prince not only received a sound yachting training but acquired a lifelong love of the sport. Edward also had the opportunity to race on several of the crack racers of the time such as *Arrow* and *Kriemhilda*. In 1876, he purchased the fine schooner *Hildegarde*, which he raced with success. In 1880, he had the celebrated cutter *Formosa*, but at about this time the measurement rule was changed so that in 1893 he or his mother had Watson design the beautiful *Britannia*, one of the most reliable racing yachts ever built.

During *Britannia*'s first five years she started in 219 races in which she often came in first, second or third, thus accumulating in this time prizes amounting to ten thousand pounds. I must note that *Britannia* under both Edward and King George V is said to have competed in well over 500 races in the some twenty-two seasons she was in commis-

Fig. 50. The CAMBRIA, in a practice race on The Solent in 1870 before sailing to America to become the first challenger for the America's Cup

sion, thus racing many more times than any other large yacht. For instance, our *Vanitie,* which has raced perhaps more than any other American large yacht, only competed 142 times.

Some of the steam yachts that Edward owned, both as prince and king, were *Princess, Zenobia,* and the large *Victoria and Albert,* built in 1899, of 5,005 tons and 11,000 horsepower. She, however, was found to be too large and cumbersome for short trips so later he also had the turbine yacht *Alexandria* of 2,000 tons. Edward was commodore of the Royal Thames Yacht Club between 1874 and 1881, and was also president of the Yacht Racing Association and did much to give that organization its present prestige. He was commodore of the Royal Yacht Squadron from 1882 until his accession to the throne when he resigned all such offices but kept up his connection with the Squadron as its admiral. Following the example of Queen Victoria, Edward gave annual trophies to four British yacht clubs and presented the New York Yacht Club with The King's Cup for annual competition. These trophies were personal gifts of Edward, paid for out of his private funds.

It will be hard for some of my younger readers to understand how a prince or king could have such an influence on a sport, but before World War I the monarch or ruler of most nations was not only adored by a large part of his subjects but almost invariably looked upon as the one to be imitated. These remarks apply particularly to the upper and middle classes who naturally were the most interested in yachting. Before *Britannia* came out the interest in racing the larger classes was practically nil throughout the world, but that year the British built four and we, five, great single stickers which were generally referred to as ninety-footers, for their water line lengths were usually a few feet less than ninety. Some of the other proportions of these yachts were roughly: L.O.A. 115', L.W.L. 85', Sail Area 10,000 sq. ft., with a displacement of perhaps 200 tons. The 12-meter boats of 1958 are approximately L.O.A. 69', L.W.L. 45', Sail Area 2,000 sq. ft., and displacement of 23 tons.

This stimulus in first-class racing yachts was to keep up until World War I in spite of changes in rules on both sides of the Atlantic, and I for one think it might well have been quite different if it had not been for Edward. While Charles II can well be called the grandfather of yachting, Edward VII was certainly yachting's greatest patron.

Edward's sister, who was fondly called Vickie (and I only use the name to differentiate her from her august mother), also must have imbibed the spirit of yachting while she summered at Osborne House, for her son William II was an ardent yachtsman throughout his life, though apparently he inherited few other English traits. The Kaiser greatly stimulated yachting in Germany, particularly in the large schooner classes. Before his time

Germany was not considered a yacht-building country, but since then she has gradually worked up to be one of the leaders.

It has been necessary to run way on to the twentieth century with Edward VII but now we may go back to his childhood to consider the effect of the schooner *America* and try to account for the first challenges for the cup that has since held the *America*'s name, and I will note that before this the cup had been called the Hundred Guinea Cup, apparently because of its cost.

The America

Many people and several writers seem to think that the schooner *America* was a unique craft, but while she was undoubtedly highly developed and designed by a great artist, she was largely the natural outgrowth of an American type that had been developing since before 1800. Some of our early rakish craft were used as colonial privateers, slave ships, privateers of 1812, and some found their way to the pirates of the West Indies. (My ancestors either owned or commanded vessels in all of these classes but the last, for they had been connected with shipping since colonial times.)

By far the greatest number of vessels which resembled *America* were the so-called packet schooners which carried mail, passengers, and light express cargoes between the towns and cities of our Atlantic coast. These packets were so common at the time that few artists painted them although they often appear in the background of ship paint-

ings. Several sets of the lines of these early schooners may be seen in Chapelle's book, "The Baltimore Clippers." Some of the New England packet schooners did not run in winter but took a cargo of onions and other New England products to the West Indies where they stayed until warmer, steady weather came.

While the sail plan and the profile of *America* was quite similar to those of our packet schooners, yet her deck line and water lines forward were much sharper, for she was one of the first vessels modeled to the wave-line theory that had been worked out by Scott Russell a few years previously in England. Presumably, Russell worked out this shape for steamships, but Steers, the designer of *America*, seems to be the first to have adapted it to sailing vessels. No doubt most sail boats of the world, with the exception of a few small French craft, had been too full forward for best performance against wind and sea. But the late Tom Ratsey told me it was the opinion of his father that it was the sails, and not the model, of *America* that gave her an advantage over other yachts. You may very well think that would be the natural reaction of a sailmaker, but the Ratseys of around 1850 were as much yacht designers as sailmakers.

Three views of *America* as she appeared in her races in England are shown in Figure 51. This painting by the accurate artist, Fitzhugh Lane, is very interesting. In the view from astern you can see that her sails are almost perfect air foils, just twisted aloft correctly for the higher wind velocities there. The usual British yacht of the time was using sails of considerable draft; they were loose-

Fig. 51. Three views of the AMERICA as she appeared when racing in English waters

footed, and often made of flax, which invariably became baggy in dry weather.

Although the *America* would have had no chance of winning under the British tonnage rules and only won the Hundred Guinea Cup because the British were kind enough to give this trophy in a race without handicap around the Isle of Wight, even then she would not have done so well if fate had not eliminated several of the larger fast yachts in the race. It happened somewhat like this—it had been the custom in races around the Wight to round the lightship called The Nab, several miles to the eastward of the island, and several of the leaders (and so probably the fastest yachts) did that, but *America* with perhaps two-thirds of the other yachts took the shorter course inshore. This was the first incident that eliminated some of the faster competitors. Then on the course down the south side of the island, when the yachts were short tacking inshore to avoid the head tide, the cutter *Arrow* took bottom and the large cutter, *Alarm,* turned back to stand by her. Shortly after this in the short tacking, the fast cutters *Freak* and *Volant* had a collision and dropped out. So, although *America* was the leader at this point, she might not have held the lead in the light weather that was to come if these other yachts had not been eliminated, for as a matter of fact the small cutter *Aurora* of 47 tons (*America* was 170 tons), finished only eighteen minutes after *America*. So *Aurora,* although not considered as speedy as some of the cutters which had dropped out, would have beaten *America* easily with the allowance she would have had under any measurement rule whatsoever. This does not sound much like the myths, "A hawk among pigeons," "There is no second, your Majesty," etc., that have been taught to American children during the last hundred years.

I will give a few notes about *America* because the various pictures of her confuse many people. Her approximate dimensions were: L.O.A. 100′ 6″; L.W.L. 90′ 4″; beam 22′ 6″; draft 11′ 6″.

America's first race was at New York May 13, 1851, and during her life she competed in 51 races, of which she won twelve. She went out of commission as a yacht on October 15, 1901. Originally she had been painted white, but after crossing the Atlantic she went to the dry-dock at Havre where she was completely refitted and repainted. This time her topsides were black, which I believe they were to remain until 1887 when she was again painted white and modernized by Edward Burgess. She was painted black once more when prepared for presentation to the Navy about 1920.

The changes in her rig were about as follows: *America* was designed as a bald-headed schooner, like our packet schooners, but while standing by at Cowes before her race around Wight, a temporary extension of her bowsprit (which might be called a jib boom), was rigged to set a jib from, and *America* carried a jib ahead of her forestaysail in the first part of this race. But the spar carried away when about halfway around the island so she is sometimes shown in pictures carrying a jib, although in most of her

other races during the first few years she appeared as in Figure 51. When only a few years old the foot of both of her masts rotted out and so the masts were shortened a few feet to eliminate the rotted section.

The *America* was about twelve years old when she was serving as a dispatch boat for the United States Navy. She then had topmasts and a jib boom complete with martingale and dolphin striker. Whether these were added by the Navy or when under British ownership I do not know. After the Civil War the Navy spent considerable money on *America* ($30,000, it is said), mostly with the aim of preparing her for the races of 1870 when *Cambria* came over to be the first challenger.

In 1875, when Donald McKay was giving her an extensive overhaul, he plumbed her masts and, though the raking masts of 1800 were out of style by then, this certainly took away much of her character. It was the last job McKay undertook, and perhaps not his best one.

At about this time, when under the ownership of Ben Butler, *America* made some very fast runs and was said to log fifteen knots or better for several hours so that General Butler decided to have her modernized in an attempt to compete with the newer yachts. Of course you must understand that *America* had been repeatedly repaired before this and almost totally rebuilt while under British ownership. She had been built to a great extent of soft woods, so as early as 1858 she suffered extensively from dry rot, hence was expensively rebuilt by a ship builder named Pitcher, who replaced her rotted frames and completely replanked her with elm below water and teak topsides so she was sound enough, at least in parts, for hard driving.

In 1886, General Butler had Edward Burgess, who was our leading yacht designer, made extensive changes. She was given a new sail plan of increased area, and her wooden outer keel was removed and replaced with nearly 60,000 pounds of outside lead. Her overhangs, which had been repeatedly changed before, were lengthened so that in the last of her sailing years she looked as in Figure 52. But *America* was too long on the keel to turn quickly, and we know today that her sharp, deep forefoot had detrimental surface resistance, though undoubtedly she always was a vessel that could be driven fast on a straight course in strong breezes. The author has designed half a dozen or so yachts of this old American type and found that they had the following advantages:

1. They are cheaper to build because of their straight keel and no thick deadwood to shape up.

2. They can be shallower draft than the modern models and still carry sail well and not make excessive leeway.

3. They carry their floorline for a long distance fore and aft.

4. They do not throw much spray because of their easy entrance and flaring bows.

5. They are most excellent sea boats, with a slow motion, and can be driven hard in a following sea without steering hard.

6. They can be driven much faster under power than the modern types on account of their long water line.
7. They are faster under sail for their cost or sail area than modern models and can make fast runs when cruising without the multiplicity of expensive head sails that require a large crew.

As a proof of the speed of this model, a signed statement of a three-day run of *Ticonderoga* in 1956 on a voyage between the Virgin Islands and Miami certifies a noon-to-noon run of 264 miles, and 667 miles in 72 hours. While you may say it is easy to get a yacht up to 10 knots occasionally, I will say it is very difficult to maintain that speed for 24 hours, for if at times she drops down to seven or eight knots, then she must go real fast to make up for it. But for a yacht 72 feet overall to maintain 11 knots for 24 hours certainly makes our modern models ridiculous.

For instance, the *Twelves* that raced the summer of 1958 and are only about three feet shorter than *Ticonderoga,* probably never made nine knots over the Cup course even though they had trained crews which could set dangerous rule-cheating sails. Consequently, as the result of measurement rules which penalize the speed-giving qualities of a sailing yacht, we seem to have gone backward in the last hundred years, and while *Ticonderoga* is no more capable of winning races under the present measurement rules than *America* was able to beat the British under their tonnage rules, this model is far superior for cruising than anything we have.

But we must go back to the effect of *America*'s visit to England. Here, although other writers on the subject have said she affected the design of the time, I would say she had little effect, for the English were to continue with their tonnage rules for another thirty years. One English cutter, *Alarm,* was extensively rebuilt, remodeled, and rerigged in imitation of *America*—Figure 53 shows her sailing. We will speak of her later. Several English yachts were lengthened and sharpened forward, and since then most British yachts have laced the foot of their sails to the boom when racing, although up until now the loose-footed sail has its advocates for cruising.

The real stimulus of *America*'s visit was to start international yacht racing, with the first races of importance those between the Swedish schooner *Sverige* and *America,* then owned in England by Lord deBlaquiere. It seems that the Swedes, who were always good sailormen, thought they at least could beat the Americans boat to boat, but they made the mistake of adopting or copying many of *America*'s features instead of sticking to their own types. *Sverige* even had a sharper and deeper entrance than *America.*

Fig. 53. The cutter ALARM was rebuilt and remodeled, imitating the AMERICA

However, most of her shape above water was quite similar, with the exception of the overhanging part of the bow which was a quite homely, overdone copy of *America*; *Sverige*, though, was a little larger and said to have been 280 tons to *America*'s 170 tons. They raced for a hundred pounds a side with an agreement that there should be over a seven knot wind at the start. The first leg of the race was to leeward when, with her size, *Sverige* took the lead and held it until the latter part of the windward leg, but *America* finally won by 26 minutes.

The small cutter *Wildfire*, of 48 tons, was also in this race and beat the two schooners quite handsomely on all points of sailing. This race was 55 miles long and held October 9, 1852.

The notoriety that *America* acquired in 1851 induced two smaller yachts to try their luck in England in the next two years; they were *Sylvie* and *Truant*. *Sylvie* was a centerboard sloop 80′ L.O.A.; 68′ L.W.L.; 24′ 6″ beam; and 6′ draft, of 68 tons. She was designed by George Steers and built by W. H. Brown—as was *America*. *Sylvie* came out in 1851. At first she had several owners and did well in races over here, but in 1853, under the ownership of Louis A. Depau, she sailed to Havre, as *America* had, where she was put in racing trim, then proceeded to Cowes where she raced with fair success.

The British yachtsmen did not like her and called her a freak with a false drop keel that swung down to some 15 feet, so they said. Indeed, although *Sylvie* appears quite good-looking in some pictures, she was somewhat of a freak, for Steers made her even sharper, or more hungry forward than *America*. She was also very beamy and shallow, so she proved very little other than causing the principal British yacht clubs to bar centerboard or drop keels. However, the British have always disliked centerboards because their yachts often lie on bottom at low tide when a centerboard invariably becomes jammed or the slot damaged. *Sylvie* could not be sold in England so she sailed back to this country in 1856, having rather a hard voyage in which she carried away her boom and bowsprit. She was later changed to a schooner and raced for many years, not being broken up until 1906.

The other yacht, *Truant*, went over in 1852 and was what would be considered very small in those days. She really was one of the first of our so-called sandbaggers only about 22′ L.O.A. She was designed by Fish, who became famous for building boats of this type, and was owned by R. M. Grinnell. Figure 54 shows *Truant* racing in England, and is taken from a lithograph by T. Dutton, who made the well-known pictures of *America*, and who drew the clipper ships better than any artist of any time.

Truant seems to have made a better record than *America,* for I think she won all her races while abroad, racing at Kingston, Liverpool and Queenstown. On the Thames on May 18, 1852, she beat the English keelboats an immense distance. Small boats were hardly recognized in those days, but now that boats of her size, and even smaller, are the principal racers, *Truant's* history should be looked up for few people know about her today.

Fig. 54. TRUANT, a 22-foot sandbagger, was raced in England in 1852

8 Ocean Racers and Centerboarders

There was little yachting activity in England in the seasons of 1854-55 because of the Crimean War, for the British Navy required all sailors and seamen who were available. Fortunately the war was of short duration. At about this time the Swedes sent down the large schooner *Aurora Borealis,* 250 tons, and that kept up interest in international racing. Also several towns and yacht clubs offered valuable trophies and large purses, often of a hundred guineas or more, so that by the season of 1857 interest in the sport of yachting was increasing by leaps and bounds.

In that year the yachts of the United Kingdom numbered 511 cutters, 138 schooners, 75 yawls, 37 other rigs, and 19 steam yachts, with an aggregate tonnage of 30,000. By this time the Fifes of Fairlie, Scotland, were becoming famous for building the fastest cutters, and the sport of yachting in the picturesque waters of Scotland was growing rapidly. During the Crimean War yachting was kept up as usual in Ireland, and several of the most important regattas were for yachts manned completely with corinthian crews, and were raced for purses of a hundred pounds sterling. So we see yachting was widespread throughout the British Isles, and corinthian racing was becoming popular. I note that from this time on, many races in Great Britain required an amateur helmsman, but in America professional helmsmen were rather the rule until about 1910.

The type of yacht in vogue for racing in England was still the so-called cutter, or a single-masted vessel quite similar to the revenue cutters of a few years previously. They were beginning to have several sizes of jibs, and forestaysails of different weights for different breezes, and several sizes of topsails, all of the type called an English topsail; that is, they were set with the yard parallel with the gaff, as the topsail is set on a lugger. So club topsails must have been in use from about 1850.

Una was a Newport catboat sent over to England as a present to the Marquis of Connyngham from William Butler Duncan in 1852. As a direct result, catboats of this type at once became popular in England and Europe for use on lakes and sheltered waters; and in these countries the catboat types for many years were called Una Boats. The catboat of this type was originated in Newport, R. I., where apparently the first scheduled races for small boats were held in this country well before 1800. At Newport these single-sailed boats were called Point Boats, for they were mostly built on a point in Newport harbor that is now called Long Wharf.

Apparently the first ocean race that had several competitors was the race from Dublin to Cork, sponsored by the Royal Cork Yacht Club in 1859. In this affair there were participating nine cutters, seven schooners and a yawl, all of good size. They had heavy, disagreeable weather part of the way, but the three leaders finished close together, within five minutes.

By this time, or around 1860, the Civil War in this country was looming on the horizon, and the political tension very severely curtailed yachting in America for some five or more years. As a consequence of the war there was little surplus money to be spent in yachting, for this country was rather hard up from 1860 to 1870. In England, however, several large schooners of between 100 and 200 tons were built, and many important regattas were held, and I would like the reader to realize that at about this time seven-eighths of the world's large yacht races were held in England. And I would like to impress on his mind that Great Britain has been the principal yacht racing country from 1650 onward.

In December, 1861, H.R.H. the Prince Consort died and as Victoria went into very deep mourning almost all regattas of 1862 were called off. Consequently, a great number of match races were held where the larger yachts, particularly the schooners, challenged one another for rather high stakes.

An Ocean Race from Ryde to Cherbourg

In the season of 1863 there were several ocean races, the most important of which was from Ryde, I.W., to Cherbourg for a prize of £100, sponsored by the Royal Victoria Club. In this race were eleven cutters, seven schooners, and two yawls, ranging in size between 30 and 175 tons. From this time on, ocean races have been held several times a year in some part of Europe, and particularly in Ireland. While it is true that ocean racing abroad dropped somewhat in popularity between 1890 and about 1910, the years when yacht racing was at its height, ocean racing never had been popular in America until the editor of *The Rudder*, Thomas Fleming Day, devoted much effort to rejuvenating it around 1905 in the hope that more sea-worthy types of boats would be developed. I am afraid Mr. Day must be pretty uneasy in his grave when he hears of the types of sail plans the present ocean racers are using, and of the price they cost.

The first important trans-Atlantic ocean race was held in 1866 and started on December 11. It came about somewhat as follows: near the end of the yachting season of 1866 the owners of the large schooners *Fleetwing* and *Vesta* were at a dinner when the question of the comparative speed and endurance of their yachts came up. These two yachts and the schooner *Henrietta* had raced two or three challenge races for $500 a side during the summer, and all three appeared to be of about the same speed and unusually fast, which made their owners a bit cocky. Perhaps also they had dined particularly well and were somewhat flush, but when one owner said to the other words to this general effect: "Your vessel may be able to hold or beat my yacht in sheltered waters, but at sea in a breeze she can never hold her"; the other perhaps quickly replied, "What do you say—Sandy Hook to Cowes?"; "Done," answered the first, "in December." And here both owners agreed to make the stakes $30,000 a side. So with the preliminaries settled, it became simply a matter of arranging dates and rules.

When Mr. James Gordon Bennett (the donor of many cups, and twice Commodore of the New York Yacht Club, and owner of large yachts for 60 years), heard of the race he requested to be allowed to enter his schooner *Henrietta* at the same stakes, so the total stakes were $90,000. Perhaps some of my modern readers will not think this is a great sum of money, but at that time wooden schooners

of this size, 200 tons and 105 or 110 feet over all, cost only about half of this sum, for at the close of the wooden ship building period there were many good ship carpenters who received $3.00 or so a day, and good materials were plentiful.

Some people think this was the most remarkable yacht race ever run, basing their opinion on the length of the course, the speed of the yachts, the amount of the stakes, and the season of the year, and I think it truly remarkable that all contestants carried their regular summer racing rigs and were on time at the start with so little time for preparation. The yachts' characteristics were as follows:

Henrietta was a keel schooner built for James Gordon Bennett in 1861 by Henry Steers (nephew of George Steers), at Greenport, N. Y., after a design by William Tooker. In 1864 she was altered and lengthened at both ends so that her dimensions were, L.O.A., 107'; beam, 22'; draft, 11'6"; tonnage 205. Her model was fine and sharp at the water line at both ends; her rig was described in the writings of the time as "sailor-like, trim, and taut-o from truck to keelson."

Fleetwing was a keel schooner built for George Osgood, Esq., from his own designs, by Van Deusen of Long Island, N. Y., in 1865. Her dimensions were, L.O.A., 106'; beam, 23'; draft, 12'; tonnage, 206. She carried 60 tons of iron ballast.

Vesta was a centerboard schooner built for Pierre Lorillard, Esq., by David Carll at City Island, N. Y. Her dimensions were, L.O.A., 105'; beam, 25'; draft, 7'6", with centerboard down, 15'; tonnage 201.

There was little time to prepare the yachts for the race but they all had square sails made for the crossing. The start of this race was painted by three or four artists. It was a bright, clear December day with a brisk northwest wind and quite a fleet of steamers ran out to Sandy Hook to see the start, for the general public's imagination had been captivated by the daring character of this winter race. The racers were towed out to the Hook but promptly cast off their tows and started the long race at 1 P.M., December 11, 1866.

The northwest wind held for the first few days, then they had some snow squalls. Up to this time they had all three led at one time or another, though they were spread out north and south as a result of holding different courses. On the 19th and 20th they experienced a heavy gale, and while running under a double-reefed foresail, a sea swept the deck of *Fleetwing*, washing eight men out of the cockpit. Two managed to grab something, but the other six were lost. In the confusion which ensued *Fleetwing* broached-to (I suppose the man at the helm had been washed away), and broke her jibboom (outer bowsprit), so she was crippled badly.

On Christmas Eve, *Vesta* made the first landfall and picked up the Scilly Isles lights at 6:55 P.M. *Henrietta* picked them up 15 minutes later but may have actually been ahead for she was farther to the south and thus farther from the lights. However, in the sail along the south of England *Henrietta* took the lead and *Vesta* lost several hours, for the English pilot whom they picked up took them to the south of The Needles light, and when he found his position had to tack back to The Needles. So *Vesta* did not arrive at Cowes until 8 hours 45 minutes after *Henrietta*. In the meantime, *Fleetwing,* which must have been close astern and sailed the proper course, slipped in between and arrived at Cowes 40 minutes ahead of *Vesta*. The time of the yachts was:

	Time over course	Distance sailed	Best day's run
Henrietta	13 dys, 21 h, 55 m.	3,106 miles	280 miles
Fleetwing	14 dys, 6 h, 10 m.	3,135 miles	270 miles
Vesta	14 dys, 6 h, 50 m.	3,144 miles	277 miles

The average speed of the three yachts was about the same, and it might be said of this race that *Henrietta* did win but *Fleetwing* would have won if she had not had the accident in the gale, or *Vesta* might have won if she had not been taken off the course by the pilot in the last few miles. But yacht races often consist of "ifs." However, the speed of the yachts was outstanding and compared very favorably with any clipper ship records over this course and was faster than some of the steamers of that time. Altogether this race did a great deal to enhance the reputation of the American yachtsman, and particularly the New York Yacht Club.

Two great characters were on that race. One was Captain Samuel Samuels, the famous captain of the clipper ship *Dreadnaught,* and author of the book "From Forecastle to Cabin." He was captain of *Henrietta,* and perhaps it was his good navigation that brought her in a position to take the best advantage of wind and tide. The other character was Neils Olsen who was steward on *Vesta*. Later in life he became superintendent of the New York Yacht Club and served in that capacity for some 35 years, becoming well known to three generations of prominent yachtsmen. He compiled one of our earliest yacht registers, covering the years 1874 to 1887, and the New York Yacht Club is indebted to him for much of its early data or history. W. P. Stephens says that Niels was a walking encyclopedia of yachting information and an authority on yachting history. He was mate on board both *Magic* and the schooner *Columbia* when these vessels defended the America's Cup.

Henrietta, Fleetwing and *Vesta* sailed back the next year at different dates, and Mr. Bennett came over on *Henrietta,* but I have been told that the owner of one of the schooners was so fed-up with ocean sailing or the sea that he did not return for two years, and then on the deck of a steamer.

To give the reader an idea of the many Atlantic crossings made by American sailing yachts of about this time, here is a list taken from Niels Olsen's American Yachting List of 1874.

Year	Rig	Name	Ton.	Ports	Time
1851	Schr.	*America*	170	N.Y.-Havre	21d.
1853	Slp.	*Silvie*	105	Halifax-Havre	16d, 12hr.
1856	Slp.	*Silvie*	105	Southampt'n-N.Y.	34d.
1857	Slp.	*Charter Oak*	23	N.Y.-Liverpool	
1858	Slp.	*Chris. Columbus*	45	N.Y.-Cowes	45d.
1863	Schr.	*Gipsey*	135	N.Y.-Queenstown	19d.
1866	Slp.	*Alice*	27	Boston-Cowes	19d.
1867	Slp.	*Alice*	27	Cowes-Boston	34d.

1866	Schr.	*Henrietta*	205	Sandy-H'k-Cowes	13d, 21h, 55m.
1866	Schr.	*Fleetwing*	206	Sandy-H'k-Cowes	14d, 6h, 10m.
1866	Schr.	*Vesta*	201	Sandy-H'k-Cowes	14d, 6h, 50m.
1867	Schr.	*Vesta*	201	Cowes-N.Y.	34d.
1867	Schr.	*Henrietta*	205	Cowes-N.Y.	36d.
1867	Schr.	*Fleetwing*	206	Cowes-New Bedford	42d, 6h.
1868	Schr.	*Sappho*	274	N.Y.-Cowes	14d.
1868	Schr.	*Sappho*	274	Cowes-N.Y.	32d.
1869	Schr.	*Sappho*	310	N.Y.-Queenstown	12d, 9h, 36m.
1869	Schr.	*Dauntless*	268	N.Y.-Queenstown	12d, 17h, 6m.
1869	Schr.	*Meteor*	293	N.Y.-Cowes	
1870	Schr.	*Dauntless*	268	Queenstown-N.Y.	23d, 7h.
1870	Schr.	*Sappho*	310	Cowes-N.Y.	32d.
1871	Schr.	*Enchantress*	253	N.Y.-Gibraltar	
1871	Schr.	*Enchantress*	253	Cowes-Newport	34d.
1872	Schr.	*Sappho*	310	N.Y.-Cowes	18d.
1872	Schr.	*Dauntless*	268	N.Y.-Cowes	25d.
1872	Schr.	*Dauntless*		N.Y.-Cowes	35d.
1873	Schr.	*Enchantress*	253	N.Y.-Cowes	22d.
1873	Schr.	*Faustine*	95	N.Y.-Cowes	18d.
1874	Schr.	*Viking*	157	N.Y.-Cowes	30d.

No one, I believe, knows where the schooner rig originated, for the principal reason that there were several almost identical rigs used by other countries well before 1700. I have seen a picture of a Roman coaster of about the year 100 that was a crude bald-headed schooner, so I take little stock in the myth that the schooner originated in Gloucester. I do have a copy of a Dutch map of 1682 which calls an inlet just north of Cape Ann "Schoon Haven," which may indicate that schooners were built or used in this region—Ipswich and Annisquam—before Gloucester was settled. However, the slight difference between the schooner and the older rig called a Ballahou, was that the schooner carried a standing or permanent stay, called a spring stay, between the mast heads, while the mainmast of the Ballahou was supported by a mainstay that ran between the mainmast head and the deck near the foremast partners, and many topsail schooners, including American slavers, had this rig. In the 16th and 17th centuries France was the most advanced in developing new rigs, and in that country the schooner was called a Goelette.

However, at the time we are speaking of, perhaps 1860, the schooner was considered our national rig and used very extensively for coasting and yachting here while in England they stuck to the cutter rig in the smaller and middle-size yachts. After the *America* and the Swedish schooner *Aurora Borealis* raced in England, the English were designing and building very fine large keel schooners, generally a more seagoing lot than ours, simply because the English schooners often spent the winter in the Mediterranean, while ours were laid up in the winters.

Many of our large schooner yachts like *Vesta* were centerboarders, and for many years the centerboarder was considered the fastest. The reason for it was that in those days all, or nearly all, of the yachts carried inside ballast, hence there was not so much difference between the stiffness of the keel and centerboard yachts. While the centerboarder might only draw about eight feet with the board up, with it down her draft might be some fifteen feet, and as the board then would be down in good stable water that was not running to leeward, the centerboarder in moderate weather was the fastest to windward, while of course in running before it with the board up she had an advantage. Speaking of the centerboard being down in stable water, I have to mention some experiments of the past, for there is at present some experimentation with bow centerboards developed from tank tests to help the balance of a yacht when carrying large head sails. I speak of this now to show the value of a thorough knowledge of the past.

Well, when the cup boats of 1893 were built, John Paine designed *Jubilee* with a bow centerboard to help in adjusting her balance. She was a rather deep finkeeler whose flat plate was down in solid water, but her bow centerboard was quite near the surface for she had a rather shallow hull. However, they were much surprised that when this bow centerboard was lowered *Jubilee* carried a lee helm instead of the weather helm that was expected. The reason is that in a good breeze in open water the surface water is moving to leeward while the deeper water is more stationary, so when close-hauled the bow centerboard of *Jubilee* was actually trying to make her head off or make more leeway.

My father was a great believer in centerboards and used them on *Vigilant* and *Resolute* and a score of other sizeable sailing yachts, and probably would have used them on other moderately deep yachts except for the expense, etc. Starling Burgess used a small centerboard on one or two of his J boats, but they were in the right place, down through the keel. Centerboards, however, are apt to jam in all sizes of yachts, so they are often a nuisance.

As I have said before, the English have always detested centerboards on sizeable yachts for they often ground or take bottom in harbor at low tide. So the large centerboard schooner was typically American and I think the largest of all was *Ambassadress,* built for William Astor in 1877. She was 146'2" L.O.A.; 130'6" L.W.L.; 28'2" beam; 11' draft.

The large centerboard schooners received a rather bad name because of the capsize of *Mohawk* in 1876. She was a large vessel with a L.O.A. of about 140'; L.W.L., 121'; beam, 30'4", and only 6' draft, but with the centerboard down, 31'6" draft, so she may have been the most extreme of the large schooners in great beam and shallow draft. The catastrophe happened about like this: *Mohawk* lay at anchor in company with several other yachts just off the New York Yacht Club station at Stapleton, Staten Island. She had a party aboard with several guests besides the owner and his wife. They were just getting under way for an afternoon's sail so had her mainsail, foresail, and both topsails set and sheeted flat. Some say the squall gave some warning and others say it was a freak twister that suddenly came down over Staten Island. At any rate, *Mohawk* capsized with several of her party below. It seems that not only her ballast shifted but some of her heavy furniture slid to leeward and pinned down some of the party, including the owner's wife. When *Mohawk* settled and sank, they were drowned. I believe five lost their lives in the accident, but all the crew, with the exception of the cabin boy who was with the guests in the after cabin, escaped and were picked up by several boats in the vicinity. W. P. Stephens in some of his writings says, and I quote, "In point of fact, *Mohawk* was as safe a vessel as ever floated. She was lost through the grossest carelessness and in consequence of the over-confidence felt in her stability. There has been no vessel built in this world that cannot be wrecked by careless handling, and that the *Mohawk* upset was in noway due to any defect of model. Properly handled she was more than ordinarily safe."

While there seem to be some doubtful statements in the above, I realize that many of Mr. Stephen's time would think *Mohawk* a safe yacht, and I agree that she should have been with the able crews that were customary in those days, but I believe the general public and myself think the larger yachts should not be capsizeable.

My purpose is to emphasize that the large centerboard schooner was a customary American type of this time, and capable of rather unusual speed; nevertheless the swing toward deeper, narrower noncapsizeable yachts in America can be dated from the capsize of *Mohawk*.

9 Developments in England

Two interesting developments in English yachting at about this time were the barring of shifting ballast and the development of the spinnaker to take the place of a square sail when running. Shifting ballast was barred in 1863 and, though the owners of almost all small craft had strong feelings in favor of shifting ballast, still the principal yacht clubs made a bold stand. Thus shifting ballast was barred in England many years before it was barred here.

That is another reason, besides the tonnage rules, why English yachts were much deeper than ours—to get the ballast low. We were to go on with our sandbaggers and semi-sandbaggers for another twenty years or so, with the final result that the smaller American yachts were half as wide as they were long, while some of the small and medium-size English cutters were only one-sixth as wide as they were long.

The Appearance of the Spinnaker

It is said or written that a sail like a spinnaker was first used by the British yacht *Niobe,* owned by W. Gordon, about 1867. The word "spinnaker" is a sailor's derivation which came about because a yacht named *Sphinx* was an early adopter of this sail. At first the sailors called the sail a "spinxer," but in pronouncing it quickly, in time it became "spinnaker."

At this time there were several types of sails tried for running before the wind, and there was strong feeling against booming-out sails, as it was called. However, apparently because the earlier cutters had used square sails when running, the boomed-out sails were not barred, though they were often protested.

The Lug Sail

I must also note that other rigs besides the cutter and schooner were tried or used in England, and the principal one was the three-masted lugger, which apparently was a descendant of the type often used by English smugglers of earlier times. It differed from the French smugglers in that the English set a large sail in one piece that was reefed from the bottom, while the French seemed to favor setting a topsail or two above the mainsail.

The *New Moon* must have been one of the largest of them for most were smaller semi-open boats and, although I have never found much written data on the English lug-rigged yachts, we do occasionally hear of them and the lugsail certainly was the most popular rig for fishermen almost from the Orkneys to Land's End. It is said that one of the large lugsailed craft was extremely fast on a reach and could get up to sixteen knots. This craft was reported to have been built at Yarmouth, was of light lapstrake construction, mostly open, and carried a large crew and shifting ballast.

While we in this country used sandbags for shifting ballast the English used the smaller and heavier arrangement of small lead shot in bags. Perhaps it was the barring of shifting ballast that knocked out the light, shallow-hulled luggers, or perhaps under the various YRA rules, which came into effect soon after this, they had no chance, for the

Yacht Racing Association was organized in November, 1875. However, the deep-hulled English cutters were a much safer type, with good head room and possibly were the fastest to windward.

I will note though that the English had a type faster than the cutter before 1850. Some of the older authorities (among them H. C. Folkard, in "The Sailing Boat"), state that the three-masted lug-rigged Yarmouth yawls of about sixty feet were the fastest sailboats in the world.

Sappho

The next American yacht of importance that made a great name and raced abroad was the schooner *Sappho*. She was a large vessel, 134′ L.O.A.; 120′ L.W.L.; 24′9″ beam; 274 tons. She was built by the Poillon Brothers, shipwrights, in Brooklyn, on speculation in 1867 but was unsuccessful in racing or in finding a purchaser so was sent to England in 1868. She made a fast crossing in fourteen days, but in a race around the Isle of Wight on August 25 was soundly beaten by the four large British yachts that sailed against her—the cutter *Oimara*, 165 tons; cutter *Condor*, 129 tons; schooner *Cambria*, 188 tons; and schooner *Ailine*, 212 tons.

As *Sappho* received no offers for purchase she returned to New York where she was bought by William P. Douglas. He apparently thought she could be improved by changes, so turned her over to famous Captain Bob Fish who seemed to know what was wanted, for he stripped the planking off her bilges and hipped, or padded out, her frames amidships so that she was wider at the waterline but had considerable tumble home amidships. *Sappho* proved on her second trip to England to be very fast, particularly on her eastward crossing with a strong breeze on the quarter and a smooth sea the whole way. Her time from Sandy Hook Lightship to Queenstown, 2875 miles, was 12 days, 9 hours and 36 minutes. And this may still be the record over that particular course, for all I know. Her best day's run was 315 miles at an average of over 13 knots, which seems remarkable, but even then her speed-length ratio was less than that of *Ticonderoga's* 11 knots average for 24 hours, mentioned earlier. It does seem that we have to go back to the older types for fast sailing.

Early in the season of 1869, Mr. Douglas, *Sappho's* owner, made arrangements with Mr. James Ashbury, the owner of *Cambria*, for a series of three races for a Fifty Guinea Cup, boat to boat, and, although *Cambria* was the smaller vessel, she had beaten *Sappho* quite handily the previous year. The three races were of approximately sixty miles each, two, windward and leeward races and one, triangular. In the first race, May 10, 1869, *Sappho* drew well ahead and rounded the mark boat first, but Ashbury claimed the mark boat was misplaced, so withdrew *Cambria* with the race little more than half completed.

The next race was scheduled for May 14, and the race committee gave the course from the Nab to and around the breakwater at Cherbourg and back. There was a strong west wind blowing so Ashbury would not start, claiming

it was not a windward and leeward course, which of course was so, for it would have been a reach each way. So *Sappho* sailed over the course alone under her four lowers with topmasts housed.

The third race was May 17 over a triangular course in which the first leg happened to be dead to windward, so *Cambria* did very well at first and led near the weather mark. On the last tack, however, she overstood the mark and *Sappho* took the lead and romped away from *Cambria* on the broad reaches to the finish. Although *Sappho* won all these races it was not a satisfactory test of the yachts, and we must remember that she was much the larger vessel and is said to have had some 3,000 square feet more sail area than *Cambria*.

The First America's Cup Challenge

Cambria was also a fine, able vessel. Ashbury simply did not ask for a handicap because *Cambria* had beaten *Sappho* so easily the previous year. This of course shows what a great difference a little change in model and management can make, and there is no doubt that Captain Bob Fish deserves the praise showered on him in those times, now nearly ninety years ago. While *Sappho* was a justly famous yacht *Cambria* did very well in a great many important races. However, Ashbury was so keyed up and enthusiastic over yacht racing that he became the first challenger for the America's Cup. But there was much controversy before terms for the race could be accepted as Ashbury never could seem to understand that the Cup must be raced for strictly according to the deed of gift— that is, in the waters and under the rules of the yacht club holding the Cup. But the challenge was finally accepted through the Royal Thames Yacht Club in behalf of Mr. Ashbury.

To me one of the interesting things of this first challenge was that *Cambria* sailed over apparently under her racing spars and sails. This came about as follows: Mr. James Gordon Bennett, who had owned *Henrietta* in the great ocean race of 1866, had acquired the large handsome schooner *L'Hirondelle* and changed her name to *Dauntless*. She sailed to England the same year as *Sappho* on her second visit and made nearly as good a crossing, but on the whole did not do particularly well in the racing there.

In the following year, 1870, the owners of *Cambria* and *Dauntless* arranged a match race across the Atlantic for a 250-Guinea cup. The start of the race was made July 4 off Gaunt Head, Ireland, and *Cambria* arrived at the finish line—Sandy Hook Lightship—1 hour and 17 minutes ahead of *Dauntless*, and it was reported they were in sight of each other at the finish. This slight victory of *Cambria* made many people think that she would take the Cup back with her, but as the two yachts had sailed quite different courses on the way over it was not a good test of their comparative speeds. Nevertheless, the season of 1870 was to see, I believe, the most racing of the large schooners we have ever had in America. In my opinion, the Cup races of 1870 were not fair for it was ridiculous to pit one challenger against a whole fleet of defenders, several of which were larger than *Cambria*. Of course people said the *America* had won the Cup when racing against a fleet of British yachts, and seemed to think that incident made it fair. But the conditions were really quite different, for in 1851 the *America* was simply invited to compete in one of their annual races around the Isle of Wight, and I suppose few of the British yachts were as keen about beating her as they were to win over their class rivals. Of course no one could foretell that the Cup the *America* won that day would be put up as an international trophy for the Mistress of the Seas.

Some people have intimated that I have been pro-British in these writings, and I would like to say that is not so, but I have read up on what we can call "the matter" and am only trying to strike a happy medium between what has been written in the past by both sides. I believe the truth is more instructive than exaggerated opinions, influenced by egotistical patriotism, and certainly the time has come when there should be no spite shown between the Anglo-Saxon races, and that true sportsmanship is best expressed by sticking to the truth. I think some of the boasting denials and accusations of the past are ridiculous and have done harm to the sport on both sides of the Atlantic.

The First Race

The one race for the Cup on August 8, 1870, was from a so-called anchor start that was then customary over here but has now long been out of vogue. The 24 competitors were lined up at anchor off the New York Yacht Club station at Stapleton, Staten Island, with *Cambria* to windward and the old *America,* which the Navy had prepared for the race, next in line; then the large schooners *Rambler, Dauntless, Fleetwing,* and so on down to the smaller leeward yachts. It must have been a long line and an impressive sight, and it is said that everybody who could get a place on anything that floated was there to see the spectacle. It was a fine day with a good sailing breeze. The schooner *Magic* was the first to get her sails up and under way and thus get away in the lead, but *Cambria*'s crew did well and she was close astern, while *America* with her Navy crew was among the last to get started.

The course was from Stapleton down the Narrows to the S.W. Spit Buoy, thence out and around the lightship off Sandy Hook with the return over the same course, making the L-shaped course used for many years by the New York Yacht Club. On the way in the wind was strong and *Cambria* made some gain on the leaders, but unfortunately carried away her fore-topmast. At the finish *Magic* was well ahead and as she was a much smaller vessel than *Cambria* she received considerable time allowance so, with corrected time, *Magic* beat *Cambria* some 39 minutes. The other yachts in the squadron which came in ahead of *Cambria* were *Idler, Sylvie, Dauntless, America, Madgie, Phantom, Alice* and *Halcyon.* While this was the only race for the Cup that year, Mr. Ashbury stayed over and raced *Cambria* in most of the season's New York Yacht Club races and gave cups for both the schooners and sloops in a race off Newport. There *Cambria* came in second in the schooner class, winning a cup put up by the club.

10 *Big Schooner Days*

There was a great deal of large schooner racing that summer and *Cambria* sometimes raced day after day. Altogether I think she raced ten times when here, and both Mr. Ashbury and Mr. Bennett were worked up to such a high state of enthusiasm that Mr. Bennett gave the fine trophies known as the Brenton's Reef Cup and Cape May Cup for which the larger yachts have raced occasionally up to World War I. It is interesting to note that the British challenger *Genesta* took both of these cups to England in 1885, but the Brenton's Reef Cup was brought back by *Navahoe* in 1893, and the Cape May Cup forfeited by H.M. King Edward VII whose *Britannia* was the last holder of the cup in English waters. The deed of gift of the cup stated that if the winning yacht could not defend it it must be returned to the New York Yacht Club, and when the American schooner *Ingomar* challenged for it it was returned to the club because the king in the meantime had sold *Britannia*. This was about 1903, if I remember rightly. Figures 55-56 show the Cape May and Brenton's Reef Cups, and in speaking of the wonderful trophies of the 1870's we should note that Tiffany at that time had designers and workmen who could adorn their work with nautical motifs in a way that has never been excelled here, but perhaps the younger generation will not call it art.

After this wonderful season of racing Mr. Ashbury was satisfied that *Cambria* was not fast enough to compete successfully with the large American schooners so on his return to England he ordered a new schooner of a more racy type. He again went to Ratsey for the design and the Ratseys at that time were probably the best yacht designers and builders in both the British Isles and in Europe. The new schooner yacht was named *Livonia* and in my opinion she was an all around handsome vessel of nice proportions. Figure 57 shows her sailing. If at times I praise some of

Fig. 55. The Cape May Cup

the English yachts it is only to emphasize the fact that our craft had to be very fast to beat them.

Now I will say something more about what the old timers used to call "the schooner days," for between something like 1870 and 1880 we had many large schooner yachts that were between 90 and 100 feet on the waterline. It would be entirely out of the question to have such large racing yachts today even if there were no income tax for these large sail area vessels required expert and hearty crews who were sailormen by profession, and who spent their winters manning the sailing ships of the merchant marine. The total crew to man the fleet of the schooners must have been over five hundred. But show me a willing professional today who could splice, reef, or take the helm with any of those boys.

I have known many men who knew and spoke very affectionately of these large schooners, among the last of them being Commodore Ralph M. Munroe and my father, Nathanael G. Herreshoff, both of whom were between twenty and thirty years old in the schooner days. Commodore Munroe was an early photographer who took pictures of these yachts, and my father was a great admirer of them. Among other things they considered them fast, safe and comfortable sea boats, and thought the centerboarders the most comfortable in a seaway. This is due to the fact that when the centerboard is partly raised a yacht will make leeway when a wave strikes her, or move to leeward when receiving the blow. These two thought that to be able to adjust the leeway by raising the centerboard was a great advantage.

Some of the large schooners of those days had fine accommodations; Figure 58 shows the cabin of *Magic,* and she was by no means a large schooner of the times.

Fig. 56. The Brenton's Reef Cup

Fig. 57. LIVONIA sailing

Over the fireplace the decorations include cutlasses and large size horse pistols, while the table is decorated with a magnum of champagne. Though *Magic* seemed to use square-bottom glasses *Dauntless,* when owned by Commodore C. H. Colt, was famous for her round-bottomed old-fashioned tumblers that required one to finish his drink before setting the glass down. I guess there were hearty men both forward and aft in those days, but while there is no space to enumerate some of the great squadron runs and match races of the great schooner days, it is my belief that the coming in of the steam yacht was the principal cause of the decline of the large schooners, for their owners were men with pressing engagements, and steam could get them there on time, fair weather or foul.

Second America's Cup Challenge

To get back to the America's Cup races. In the winter of 1871 Mr. Ashbury tried several times to arrange a challenge under other terms than the original deed of gift of the cup, and has always been somewhat criticized for the negotiations of both of his challengers, but the New York

Yacht Club had accepted the custody of the cup under the deed of gift and did not see how they could disregard this document. It was finally arranged that there would be a series of races instead of one race, and that only one yacht at a time should be the defender of the cup. This gave the New York Yacht Club the opportunity of choosing the defender the day of the race, and the advantage of using a heavy or light weather boat under the conditions. Thus they had four yachts stand by ready to sail as defenders. They were the centerboard schooners *Columbia* and *Palmer,* and the keel schooners *Sappho* and *Dauntless.* While this does not seem quite fair it is likely that several of our schooners could have defended the cup successfully that year for in the five official races for the cup *Columbia* and *Sappho* each beat *Livonia* twice while *Livonia* beat *Columbia* once when the latter's steering gear broke down. However, Mr. Ashbury was not satisfied and imagined he had technical claims on the cup so to give him further satisfaction James Gordon Bennett, who was commodore of the New York Yacht Club that year, arranged a private match race between the flagship *Dauntless* and Mr. Ashbury's *Livonia* in which *Dauntless* proved to be the faster

Fig. 58. Cabin of MAGIC

yacht. While I have said that *Livonia* was a handsome, well-proportioned yacht, still under the rules of the New York Yacht Club of that time our lighter displacement schooners seemed to be faster, and it is interesting to note that the schooner *Columbia* that year made a record over the cup course that stood for many years, and I think has only been surpassed by modern cup yachts two or three times.

The Cutter vs. the Sandbagger

While it is true that there has always been considerable difference between European and American yachts, perhaps there was no other time when the difference was so great as between 1870 and 1880 for, while they had barred shifting ballast and rated their yachts by a tonnage rule that measured beam twice and depth not at all, we were racing sandbaggers and using shifting ballast on quite sizeable craft whose principal measurement for rating was the length over all. The cutter, of course, was non-capsizeable and with her topmast housed and bowsprit run in perhaps she was more comfortable than any modern craft for they generally were flushed decked with bulwarks and hand rails all the way around.

So, perhaps now we should say something about the development of our small craft which were so different from the English. While it is generally conceded that the catboat and catboat racing were developed at Newport, Rhode Island, well before 1800, this type of small craft, but using a centerboard, soon became popular in shallow water regions around New York where very fast small sailboats were finally developed. By 1850 or so there were several famous builders and modelers of these shifting ballast craft at such places as Weehawken, Gowanus Bay, Bayonne, Staten Island, and other places that were then farm land but now are all built up with large industrial plants. Up the Hudson at Nyack, down the Sound at City Island, Mystic and Noank there were good yacht yards, and on the north side of Long Island shipyards in most every port that could build large or small craft. Some of these places at first only built racing catboats of various sizes, perhaps between sixteen and twenty-four feet long, but soon after 1850 a type using a jib on a long bowsprit came into vogue for shallow water racing.

Both Steers of the *America* fame, and Fish of equal fame in modeling and sailing, designed these craft, and at first these craft were simply measured or rated by their length on deck, but later, because some had adopted a ram bow, the mean of the length on deck and the length of waterline was adopted. At any rate, when length was the only measurement and beam and sail area went free it was quite natural with shifting ballast to use large sail plans and sometimes a beam on deck of nearly half their length. These boats generally ranged in length between eighteen and twenty eight feet; they usually had two mast holes and sloop and cat sail plans for racing in the two classes. For a while, perhaps around 1860, the fastest or most extreme of these craft were called Penny Bridge Boats, for quite a

fleet of them anchored near a toll bridge at the head of Gowanus Cove. In time these fast boats became popular for racing all along Long Island Sound, up the Hudson, and in Great South Bay and Delaware Bay, so they are called sandbaggers. The best collection of the lines and sail plans of sandbaggers that I know of is in the latter part of the book "History of American Sailing Ships" by Howard I. Chapelle. The sandbaggers were beautifully built and of very light construction so by far their greatest weight was their crew and shifting ballast.

The Crews Were Tough

For many years a great deal of the sporting element was fascinated by these craft for in their time there were few other sports worth watching, and as the sandbaggers often sailed match races close to shore they drew great throngs of spectators and were the cause of much betting. In those days there were many sporting inns, taverns and saloons along the shore within a reasonable driving distance by carriage of New York City, and the proprietors of these public houses were quick to see the business they could attract by holding sandbagger match races in the waters directly in front of their property. These match races were much advertised by their promoters and the innkeepers often promised large purses for the winner. These races were said to be the hottest, most spectacular sailboat races ever held. The captains were great heroes in their home ports, and the rivalry between ports was very hot. Some of the sandbaggers were actually owned by saloon- and innkeepers of the type that held boxing matches and cock fights, etc. While there were exceptions to the rule, the sandbaggers were generally manned by the toughest individuals imaginable; many of them were New York watermen who had spent their lives in the small, fast sailboats that were then used for ferrying purposes. Under these conditions, and because the sandbaggers raced under few rules or restrictions, the match races were often a real fight all around the course and there were many capsizes and a few fatalities. In other words, the sandbaggers close to New York were manned by professional crews who, if they could not beat you on the water, would beat you up when they got you ashore later.

Mr. C. Oliver Iselin, who started his racing in sandbaggers, said about the sport some years later, "You had to fight all the way around the course, and if you should win you had to fight again to get the prize." I believe the sandbaggers had the fastest average speed for their length over all of any type of boat that has been accepted as a type. The catboat *Gleam* had some outside ballast and thus could get along with less shifting ballast and crew. *Gleam* was the first American yacht or boat to have screw fastened planking, all previous ones having their planking fastened with boat nails, clout nails, rivets or trunnels.

Shifting Ballast

About this time my grandfather experimented with shifting ballast. He had his catboat *Julia* equipped with a sort of track that ran athwartships. On the track was a car loaded with about five hundred pounds of lead. The car was held in its weather position by a ratchet arrangement. In tacking ship, as *Julia* righted or nearly righted, the car of lead was lowered to leeward by a tackle and the opposite ratchet held this weight there after the tack was completed and the leeward side had become the weather side. This arrangement was said to have made *Julia* faster than any boat of her size in Narragansett Bay, but this shifting ballast box was only used on three boats and was given up as it was thought that lower ballast or outside ballast was safer. The reason for this of course is that when ballast is above the center of flotation it loses power as the vessel heels. But when the ballast is below the center of flotation it gains power or leverage as she heels, so at that time most all American yachts were capsizeable while the deep English cutters were non-capsizeable.

While I am sorry to have perhaps bored the Gentle Reader with the different methods of gaining sail carrying power, and remarks on the professional crews of the sandbaggers, it still has been necessary before taking up the so-called cutter-sloop controversy.

Fig. 59. Schooners at Newport in 1872

" Peerless "   " Wanderer "   " Rambler "   " America "   " Dreadnought "   " Tarolinta "   " Madeline "
      " Fleetwing "   " Magic "   " Clypso "   " Sappho "
" Dauntless "   " Palmer "   " Columbia "

THE YACHT SQUADRON AT NEWPORT, 1872. LITHOGRAPH IN COLOUR. (Macpherson Collection)

11 Cutter-Sloop Controversy

The Seawanhaka Yacht Club was formed in 1871 by men who were interested in amateur yacht design and amateur sailing. Their principal object was to try to improve the type of sailboat then in use in this country which, as we see through the sandbaggers, was not suitable for amateur sailing or racing. So, with their interest in amateurism, the club changed its name to The Seawanhaka-Corinthian Yacht Club a few years after it was formed, and was the first American club to bar shifting ballast, a move that most all other clubs soon followed. The early members of the club were mostly capable men of means who owned yachts and took a great interest in yacht design. The most influential of them seems to have been Robert Center who had been one of the afterguard on the schooner *Fleetwing* in the famous ocean race of 1866. Schooners at Newport in 1872 are shown in Figure 59; the *Sea Fox* in Figure 60. He stayed abroad for a few years studying English yachts and yachting and became very much attached to the English cutters of the time.

Cary Smith Designs Vindex

On Mr. Center's return he brought over the best books on yacht architecture that he could get, and with his actual experience on the cutters he was able to gather a knot of friends who were very cutter minded, so he decided to design a cutter to be built in this country and had A. Cary Smith associated with him in this undertaking. At that time Mr. Smith was a young marine artist who was later to become one of our leading designers. Perhaps he did the drawing and Center furnished the enthusiasm and specifications; however, they and their friends were so enthusiastic about the design that Mr. Center had the yacht built and she is said to have been one of the first sailboats built in this country from drawings alone without a model. From that time on many American yacht designers drew all their plans on paper as had been done for centuries in Europe. The name of the yacht was *Vindex*; she was about 62′ L.O.A.; 56′ L.W.L.; 17′ beam, and 9′ draft; of 53 tons, and built of iron. There were heated controversies over the performance of *Vindex,* and this developed into a set of men who were commonly called cutter cranks, and I am not sure I would not have been one if I had been around in those days. However, Cary Smith took up yacht designing on his own and soon designed several yachts of different rig, built of iron and shaped much like the English yachts, but slightly wider. One of them, the 100′ L.W.L. schooner *Intrepid,* was a very fine vessel.

The Seawanhaka-Corinthian Yacht Club had Cary Smith give a series of lectures on yacht design in the winter of 1877. Soon after this Mr. W. P. Stephens, who was editor of the yachting section of *Forest and Stream,* wrote several illustrated articles about yachts, and C. P. Kunhardt began publishing his books about small yachts. As those gentlemen were at heart cutter cranks the general public became quite cutter conscious, and the sloop-cutter controversy was in full swing and American yachtsmen began importing English and Scottish cutters.

Shadow *Stops Stampede*

In about 1881, Mr. James Coats of Paisley, Scotland (a textile manufacturer with interests in this country), decided to send over his crack 10-ton cutter *Madge*. *Madge* was designed by George L. Watson at the beginning of his career, or about 1879. *Madge* came over on a steamer and arrived in August; she was a beautifully kept up craft with capable captain and crew dressed in neat uniforms, quite in contrast to the nondescript crews manning the usual small yacht of that time over here. *Madge* at once became very popular, and this lifted the cutter cranks to the very height of their enthusiasm. Matches with the New York sloops of about her size were soon arranged and she beat three or four of them quite handily, partly because she could set a very large light club topsail in light weather, and quickly shorten down to appropriate area for strong breezes. I believe some of these races were arranged by the Seawanhaka-Corinthian Yacht Club. After this *Madge* sailed to Newport to have some matches with the sloop *Shadow* that had been designed by N. G. Herreshoff some ten years before.

Shadow, though a centerboarder, was deep and full along the garboards and thus carried her ballast down quite low as had been the custom in Narragansett Bay boats from colonial times. *Shadow*'s dimensions were 37′ L.O.A.; 34′ L.W.L.; 14′ beam, and 5′4″ draft with centerboard up. She carried five tons of ballast. In their two match races at Newport *Shadow* won one by quite a margin and *Madge* won the other by a short distance, thus *Shadow* partly saved the honor of the American sloops and created what was called the Compromise type, that is a model somewhat between the English cutter and the wide, shallow American type, and for the next twenty years or so many of our yachts were of this Compromise model, including *Puritan* and *Mayflower*.

Length and Sail Area Rule

While *Shadow* peaceably concluded the cutter-sloop controversy, the Seawanhaka-Corinthian Yacht Club was to go on with its interest in amateur design until finally its commodore, A. Cass Canfield, designed the beautiful schooner *Sea Fox,* which many say was the best amateur

Fig. 60. SEA FOX

design ever made. The club was becoming very rule-minded and tried out several measurement rules to try to improve the type of yacht being built until finally their member and measurer, John Hyslop, got up what is called the Length and Sail Area Rule, which was first adopted by the Sea-wanhaka-Corinthian Yacht Club in 1882, and with minor adjustments, was used by most American yacht clubs during the next twenty years or so. Altogether, perhaps the Seawanhaka-Corinthian has done more to promote yacht design and amateur sailing than any American club.

I suppose I should point out the difference between a cutter and a sloop for the benefit of my younger readers who must be rather confused with the cutter-sloop controversy in which sail plan had little effect. The argument could have been called the keel-centerboard controversy, or the deep-or-wide hull controversy, but as the cutter, or English cutter, was considered the national rig of England, and the sloop the national rig of America, perhaps the choice of these names added a heating patriotic effect to the argument.

Cutter—Defined

A cutter yacht is a one-masted vessel always rigged with a gaff, a topmast and topsails. She always carries three headsails, and always has a housing topmast and a bowsprit that can be reefed or run in on deck. The cutter usually has a loose-footed mainsail and is a rig that was developed by the Revenue services of both France and England well before 1800. After the cutter yachts had been used many years for racing under a tonnage rule that measured beam twice and depth not at all, they became very narrow and deep and this was their principal peculiarity at the time of the cutter-sloop controversy.

Sloop—Defined

A sloop is a single-masted vessel which can carry a topsail or not; it can be without a gaff if a leg-o'-mutton sail is used; it can have one, two or three headsails. The older ones carried a fixed bowsprit and often had the mast stepped well amidships. The American sloop and its name were descended from the early vessels the Dutch had developed for plying up and down the Hudson River. Between 1800 and 1880, a large proportion of the American sloops were wide, shallow centerboarders, and that is the reason why the word "sloop" was used in opposition to cutter in the controversy.

I note further that there is now no true cutter in use in this country that I know of, and our present single-masted sailboats that carry headsails can only correctly be called leg-o'-mutton sloops for they have no gaff, bowsprit, or topsails—the principal features of a cutter. The small fry at the time of the Penny Bridge boats were called jib-and-mainsail boats, and that would be a quite correct term for most of our small craft today. I'm often amused at some owners of late years who prefer the harsh word "cutter" to describe their pot-bellied tubs, most of whom have never seen a cutter and do not know that the sloop is our national rig.

Canada's Challenge for America's Cup

While we have gone up to beyond 1880 with the cutter-sloop controversy, we must go back to the first of the Canadian challengers for the America's Cup. In the spring of 1876 the Royal Canadian Yacht Club challenged for the America's Cup under the name of their vice-commodore Gifford, and named the *Countess of Dufferin* as the challenging yacht. They requested that the six months' notice clause in the deed of gift be waived. The New York Yacht Club promptly accepted the challenge. Vice-commodore Gifford requested that only one yacht was to be used as defender, which of course was very reasonable and has been the rule ever since. So the New York Yacht Club named the schooner *Madeleine* as their defender. It is said the Canadians challenged for the reason that one of their builders, Alexander Cuthbert, had designed a sloop which finally beat the sloop *Cora* modeled by "Pat" McGiehan of Ramapo, New Jersey, one of the famous modelers of Penny Bridge type boats. *Cora* had been built for a Canadian yachtsman and beat everything in her class at first, but soon Mr. Cuthbert built a sloop named *Annie Cuthbert* which beat *Cora,* and this stirred up the ambition of the Canadians to build a cup challenger. It is doubtful if Cuthbert had had experience with the larger craft for the *Countess of Dufferin* seems to have had defects, one of which was the required stiffness to carry sail well. Otherwise she was quite similar to our schooners of the time. The challenger, *Countess of Dufferin,* was named for a yachtswoman of the highest degree, the wife of the Governor General of Canada, and if I remember rightly she and Lord Dufferin had made cruises in high latitudes in a large schooner.

The challenger sailed down the St. Lawrence River, along our coast to New York, arriving there by July 18. She was a sizeable vessel, 107' L.O.A. and 24' beam, though with her centerboard up she only drew 6½'. After the challenger was extensively refitted at New York she sailed with the other large schooners in the Brenton's Reef race of that year. The race took place between Sandy Hook light vessel to Brenton's Reef light vessel and return, a distance of some two hundred and seventy-five miles. In the first part of this race they had a nice breeze, wind on the quarter, and the large schooners averaged nearly fourteen miles an hour under full sail. *Countess of Dufferin* kept up with them for a while with no topsails set which showed she was capable of considerable speed under some circumstances.

An account of this race is given in the July number of the *Aquatic Monthly* of 1876, and the publishers make this comment as an introduction:

"The following account of this grand yachting contest is from the pen of R. C. Coffin of the New York World; a gentleman who has no equal in this country as a writer on yachting subjects."

The publishers seem to be right for Coffin certainly has written an account which covers all of the details, yet holds your attention to the end. The modern writers of yacht races have usually concocted such uninteresting accounts that modern editors seldom publish them, and a good, interesting description of a race is rare. Perhaps this Brenton's Reef Race is interesting because of the fine large yachts that were in it, and to give the readers an idea of the approximate cost of some of the schooners we have spoken of I list them below:

Dauntless	$70,000.00
Sappho	50,000.00
Vesta	45,000.00
Henrietta	40,000.00
Fleetwing	48,000.00
Magic	33,000.00

Although the value of the dollar then was some four times what it is now, because of poor management of the present yacht yard these schooners would cost from ten to fifteen times as much today, or would average half a million dollars apiece. So, while there may be many more millionaires today, few, if any, of them could afford such vessels as were common in the great schooner days. And where would you find an architect to design them?

But let us get back to the races of 1876. After the Brenton's Reef Cup race, in which *Countess* dropped out when about halfway around, it was found that her sails and rigging were so strained that she required new sails and quite a lot of refitting, but as the Canadians did not have the money to do this properly the challenger never was in proper racing trim.

The defender, *Madeleine,* was a schooner of almost the same size as the challenger, but of more displacement and, under the New York Yacht Club rules of the time, rated slightly less than *Countess of Dufferin. Madeleine* had proved herself to be very fast and, although she was the flagship of the Brooklyn Yacht Club, her owner, Mr. John S. Dickerson, was a member of the New York Yacht Club.

The first race was on August 11, and this time there was a flying start in which *Madeleine* got over the line first and stayed in that position throughout the race. The course was the usual L-shaped course of the New York Yacht Club at that time. The wind was moderately strong from the south. At the finish *Madeleine* had a good lead and won by nearly eleven minutes.

The second race was on the following day. It was supposed to be a windward and leeward race but the wind shifted which reduced the amount of windward work and, although this should have been favorable to the challenger, still *Madeleine* beat her some twenty-seven minutes by corrected time.

A third race was not necessary for that year the match was for the best two out of three races. *Countess of Dufferin* was layed up at Staten Island and had financial difficulties, finally being sold at a sheriff's sale. She was later owned by a Chicago yachtsman who shortened her name to *Countess*. Before finishing with this yacht it is interesting to note that she lay at anchor near *Mohawk* when that yacht capsized at Stapleton, and her boats helped to pick up the survivors. *Mohawk*'s proportion of draft to sail area was similar to *Countess of Dufferin*'s, but the latter was probably a less stable craft.

Rowing Clubs

This was the centennial year and there was an unusual number of prizes offered for the smaller classes of sailboats in various places, but by far the most medals and prizes were for rowing races, for perhaps in America rowing was then at its height. Most every eastern town that was on a river or a suitable sheet of water for rowing had its rowing club. The rowing clubs then probably outnumbered the yacht clubs three to one, and while today most of the important rowing races are in four- or eight-oared shells then there were many single sculls and nice open working boats, for rowing was thought to be a manly and healthy sport.

12 *English Cruisers*

I must not forget to mention the cruising sailboats of these times—between 1860 and 1890—for in England perhaps they were more numerous than now supposed, but if one studies the English yacht registers of those times one will be impressed with their numbers. Figures 61 and 62 give you an idea of typical English cruising sailboats of, say 1870. While they retained the plumb bow of the racing cutters, they were wider and shallower, almost always had good bulwarks all the way around, and sometimes a life rail or life line above the bulwarks. The larger ones were flush decked so they had plenty of deck space to carry their rowboats inboard. These types, outside of being wet forward, were much more wholesome vessels than anything we had over here at the time.

Makes Men of Boys

Many of these boats would sail around England and Scotland most every year, and rounding the north of Scotland called for able boats and good navigation because of the strong, variable tides, et cetera, but the after guard often contained a naval officer on leave, and the professional crews of the time were real sailormen who had been trained in the fishing fleets or the merchant marine. Some of these cruises were leisurely and thus allowed the after guard to visit most of the picturesque places, and wait for suitable weather to make a passage which would be through the beautiful islands off Scotland with grand mountain scenery in the distance. One of the books which describes such a cruise is *A Yacht Voyage Round England*

by William H. G. Kingston. Although it is supposed to be a boys' book, it is particularly well illustrated. It is also noteworthy that in those days it was thought to be very desirable for a young gentleman to make this circumnavigation of his homeland, both for educational and patriotic reasons, and somebody of those times said, "There is nothing like yacht cruising to make a man out of a boy."

The larger English yachts were often in commission most of the year, and frequently spent the winter months in the Mediterranean. The smaller cruisers usually were laid up in some small sheltered cove and there were several places in southern England where many could lay up in company with no danger from ice. Some of these yachts or cruising sailboats would stay half in commission all winter, keeping a man aboard and a fire going all the time for some of their young owners thought it was fun to spend an occasional weekend aboard, and as spring comes so much earlier in Old England than New England they often got under way by the Easter holidays. Perhaps in 1870 there were ten times as many good, comfortable cruisers in England as here, and, although this statement may surprise some modern American readers, there were several reasons for it, the first of which was that the upper and middle classes in England had much more leisure; in fact many did not work at all. But for several years after the Civil War almost everyone here was working hard and had very little leisure. While it is true that there were tycoons in New York who owned the large schooners of the eighteen sixties, even these men did their yachting so

Fig. 61. Typical English cruisers

hurriedly that a time-consuming thing like a cruise was hard to arrange.

The yachting season in England is nearly twice as long as here. Besides this, during most of Victoria's reign you could hire good, reliable men to build or crew a boat for one pound a week or less. So, together with their strong non-capsizeable vessels, it is not surprising that they did much more cruising than we did. Some of the English cruisers were very comfortable with good galleys and a cabin heater or semi-open fireplace. Most of the older ones had a well locked meat safe on deck where a haunch of venison or some game birds were aged. While they did not vary much in model and continued to resemble the Revenue Cutters of 1800, whose depth of hull was about half the beam, they were rigged as cutters, yawls, ketches, schooners and luggers. Many lasted a long while and I have seen one in commission that I was told was eighty years old.

Good American Cruising Yachts Scarce

The reason we have had so few comfortable cruisers in this country is that at first we used shallow center-boarders whose principal measurement was length over all (which eventually became the sandbagger), or the larger capsizeable craft. Then, after the length on water-line became the principal measurement and we had developed the short waterline scow type with its deep keel, we had hulls entirely unsuited to cruising. While their hulls were too shallow for accommodations below deck, their deep keels prevented them from being cruisers. Now that measured sail area is a principal factor in rating and we have found ways to carry actual sail areas of twice the measured sail area, we have freak types that are called ocean racers which amount to windbags trying to propel submerged lead mines. So today there are very few in this country who even know what a cruising yacht is.

However, one of our good cruising sloops of the eighteen sixties was *Alice*, built by Townsend of Portsmouth, N. H., in 1866, for Thomas G. Appleton of Boston. She was a keel sloop, L.O.A. 66′ 6″; L.W.L. 58′ 8″; beam 17′ 6″; draft 6′ 4″, and she was a very strong little vessel mostly built of oak. She was sailed to England in the summer of 1866, a few months before the famous race between *Henrietta, Fleetwing* and *Vesta,* which seems to have overshadowed the feat of *Alice.* Up to her time I believe *Alice* was the smallest American yacht to make the crossing both ways. She was commanded by the famous Captain Arthur Hamilton Clark, who had gone to sea at sixteen and had worked his way up to the command of clipper ships and was to be one of the first Americans to command the early steamers in the China Trade. He was the author of the fine books, *The History of Yachting (1600 to 1815)* and *The Clipper Ship Era.* Mr. Clark in his residence in London and other parts of the world picked up the fine collection of marine prints, models and books that are in the Clark Collection at the Pratt School of Naval Architecture of the Massachusetts Institute of Technology.

Mr. Clark sailed *Alice* to England while on vacation between voyages as a ship captain, and made the crossing from Boston to Cowes in nineteen days, which was considered very fast for so small a vessel. The crew consisted of four men before the mast and two besides himself in the after guard, one of whom was Charles A. Longfellow, son of the famous poet. *Alice* was well received in England and Figure 63 shows her at Torquay. This is a water color painted for Captain Clark by Fred S. Cozzens and is now in the author's possession.

Edward Burgess

In about 1882 the great yacht designer, Edward Burgess, suddenly came into prominence and, although his career was abruptly cut off by his untimely death in 1891 at the age of forty-three, he designed several large fine yachts in these few years, including three cup defenders. He was remarkable in acquiring such success for he had had practically no training in this exacting art. Nevertheless it seems that the natural instincts of an artist can take the place of scientific training.

Edward Burgess' father was descended from one of Boston's old families and was a man of means, said at one time to be one of Boston's most prosperous merchants. He had counting houses in both Boston and the West Indies, with a winter residence in Boston and a summer

Fig. 62. Another English cruiser

Fig. 63. ALICE at Torquay

13 *America's Cup Challenge of 1885*

But we must go back to the two challenges for the America's Cup in 1885, one from the Royal Yacht Squadron named *Genesta,* owned by Sir Richard Sutton as a challenger, and the other from the Royal Northern Yacht Club, named *Galatea,* owned by Lieutenant William Henn of the Royal Navy. These two challenges were inspired by Mr. Beavor-Webb who had designed both yachts. At first it was expected that both sets of races would be the same year if the first challenger, *Genesta,* were unsuccessful. The New York Yacht Club promptly accepted these challenges, but after a cup defense committee was selected the club thought it would be best to arrange one set of races for 1885 and the other for 1886, which turned out best, for *Galatea* had trouble during construction and would not have been completed in time.

Genesta and *Galatea* were very much alike, which was quite natural for two vessels designed by the same man at about the same time. Many Americans think of John Beavor-Webb as an American designer because he designed several of our large auxiliaries and steam yachts including the good looking, famous *Corsair,* but Beavor-Webb did not come to this country until shortly after designing *Genesta* and *Galatea.* In fact, he was born in Ireland in 1849 and came here in 1885 and died in 1927, so by far the greatest tonnage of yachts he designed was in America. Beavor-Webb always designed wholesome vessels that were of strong construction and of heavy displacement, and *Genesta* and *Galatea* were no exceptions to this. They were typical English cutters in model and rig; in fact, they were quite similar in outer appearance

to the typical racing yacht that had been popular in England since about 1840, but were wider than some of the extreme cutters. *Genesta* was of composite construction with an outside lead keel of fifty-one percent of her displacement. *Galatea* was steel plated with her lead run into her trough keel. She was said to have eighty-one tons of ballast so must have had a high percentage of ballast.

Priscilla *by Cary Smith*

These were only plumb-bowed yachts or true cutters to challenge for the cup, but all together we had three plumb-bowed defenders. They were *Mischief, Puritan* (Figure 68) and *Mayflower;* all other cup boats were clipper bowed or had the overhanging spoon bow. The flag officers of the New York Yacht Club, James Gordon Bennett and William P. Douglas, decided to build a sloop for defense and naturally turned to A. Cary Smith for the design because he not *only* had designed the last defender *Mischief,* but was then considered the leading yacht designer of this country. This yacht that was named *Priscilla* (Figure 69) was a larger and improved *Mischief* with frames and plating of iron.

Puritan *by Burgess*

In Boston at a meeting of the Eastern Yacht Club where their secretary, Edward Burgess, was present there were some interesting discussions about the coming cup races, and some of the members were so much impressed by Mr. Burgess' discourse on the matter that a syndicate, headed by General Charles J. Paine and J. Malcolm Forbes, decided to build a trial sloop for defense designed by Mr. Burgess. This was truly challenging for Mr. Burgess, for he had not designed large yachts before, and had only a few years' experience in the art. The yacht was named *Puritan* and was built by George Lawley almost entirely of wood. Mr. Lawley was an English boat or yacht builder who had come to this country several years before and produced very high-grade work. *Puritan* was a compromise cutter, perhaps a little wider than necessary; she had a large centerboard passing down through her ballast keel and was certainly a beautiful model of her type. Her manager was General Paine who had had quite a lot of racing experience in his schooner *Halcyon*. He was not noted for keeping his yachts polished up; rather he had the crew spend their time improving all matters that had to do with speed and proper functioning of parts. He was ahead of his time in realizing the importance of sails of exactly the right draft, and perhaps much of his success can be counted from the sails that he acquired and had worked into perfect shape. General Paine was perhaps the most able cup boat manager we have ever had. *Puritan*'s professional captain and helmsman was Aubrey Crocker who won so many races in the little sloop *Shadow* that we have spoken of.

The New York Yacht Club gave three official trial races that year to select a defender in which the following yachts competed:

Puritan	84'	rating
Priscilla	85.30'	"
Gracie	71.60'	"
Bedouin	71.45'	"

At that time the New York Yacht Club rated its yachts by taking twice the waterline length and the square root of sail area added together, and this sum divided by three. *Puritan* won two of these races and, as she had come in so far ahead in one, it was quite plain that she was the fastest yacht, so the wooden Boston boat was chosen to defend the cup.

The Cutter-Sloop Controversy Again

The final races for the cup were in September, 1885, and one writer of the time says, "The interest in the races had been continually increasing, and at the time had reached a pitch wholly unparalleled in yachting history." To which I will say there were few sporting events in those days that were worth space in the papers, but an international contest like the cup races of 1885 gave scope for headline news and no doubt there was very great interest in the races that year. We also must remember that the cutter-sloop controversy was still in the minds of most yachtsmen, and this was a contest between a pure English cutter and an American centerboard sloop.

The first race was called off for lack of wind while *Puritan* was well ahead. Unfortunately in the second attempt the yachts had a collision just before the start. It

seems that *Puritan* tried to cross the bow of *Genesta* while the latter was on the starboard tack and just failed to do it, so *Genesta*'s bowsprit went through the after part of *Puritan*'s mainsail, and before the two yachts could be cleared *Genesta*'s bowsprit was carried away. The race committee promptly disqualified *Puritan* which automatically gave the race to *Genesta,* but her owner, Sir Richard Sutton, very sportingly refused to accept this win declaring that he had come to America to test the relative merits of the cutter and centerboard sloop and not to claim races on technicalities. The afterguard of *Puritan* was profuse with apologies and offered to pay for all repairs, but Sir Richard very sportingly assumed the expenses of repairs to *Genesta*. While one seldom hears of this incident nowadays, it is my opinion that if *Genesta* had fouled *Puritan* it would still be noised about.

I, too, will express my opinion in order to minimize the bad behavior of *Puritan* that day. The yachts of that time were very slow turning and were unwieldy and carried long stingers some thirty feet ahead of their bows. Edward Burgess' designs were all characterized by very small rudders. Apparently he thought that the rudder was a source of resistance while later designers thought that a rudder of good size gave very effective lateral plane to reduce leeway. The captain and helmsman of *Puritan* was used to maneuvering *Shadow*, which was perhaps one third the length of *Puritan* from bowsprit to boom end. Maybe a quarter of a mile back he had planned this maneuver to get on *Genesta*'s weather quarter, but, because of *Puritan* turning slower and being so much longer than he was used to, he miscalculated by a small margin. At any rate in a few days both yachts were ready for the third attempt. This also was a failure for there was quite a ground swell running, and when the wind went down the yachts were progressing too slowly to finish within the time limit, but *Puritan* was again in the lead.

Many Delays

The fourth attempt was also called off because of calm weather, so the first completed race was not until September 14, seven days after the first attempted race. On the first try there was said to be a spectator fleet of over four hundred good-size vessels, but this fleet was much reduced in consequence of the several failures to complete a race, and I imagine this rather pleased the competitors for the courses were not patrolled in those days. The race of September 14 was a so-called inside race over nearly the same course as had been used in some of the previous cup races. The wind was changeable and flukey, but *Puritan* proved herself the faster boat under all conditions, finishing with a lead of some sixteen minutes' corrected time.

Third Race a Thriller

The next race on September 16 was one of the most exciting of all the cup races. This time it was an outside race starting at the Scotland Lightship off Sandyhook.

then rounding a mark twenty miles to leeward, and return. It was a typical autumn day with a strong and puffy northwest wind blowing, and all the cutter cranks were quite sure *Genesta* would win, and she did lead much of the way around the course. *Genesta* got the start and the two were running to leeward very evenly when she decided it would be advantageous to jibe over, but before she got her spinnaker out and on the other jibe *Puritan* passed her. However, *Genesta*'s sails worked so much better after the jibe that she rounded the leeward mark first. The wind was blowing hard by that time so *Puritan* housed her topmast for the beat back while *Genesta* carried a working topsail that made her heel excessively and probably did not help her, for when cutters are heeled way over they have a lee helm which is not good for windward work. So, as the yachts approached the finish line, it was seen that *Puritan* had a slight lead, and she won by one minute and thirty-eight seconds. Right after the finish *Genesta* ranged alongside *Puritan* and her crew gave the American yacht three hearty cheers to which Captain Crocker and his crew replied in like manner. This race demonstrated that an American centerboard sloop could be driven to windward as fast as a cutter in strong wind and choppy sea, and very much dampened the ardor of the cutter cranks.

These victories of *Puritan* at once put Mr. Burgess at the head of all American yacht designers, and he was swamped with work the rest of his short life. There was nothing radically different about the design of *Puritan*, but she was an exceptionally beautiful model; however, she did change the style of painting sailboats. Prior to that time a large percentage of our boats were black or dark green with only an occasional white one, but since the victories of *Puritan* American yachts large and small have usually been white.

Puritan was owned for several years by Malcolm Forbes rigged as sloop and schooner, and ended her days as a Bravos boat carrying passengers and freight between the Cape Verde Islands and New Bedford, Mass., up until about 1905.

Sir Richard Has Good Season

Genesta did not sail for home until October 9, and in the meantime won a $1,000 cup offered by James Gordon Bennett and Mr. Douglas, and won both the Brenton's Reef and Cape May Challenge Cups, which apparently pleased everyone for her owner, Sir Richard Sutton, Bart., had become very popular through his good sportsmanship.

Fig. 68. The Edward Burgess designed PURITAN stepping out lively, hard on the wind

Fig. 69. PRISCILLA, designed by A. Cary Smith. The men shown forward give a good idea of the size of the bowsprit

Mayflower and *Galatea* races of 1886: General Paine must have had a good time racing *Puritan* for in the latter part of 1885 he decided to have a large sloop built, incorporating the ideas that had occurred to him from his experience with *Puritan*. Edward Burgess was commissioned to make the design that was turned over to Lawley, the builder, early in the year 1886. The new yacht was named *Mayflower* and did not differ in model much from *Puritan*, but was longer while her draft and beam remained about the same as *Puritan*. However, her construction was carefully worked out to get the weights lower. She was built mostly of wood but had some very heavy iron floor timbers to serve as ballast as well as to give strength. *Mayflower* was built quite quickly and was ready for her trial trip by May 30. This time the General had for sailing master Captain Martin Stone who had done so well in handling his schooner *Halcyon*. Perhaps this was lucky for it happened that *Mayflower* had rather bad setting sails at first, and in the beginning of the season was beaten by *Puritan* several times, though after she got straightened out nothing could touch her.

Mayflower *Chosen*

A syndicate of New York Yacht Club members had the sloop *Atlantic* built that winter as a trial cup boat so in the trial races there were four yachts quite similar in looks which rated as follows:

Puritan	83.85
Mayflower	87.99
Atlantic	86.31
Priscilla	85.97

They all were centerboard sloops with quite shallow hulls. In the two trial races *Mayflower* won quite easily and the new New York boat did not do particularly well so it was easy for the cup committee to choose *Mayflower* as the defender which is quite in contrast to the many close races of the season of 1958.

We have partly described the challenger *Galatea* together with *Genesta* for they were quite similar and both designed by John Beavor-Webb at about the same time. The owners of *Galatea* were Mrs. William Henn and her husband, Lieutenant W. Henn, R.N., retired who had served aboard the crack frigate *Galatea*. They were both great yachting and cruising people who had cruised some forty-nine thousand miles in their eighty-ton yawl *Gertrude,* which was for some time kept in commission the year around, and they had won a great many races both in England and on the French Mediterranean coast. Mrs. Henn had *Galatea* built to be their floating home, and she was a fine, wholesome vessel. Both Lieutenant and Mrs. Henn are said to have been the most popular characters who challenged for the cup, and Mrs. Henn is the only woman who paid for a cup challenger or sailed over and back on one. Unfortunately *Galatea* did not turn out to be very fast either in England or here, and I believe it was partly because her sails were very heavy and logy in light and moderate weather. *Mayflower* and *Galatea* were about the same size in linear dimensions though they differed much in beam and draft. *Galatea* was a little heavier and had the least sail although they rated nearly the same.

Off in a Roar

The first race between *Galatea* and *Mayflower* was over the inside course on September 7, and the neighboring waters were crowded with craft of all kinds including some fast steam yachts, and the start was a magnificent one with both craft on the starboard tack with *Galatea* having a lead of two seconds. This sight so stirred the attending fleet that there were shrieks of whistles and a deafening roar of cannon, for in those days most every yacht had a saluting cannon on board. The wind was light to moderate from the south so the first leg was a beat down the Narrows with many short tacks, and *Mayflower* began to draw ahead. After passing the Narrows and rounding buoy #10 the race became a reach to Sandyhook Lightship, and as they passed the lightship *Mayflower* had a substantial lead which she seemed to increase in the reaches and run to the finish, winning by twelve minutes.

The second attempted race was called off as the yachts failed to complete the race within the time limit. But on September 11 they had a windward and leeward race starting from Scotland Lightship and rounding a mark twenty miles to leeward in a moderate northwest wind. *Mayflower* went over the starting line first with such good way on that she soon drew well ahead and could not be blanketed on the run. She had something like a fifteen minute lead at the leeward mark, and in the beat back in

a dying wind she managed to pick up some light airs which allowed her to finish within eleven minutes of the time limit of seven hours. In this last race *Mayflower* beat *Galatea* some twenty-nine minutes which seems a lot, but as we look at it with more modern knowledge it was not strange for *Galatea* had the most displacement and least sail. She undoubtedly had considerably more wetted surface, and while *Mayflower*'s bottom and much of her topsides were carefully polished with pot lead, *Galatea* was painted steel which usually has quite a little surface tension or resistance.

Galatea *Was a Strong, Able Craft*

As for sails—*Galatea*'s were too heavy for light weather, and when it is very light, as it was part of that day, a loose-footed sail will often hang straight up and down. I suppose *Mayflower* heeled slightly more which allowed her sails to take up a good draft, and as her mainsail was laced to the boom there was not much escape of air there, and it is my opinion that up to 1893 American defenders have had the advantage over the challengers in having the mailsail laced to the boom. *Galatea* was a heavy, seagoing vessel with high bulwarks all around. So, all things considered, she did quite well. Lieutenant Henn thought *Galatea* would do better at sea in a breeze so challenged any American yacht for a race around the Bermudas and back, but there appeared to be none to take the challenge. Perhaps she would have been hard to beat in the Gulf Stream.

Mayflower *Wins at Marblehead*

Failing to get the satisfaction of an ocean race, Lieutenant Henn challenged *Mayflower* to a match race off Marblehead in a strong breeze, and General Paine accepted. Both yachts lay at Marblehead ten days that fall as we happened to have one of those autumn calm spells so the race was put off until the following spring when they had a race in a strong breeze which *Mayflower* seems to have won easily. Lieutenant Henn was satisfied and said he had had the test he wanted. *Galatea* stayed in this country until the matches between *Thistle* and *Volunteer* were over, and both he and Mrs. Henn became greatly liked by everyone, and were perhaps the most popular yachting people of their time.

14 *The Thistle-Volunteer Races*

We have seen that the model of sailing yachts has been continually changing, the reason of course being the change in measurement rules, so by 1885 or so the clipper bow was taking the place of the plumb stem both in Great Britain and here. This was due to the fact that in both countries the length of waterline was a principal factor in the measurement. The clipper bow had been the usual forward arrangement of most all large sailing vessels since approximately the fourteenth century, and, while in the older vessels most of the overhang forward was composed of the figurehead, trail boards and gammon arrangement, not to mention the head, or sailors' watercloset, in the new clipper bows all this lattice work was filled in with the planking faired out to the very figurehead or fiddle head. Designers had long been aware of the advantages of the long overhanging stern on the cutters, and now that waterline length was a more important factor in the length and sail area rules used on both sides of the Atlantic they tried to get the benefit of longer lines by using a bow overhang.

Ulerin, Figure 70 might be considered a typical English or Scottish yacht of this type of 1884, but we were to see these bows on the next cup boats, and that brings us to the *Thistle-Volunteer* races of 1887.

Thistle—*a Beautiful Yacht*

During the winter of 1886-7 the New York Yacht Club received a challenge for the cup from the Royal Clyde Yacht Club naming *Thistle* of 86 feet waterline as the challenger. *Thistle* was a very handsome yacht of rather more beam than usual with the cutters. She was built purposely as a challenger by a syndicate of Scottish yachtsmen from a design by G. L. Watson, and she was built of steel. As one looks at the rigged models of *Thistle* (Fig. 72) and *Volunteer* (Fig. 71) at the New York Yacht Club he cannot but think that *Thistle* is the most modern or advanced of the two. She was beautifully finished off both above and below deck, and had a large main saloon paneled in walnut, for in those days it was customary to have the below-deck area dark as a relief to the eyes which often were exposed to too much bright sunlight above deck. She had a forecastle for twenty men with pipe berths; a fine galley and several staterooms. In her racing in England she proved faster than all other yachts. In 1887, she was commanded by Captain John Barr of Gourock, Scotland, one of the foremost racing skippers of Great Britain. *Thistle* sailed for this country on July 25, 1887, with the Scottish people confidently believing that their beautiful creation would return with the cup.

Volunteer—*Fastest Yacht of Her Time*

Volunteer was a steel centerboard sloop designed by Edward Burgess, and this was to make the third successful cup boat he produced. She was built for General Charles J. Paine and this was to be the third time that the general successfully managed a cup defender. I think that General Paine is the only one who has personally paid for more than one successful cup boat: he was the principal owner of *Puritan,* the sole owner of *Mayflower* and *Volunteer,*

92

Fig. 70. ULERIN

and also paid the cost of building *Jubilee,* one of the trial boats of 1893. *Volunteer*'s hull was built by Pusey and Jones of Wilmington, Delaware, because the George Lawley Company (who had built *Puritan* and *Mayflower*), were not then building metal yachts, but I believe her spars and much other racing gear were produced by them. Although *Volunteer* was about the same proportion of beam and draft as the two previous defenders, she was able to stow her lead ballast two or three feet lower than *Puritan* and *Mayflower.* This was because she had a steel centerboard box and steel trough keel into which her lead was run. This lowering of the lead ballast seemed to make her a very fast vessel, and many people believe that she was the fastest yacht of her time. *Volunteer* had a good useful interior, and if not as luxurious as *Thistle,* and if her interior was somewhat cut in weight, I do not infer that she was a mere racing machine like some of the later defenders. The sailing master of *Volunteer* in 1887 was Captain Henry Haff of Islip, Long Island, who had been very successful in racing around New York.

The principal dimensions of the two yachts were as follows:

	LOA	LWL	Beam	Draft	Displ.	Ballast	SA
Thistle	108.5′	86.46′	20.35′	13.8′	138 T.	70 T.	8,969
Volunteer	106.23′	85.88′	23′2″	10′	130 T.	55 T.	9,260

You see that there was quite a difference in the percentage of ballast, but *Volunteer* may have had a quantity of loose ballast, or an extremely heavy hull.

There was no real set of trial races in 1887, but *Volunteer* proved herself the fastest American yacht on the New York Yacht Club cruise of that year. I think she was an unbeaten boat throughout the year and won over $4,000 worth of prizes. It had been planned to have trial races but the attempts on September 13 and 15 were held up for lack of wind. In the one trial race on September 16, the only competition were *Mayflower,* then owned in New York, and *Volunteer.* This race was sailed over an L-shaped course off Sandy Hook in a good northwest breeze, and as *Volunteer* won by some sixteen minutes the committee immediately notified General Paine that she had been selected to defend the cup.

Able Management

I will not say that *Volunteer* did not have some of the difficulties in getting tuned up that most all other cup boats have had, but I do think General Paine, with his experience with *Puritan* and *Mayflower,* was a most able manager. It also is an advantage when the owner and manager are the same person for then quick decisions can be made. Mr. Burgess, with his experience with the two previous cup boats, seemed to have furnished a fine design for, although *Volunteer* came out rather late in the season, she evidently went to the starting line of the final races in a highly-tuned condition, and I believe never showed defects other than sails throughout the summer. Mr. Burgess credited the success of *Volunteer* mostly to General Paine and said the general's suggestions during the design and his superb management were the principal reasons for her success.

The first of the final races was on September 27, 1887, sailed over an inside L-shaped course of thirty-eight miles before a spectator fleet of hundreds of steam and sail yachts massed about the starting line, for this was expected to be a close competition with many people believing *Thistle* the better boat. The race was postponed some two hours for lack of wind, but finally in a light breeze soon after twelve o'clock they went over the line with *Thistle* slightly in the lead. While light weather was supposed to be *Thistle*'s best chance she made the mistake of sailing in the head tide of mid-channel, and her loose-footed mainsail seemed to hang up and down with little draft or life. Perhaps she was being sailed too close to the wind, or perhaps her sails were too heavy. Some say *Volunteer* had more wind as it often appears when a yacht is footing well, but at any rate *Volunteer* soon forged ahead which caused a great outburst of cheers for in those days the general public here was almost unanimously back of the defender. As the afternoon breeze increased an account of the times says, "The *Volunteer* now seemed to get a stronger breeze and increased her pace, while the *Thistle* sailed lazily with her sails hardly filled."

After rounding the first mark there was a reach to Sandy Hook Lightship, then as the course was reversed in the return over the same water, another reach in which *Volunteer* seemed to sail very fast, so that she was apparently some two miles ahead of *Thistle.* On the last leg of the course *Volunteer* set her spinnaker and romped home over nineteen minutes ahead, and as both yachts rated almost the same she won by practically this amount. The average force of wind in the race was said to be eight knots.

Keep Astern!

This was the last race for the America's Cup over an inside course for the many steam yachts and excursion steamers crowded and interfered with the racing yachts. General Paine had anticipated this trouble and had two large canvas signs painted to hang over the sides of *Volunteer* which said in large letters, "Keep Astern." (Apparently *Thistle* thought this meant her, too, for she also kept well astern.)

The next race was on September 30 over a windward and leeward course of forty miles, starting at Scotland Lightship. There was a twelve to fifteen knot breeze from the east with quite a sea running and it was raining, so this time the general did not have to hang out his "keep astern" signs. *Thistle* again got the start, probably because she was a quicker turning vessel with a proper sized rudder while *Volunteer*'s rudder was quite small, but *Volunteer* was on *Thistle*'s weather quarter close astern. At first the two yachts seemed very evenly matched and made a beautiful picture but *Volunteer,* perhaps because of her large centerboard, worked to windward of *Thistle* without outfooting her. In the latter part of the beat to windward *Volunteer* set her club topsail over her working topsail, and as the yachts split tacks she may have got a lift, for the wind varied its direction quite a little during the race. However, at the windward mark *Volunteer* had a lead of about a quarter of an hour. On the run home under spinnaker and ballooner *Thistle* picked up about two minutes so that *Volunteer* won by approximately eleven and one half minutes corrected time. At the finish cannons and steam whistles rent the air while cheer after cheer added to the tumult. That year it was the best out of three races so *Volunteer* was proclaimed winner of the America's Cup.

Handshakes for All Hands

These three Boston cup defenders had made the home city of General Paine and Mr. Burgess very proud and appreciative, so in the winter of 1888 the City of Boston gave a large reception for them in ancient Faneuil Hall, "The gathering at Faneuil Hall was a most remarkable one, not only in point of numbers, but in character, in the general good feeling displayed, and the enthusiasm expressed throughout. At intervals during the meeting His Honor the Mayor would call a halt in the speeches giving the assembled multitude an opportunity to greet the guests of the evening with a handshake. The crowd passed over the platform in single file and it is estimated that at least seven thousand persons shook hands with Messrs. Paine and Burgess."

Volunteer and *Thistle* were both strongly built yachts that lasted well. *Volunteer* was used as a yacht for about twenty-five years during which time she was twice rigged as a sloop, and for some time as a schooner. For many years she was owned by the Forbes family who used to keep a fleet of yachts in the snug harbor at Naushon near Wood's Hole, Massachusetts. *Thistle* was sold to Kaiser William and renamed *Meteor* and raced with fair success until the Emperor had G. L. Watson design the superb *Meteor II* in about 1896 when the ex-*Thistle* was turned over to the Imperial Navy for use of the naval cadets.

Barr Blamed

I must say a few words about Captain John Barr of *Thistle*: he was born at Gourock, Scotland, in 1846 and in his early life went fishing and learned the boat building trade and built many small sailboats for the Clyde. He

Fig. 71. VOLUNTEER

Fig. 72. THISTLE

became famous as a racing helmsman in Scotland between 1875 and 1884, and in 1885 sailed the small cutter *Clara* to this country with which I believe he won fifteen firsts out of fifteen starts. So, with his reputation as a racing skipper and his experience in this country, he was chosen to sail the challenger *Thistle*. When he took *Thistle* back to Scotland in October, 1887, the Scottish people in their disappointment put the blame on Captain Barr and could not believe that their beautiful *Thistle* was beaten. Some even said that he sold out to the Americans, and in general they made it so disagreeable for the captain that he came to this country and settled in Marblehead, Massachusetts. He was sometimes spoken of as a second Paul Jones for they both had the satisfaction of licking their mother country which had not appreciated them.

Captain Barr did this when he was captain of the fin keeler *Niagara* which Howard Gould sent to England in 1895 to race in the popular British 20-rater class. *Niagara* won forty-one prizes in fifty-three starts and I believe never came in worse than third in a big class. John Barr was captain of several famous American yachts including

Gloriana and the trial cup boat *Jubilee,* but he has been rather overshadowed by his younger half-brother Charlie Barr who sailed on *Clara* as cook and cabin boy and rose to be the greatest yacht captain we ever had. Captain John Barr died in his home at Marblehead January 11, 1909. He was a kindly, plain-spoken, straightforward man universally respected. He had five sons, all of whom were first-class yacht captains in this country.

Most Important Years of Yachting

We are now coming to the greatest or most important years of yachting which roughly were between 1890 and 1910. There were several reasons for this. First of all there was considerable prosperity in England and here at the close of Victoria's reign. In England there were many landed proprietors who had inherited large tracts of land which they let to hundreds of tenants. There were those who had made fortunes in India, and those who became wealthy as shipowners and shipbuilders; and the heavy industries of locomotive building and naval armament

96

were booming. Part of this prosperity was due to the fact that England was the leader with the heavy machine tools thus could make rolling mills and other types of large machinery for the manufacture of textile machines, mining industry, et cetera. In those days England exported large quantities of machinery to many parts of the world. Some of her large manufacturing concerns made great profits, for in those days the workmen's wages were in the neighborhood of one pound a week, so most of England's wealth was in the upper classes and many of them could take time off for yachting.

In this country we were lucky to have vast tracts of fertile prairie land that was so level that large steam traction engines could draw whole gangs of plows across fields as far as the eye could reach, and for many years we exported large quantities of wheat. Our mineral deposits were remarkably good with such raw metals as copper at ground level. We were the first to go into quantity production in a large way and so could outsell the world in cheap clocks, watches, bicycles, agricultural machinery, fire arms, et cetera. We were beginning to make very ingenious machine tools which have contributed to our prosperity perhaps more than is generally realized. While our workers were paid more than in Europe, still Yankee ingenuity was able to run some of our manufactories at great profit during the time that we speak of. During that time also railroads running in most every direction paid well. While our wealthy citizens did not enjoy the leisure of the European upper classes, still during these times we were making millionaires also in quantity production, and were to produce several of the world's wealthiest individuals before the income tax started in 1913.

Another thing that made yachting then the principal sport of the wealthy was that there was practically no other sport that one could personally indulge in, particularly if he were over fifty by the time he had made his million. In those days the papers devoted a lot of space to yachting, but presumably the introduction of new measurement rules for the racing sailboats had its important effect for, although changes in rules are generally frowned on by those who have vested interests, still history shows that right after a new measurement rule is introduced there is a general acceleration in yachting. It was during this time that England changed from the tonnage rules to what she called the rating classes, which means that soon after 1890 most British yachts were rated by complicated rules that were based on length and sail area but also had many restrictions to keep the yachts of a healthy type. One of these rules was evolved by Dixon Kemp, the yacht designer who published several books about yacht design around 1890. Another prominent rule maker was Mr. Froude who, I believe, was the son of the eminent William Froude who worked out the laws of comparison and similitudes still used today for testing towing models in tanks. William Froude was, I believe, the first Englishman to have a towing tank. This was in his garden at Torquay about 1870, though there were tanks earlier in Europe. Of course the greatest stimulus of the time was Prince

Edward's patronage of yachting, and he was soon followed by his nephew, Kaiser William, and many of the titled men of Europe who often had large racing sailboats as well as their steam yachts.

The greatest interest here between 1888 and 1890 was for the so-called 40-foot class. Figure 73 shows one of the 40's. They were wide, powerful boats of considerable draft, heavily ballasted, and carried a very large sail plan that was rather copied from the cutters and included several sizes of topsails, many head sails, and large spinnaker. There were quite a number of the 40-footers, mostly designed by Edward Burgess, but others by Cary Smith and William Gardner. Some of the 40-footers had centerboards in their keels which did not come above the cabin sole. Most of them were owned by men who were used to much larger craft, but apparently all of the American designers made the mistake of giving their 40's too much displacement and sail area. In other words, some of their hulls were nearly as wide as sloops, and deep as cutters, so they were too bulky to drive fast. In a breeze they were apt to look something like Figure 107 without going ahead very fast. Figure 74 shows *Baboon* owned by Charles Francis Adams and his brother, and this was perhaps the best of the American 40's. But all of these 40's were to have a great surprise and disappointment which came about somewhat as follows.

Charlie Barr

We have spoken of the cutter *Clara* that Charley Barr came over on in 1886—well, she was owned by Mr. Tweed, a New York lawyer who, though not a racing man, did love the looks of handsome sailboats and enjoyed afternoon sailing, so in 1888 he ordered from William Fife, Jr., of Scotland, a forty-foot sailboat for pleasure sailing off Beverly, Massachusetts, where he had his summer home. In the meantime young Charlie Barr had been captain of Mr. Tweed's little cutter *Shona,* five tons, and had attended classes in navigation at Boston during the winter, so Mr. Tweed sent young Charlie over to sail back the new boat named *Minerva.* They had pleasant weather and Charlie enjoyed himself very much. I think this was the crossing he told me about when they were on one tack so long in moderate weather that the topsides above the copper began to get slightly foul.

However, *Minerva* might never have entered racing if it had not been for a queer circumstance. She was at the head of the Sound when the Gardner-designed 40, *Liris,* carried away her mast. By the way, *Liris* was about the first of our racers to have hollow spars. This dismasting set the use of hollow spars back several years in this country. The crew of *Liris* was mostly Corinthian and were much disappointed that they would be out of the racing until a new spar was produced, so Mr. Tweed was approached to see if he would lend them *Minerva* for a race, which he very readily consented to do, and two days later in the Seawanhaka race *Minerva* started with a Corinthian helmsman and crew. They had varying

Fig. 73. One of the 40's.

Fig. 74. BABOON

98

weather with calms and a squall, but *Minerva* slipped along well under all conditions and won easily.

This was a great surprise to everyone for *Minerva* was not designed for the class and only had about three quarters the sail area of the others, but she was narrower and of a very beautiful form. During the rest of the season Charlie Barr raced her regularly, winning most all races with tiresome monotony, and this started him on his career of fame, which rather broke up the 40-foot class. It is probable that Charles Francis Adams, owner of the 40-foot *Baboon* was just as good a sailor, and I say this because I have raced with them both as skippers of the crack sloop *Avenger* in successive years, and that now is some fifty-one or -two years ago. However, there was a great deal of difference in the way they sailed.

Charlie Barr was perfectly relaxed during a race and kept up a conversation with the owner and guests, or even might tell an interesting story of some other race under similar conditions. He seemed to race a boat by some natural instinct without much apparent thought, as some people can drive an automobile. C. F. Adams was very different and appeared as if he were performing a solemn ritual like burying the dead, so there was no conversation other than orders, and to my young ears and eyes this did not seem like yachting or sailing for pleasure. By the way, the year C. F. Adams steered we did not win the Astor Cup, but the year Charlie Barr was at the helm we did.

At any rate, the next summer, 1889, C. F. Adams and his brother, George C., went to England to study the British yachts and had an opportunity to sail on some of the best of them. On their return they ordered from Mr. Burgess a new boat expressly to beat *Minerva*. She was named *Gossoon* and was very carefully and lightly built, but in my opinion not of as sweet a model as *Minerva* for, although *Gossoon* had much the most sail area, they were tied at the end of the season, each having won five races.

The 40-footers were a great class and numbered about twenty good ones, all but five being designed by Edward Burgess. Several of them lasted a long time and were used much for cruising. Their first cost was very little—about six thousand dollars—and they usually held a good second hand price. I believe the 40's made up the biggest open class we have ever had in what we can call yachts with good cruising accommodations, but of course we have had many small one-design classes, and small open classes, like the R boats and 6-meter boats which outnumbered them. The things that probably broke up the class were *Minerva* and the interest in a new and larger class that was being talked of in 1890. Certainly several of the owners of the 40's could afford larger craft, so the 46-footers came out in 1891 with yachts designed by Burgess, Fife, and Herreshoff.

This new class, like the 40-footers, was to be measured under the Seawanhaka rule of length and square root of sail area divided by two, with some modifications. Burgess and Fife produced clipper bowed yachts of

similar proportions to the 40's, but the Herreshoff design was quite different, being shorter on the waterline and carrying more sail. This yacht was named *Gloriana* and was developed as follows: E. D. Morgan of Newport, owned among other yachts, large and small, the 40-footer *Moccasin,* and he became very much interested in the way *Minerva* had performed, so in 1890 he ordered two sailboats from Mr. Herreshoff who had been designing and building small steam yachts for him. These two boats were to be built on the same molds but of different lengths. The first one was named *Pelican* and was launched on November 11, 1890, the same day that this writer was born. She was 26.6 feet long on the waterline. The other was named *Gannet,* 29.6 feet on the waterline. They were both rigged as cat yawls and had bows somewhat halfway between the clipper type and what was to come out in *Gloriana*. These boats were of light construction with all outside ballast lead keels. They proved fast and were much liked by Mr. Morgan.

Captain Nat Introduces Spoon Bow

Another gentleman who owned one of the 40's was Royal Phelps Carroll. One day he told Mr. Morgan that he was thinking of building a 46-footer whereupon Mr. Morgan advised him to have the Herreshoffs design and build her, so Mr. Carroll ordered a 46-footer and Captain Nat Herreshoff, who had been thinking over the design of *Pelican* and *Gannet,* decided that if he cut off the sharp forefoot of these models they would go nearly as well, and because the waterline would be much shorter this would allow more sail area under the length and sail area rule. In this way he evolved, or rather invented, the spoon bow which was practically to take the place of all other bows on racing sailboats for the next sixty years. Captain Nat's next problem was to get the required stability to carry this extra sail which he did by adopting the very light methods of construction he had worked out for fast steamers and torpedo boats, creating a light scientific rig so that all of this saving in weight could be put into the lead keel. Mr. Herreshoff had a great advantage over other designers in having his own yacht building establishment with its forge shop and machine shop capable of building the power plants of the first steam torpedo boats. Thus he could design and have made very special fittings, and this 46-footer, which was to be named *Gloriana,* had steel frames, diagonal strapping, double planking, and very neat deck and spar fittings, while the other craft of the class were built much as the older yachts had been and had to depend on stock fittings.

Before work started on *Gloriana* Mr. Carroll requested in writing that the contract be canceled as he was to be married and the Herreshoffs agreed to do this. I suppose Mr. Carroll was a little alarmed at the radical design and that was the real reason for not going ahead with it. That winter E. D. Morgan was having the high-speed launch *Javelin* built by the Herreshoffs and when he came to look at her about New Years he asked to see the design that had been started for Mr. Carroll. Mr. Morgan liked the design so much that he decided to take it over, so *Gloriana* was built for him. She entered eight races in the season of 1891; in the first race Mr. Morgan was helmsman and in the following seven races she was steered by her designer. She came in first each time, and at times seemed much faster than her competitors. Mr. Morgan then very sportingly withdrew *Gloriana* to let the other ten or eleven yachts in the class fight it out, and I think C. F. Adams' *Harpoon* (Fig. 75) turned out the best of them.

Edward Burgess died of typhoid fever on July 12, 1891, just in time to be spared the news that his 46-footers have been outmoded. It was said that Mr. Burgess had become so run down from the strain of designing so many yachts and vessels in so short a time that he did not have the strength to recover. He was only forty-three at the time of his death.

Spoon Bow Rates Lower

Not only was the spoon bow at once adopted in this country, but in a year or two England was modeling far more advanced spoon bows than we had as the next cup challenger, *Valkyrie II,* will show. But perhaps it was a mistake to make most everything from catboats to three-masted schooners spoon bowed for the clipper bowed, or long waterline, craft are really the fastest for their general size. The spoon bow simply rates lower under rules where waterline is an important factor in the rating.

Fig. 75. HARPOON

15 *Dunraven's Second Attempt*

When the designer of *Gloriana* was steering her in the races of 1891, his thoughts and imagination were stimulated and he conceived both the fin and bulb keels as means to acquire the stiffness to get more driving power from the sails, or to be able to carry more sail. And while Uffa Fox acquired world renown for thinking of the same thing in the bathtub (the fin keeler *Flying 15*), some fifty years later, we will give the fin keelers a slight review for the effect they have had on design.

The first fin keeler was named *Dilemma*. She came out late in the season of 1891 and must have been built very quickly, but, as Mr. Herreshoff designed her for himself and had her built in his own yacht yard, I suppose they could proceed with the work at once without the delays of contracts, specifications, et cetera, but it seems remarkable to me that two such yachts as *Gloriana* and *Dilemma* should come out in the same year. *Dilemma,* although her low, long sails look old-fashioned today, was a very fast boat for her time. While Mr. Herreshoff said he did not invent the fin keelers, still everyone at the time considered *Dilemma* the first successful full-size yacht to have a fin keel. It is probable that model yachts and toy boats had been made with fin keels before, and experiments had been tried with weighted centerboards, but Mr. Herreshoff was the first to work out the problems of construction which allowed the fin keel to be safe and satisfactory on a sizeable boat.

Fin Keels a Success

Both England and the United States were using measurement rules at that time which are generally spoken of as length and sail area rules in which, if you used a short waterline, the sail area could be much increased. Under these conditions the fin keelers were very successful for they could carry a large sail on a short waterline. Besides the usual yacht of the time had to be very beamy or of large displacement to carry her sail well, but the fin keelers were narrow and of light displacement so it could be driven fast in a breeze. Thus the fin keelers were quite the rage during the next five or six years and cleaned up almost all of the smaller classes both here and abroad for the English and Scottish yachtsmen were quick to import these American innovations which rather reversed the trend of the previous ten years when we were importing English and Scottish yachts. The *Wee Winn* which Herreshoff designed in 1892 for Miss Cox of England, proved so exceedingly fast that she was the talk of The Solent for many years, and her hull was preserved carefully stored in a boathouse on the Isle of Wight until recently. Figure 112 shows the Herreshoff-designed fin keeler *Dakotah* which cleaned up in the 10-rater class on the Clyde in 1894.

Fin Keels Banned

You can see that by this time the spoon bow was fully developed, and British designers were building very similar craft during the next few years. I think there were about two hundred fin keelers built in this country and of these the Herreshoff Company built a hundred. However, steps were soon taken to put the fin keelers out of racing. In this country they were simply barred from competition by many clubs and in England they were put out of the racing by what was called the girth difference rule. This rule measured the girth amidships in two different ways—one was called the skin girth and was the distance from rail to rail along the boat's skin or surface, while the other girth measurement was called the chain girth and was the distance from rail to rail that a tight chain or string would measure. The difference in these two measurements was called the girth difference, and this amount, or a fraction of it, was added to the other linear measurements of a yacht. But there was really no need of barring fin keelers for later on it was pretty well proved that the bulb keelers were the faster, particularly in the larger sizes, for the fin keelers had too much wetted surface or surface resistance.

In 1892, Mr. Herreshoff designed *Wasp* which is shown in Figure 76, and I think she was the first yacht to have a fully developed bulb keel. I say "think" because some other yachts had the same section of keel but did not have a profile with the spur of the keel dropped to near the extreme draft. *Wasp* and *Gloriana* had hot racing in the season of 1892 with the others in the 46-foot class quite out of it. *Gloriana*'s skipper and helmsman was John Barr who had been captain of the Scottish challenger *Thistle,* while his younger half brother, Charley Barr, who had won a reputation sailing the English cutter *Minerva,* sailed *Wasp.* There was not a great difference in their speed, but *Wasp* had a good lead at the end of the season. After a few years in which the bulb keel proved to be faster than the fin, practically all of the larger racing sailboats, both here and abroad, were bulb keelers.

Fig. 76. WASP

Fig. 77. VALKYRIE I

Lord Dunraven

Lord Dunraven was a famous Irish sportsman who had shot and fished over most of the world. He had inherited large estates in Ireland and Wales for he was partly of Welsh descent, had been educated in England and for some years was an assistant secretary of state for the colonies under Mr. Gladstone. He was an authority on Irish architecture and seamanship and wrote books about these matters and other subjects, so altogether he was a sportsman, statesman, and author. I believe his whole name with its title was Wyndham Thomas Wyndam Quin, Fourth Earl of Dunraven, but as his title was Irish he did not have a seat in the House of Lords. He was very wealthy and had fine residences in Ireland, England, and Wales. He usually had several yachts, large and small, at the same time and perhaps altogether won as many important yacht races as anyone in any country, for, although he was racing large sailboats as early as 1887, he won the Cowes Town cup in his 152-ton ketch *Cariad* in 1921. In 1888, he had the fine Watson-designed *Valkyrie I*

built as a cup challenger, but as he and the New York Yacht Club could not agree on the terms of the race she was not used for that purpose. *Valkyrie I* was very similar to *Thistle,* the challenger of 1887, and Figure 77 shows her sailing.

Challenge Accepted

In the fall of 1892 Dunraven again tried to challenge in behalf of the Royal Yacht Squadron, and this time, after some controversy, the New York Yacht Club accepted the challenge, but in the meantime, what with the advent of the spoon bow and bulb keel, *Valkyrie I* was outclassed, so Dunraven ordered from Watson a new and larger yacht which was named *Valkyrie II.* She was an exceptionally well modeled vessel and in some ways more advanced in shape than the spoon bowed, bulb keelers and fin keelers the Americans were to produce for the season of 1893. That was the year so many large single stickers came out: in England they built the *Britannia, Valkyrie II, Calluna* and *Satanita* while we built *Navahoe, Colonia, Vigi-*

lant, *Jubilee* and *Pilgrim,* all over 85 feet waterline. *Valkyrie II* was practically a sister ship to *Britannia* and quite similar to *Meteor* designed by Watson for Kaiser William in the next year or two, but *Valkyrie II* had a swept or raised waterline with her copper sheathing coming well above water at the ends, so appeared a little different from *Britannia.*

In the trial races to select a defender the two fin keelers *Jubilee* and *Pilgrim* proved dull in light weather because of their excess wetted surface, and were apt to break down in a breeze, so this left the two Herreshoff-designed yachts *Colonia* and *Vigilant,* both of which were shallower than should be for the depth of water at the Herreshoff Company was too little for racing yachts of this size. However, *Vigilant* (Fig. 78) had a large centerboard and considerable beam which seemed to allow her to carry her sail well and make little leeway. She was the first vessel to be plated with bronze which gave her the advantage of a polished bottom, and since her time every cup defender up to *Columbia* of 1958 has had a polished bronze bottom. *Colonia* won the first trial race but after that *Vigilant*'s designer was persuaded to steer her and she proved the fastest of the four trial boats during the summer and was chosen to defend the cup.

The first race of the *Valkyrie II-Vigilant* series came off on October 5, 1893. It was intended to be a windward and leeward race. The wind was very light and *Valkyrie II* got much the best of it, rounding the first mark some twenty-six minutes ahead of *Vigilant.* Part of *Vigilant*'s poor showing was because she was said to have been in a flat calm for some of the time, and perhaps her greater beam made her roll more in the light weather which would have knocked the wind out of her sails. And, too, *Valkyrie II* (Fig. 79) had the best light weather sails. At any rate the race had to be called off since neither yacht could have finished within the time limit, but *Valkyrie II*'s good showing made many think she was the fastest yacht, and there is no doubt she was a good drifter.

The first race to be finished was sailed on October 7 in a light breeze which shifted from northwest to southwest during the race, and this may have favored *Vigilant* for the race was intended to be a windward and leeward one of fifteen miles to a leg, and *Valkyrie II* was at her best going to windward, while *Vigilant* was a great reacher. It was a very close start with *Valkyrie II* having a lead of only about two seconds, and she held the lead for about half an hour, but as the wind shifted to make the course a reach *Vigilant* sailed by her and rounded the first mark with a lead of over eight minutes. On the way to the finish *Valkyrie II* picked up perhaps half a minute but the lead of *Vigilant* was sufficient to make up for her handicap with some five and a half minutes to spare.

The next race was on October 9 over a triangular course of ten miles to a leg. There was a good breeze that day that shifted and increased to a strong breeze before the finish. This time *Vigilant* got the start and stayed to weather of *Valkyrie II* through the first leg of the course which was to windward most of the way, but the direc-

tion of the wind was shifting so that the next two legs became reaches. *Vigilant* was a notably fast reacher, as I have said, and on the second leg averaged twelve knots and left *Valkyrie II* well behind. Both yachts had their rails under and on the last leg were traveling like steamers, but *Valkyrie II* continued to drop behind so *Vigilant* won by over two minutes corrected time and made one of the fastest times over the cup course that has ever been recorded.

An attempt was made to sail the third race on October 11, but it failed because of lack of wind. The start was postponed until 1:25. It was a windward and leeward race with the first leg to windward. This time *Vigilant* proved the best drifter and rounded the weather mark some seven minutes ahead, but the days in October are short so that it began to get dark and the spectators had the novelty of watching a cup race by starlight and the time limit expired with the yachts far from the finish line.

The third and last race was held on Friday, October 13, and as a sailor man would expect, unusual things happened. The course was to a mark fifteen miles to windward off Sandyhook Lightship and return. The wind was strong from the east with quite a slop of a sea and rose to gale force before the finish. Both yachts were late at the start for they decided to reef their mainsails which seemed to delay *Valkyrie II* the most. *Vigilant* had trouble with her centerboard and could not get it all the way down which handicapped her on the weather leg. The two yachts were not ready until more than an hour after the scheduled time for the start, then went over the line quite evenly with *Vigilant* behind but to weather. Going to windward in a strong breeze and sea *Valkyrie II* slightly outsailed *Vigilant;* this was perhaps because *Vigilant* did not get her centerboard way down, and also a narrow, deep-keeled boat is usually at her best on a beat against a strong wind and sea.

Valkyrie II rounded the weather mark with a lead of about two minutes, then tried to set her spinnaker flying, but it caught on the bitts forward and was slightly torn. In the wind that was blowing at that time the rip soon increased and the spinnaker went to pieces and had to be taken in. The *Valkyrie II* tried to set a light weather spinnaker of very light cloth, but the wind was too much for it and it, too, soon went to tatters. They then set their balloon jib to partly take the place of a spinnaker and settled down for the run to leeward. Things were quite different on *Vigilant* for they set her spinnaker in stops and broke it out successfully. Then her balloon jib was set but it fouled, or caught aloft, and a man was sent aloft to clear it. They changed then her topsail for a larger one and shook the reef out of her mainsail which was a very difficult and daring thing to do when running before a gale of wind, and to quote the eyewitness, W. P. Stephens, "By dint of this work, such as was never before witnessed in yacht racing, at the imminent danger of losing mast and the race, *Vigilant* sailed past *Valkyrie II* near the finish line and led her across by over two minutes, finally winning by forty seconds, corrected time."

Lord Dunraven had requested that the races that year should be for the best out of five so *Vigilant*'s three firsts ended the series, but it is my opinion that if there had been more races *Valkyrie II* would have won some of them for she seems by modern standards to be a better all-round model. Perhaps *Vigilant*'s bronze bottom and scientific construction gave her advantages and she always proved herself fast on a reach.

These were the great days of the large single stickers —(the British called them cutters and we called them sloops)—and in 1893 the American sloop *Navahoe,* about the same size and shape as *Vigilant,* went over to race several large cutters in England. She did quite well, considering all the odds that were against her. In the first place she was too shallow to carry her sail well, and on the first day of her intended voyage to England she ran into Nantucket Lightship in a thick fog when under full sail including her spinnaker. This strain sprung her mast and she had to limp into Boston for repairs where a heavier mast was made for her, and this was to count against a yacht that was lacking in stability. Her captain, Charlie

Barr, although the best professional we ever had, was then very young and *Navahoe* was his first large command so that he was at a disadvantage compared with the skippers of *Britannia, Calluna* and *Satanita* who had been racing together. It is also very difficult for a stranger to race a large yacht in England for many of their courses are in shallow water with strong tides. However, *Navahoe* won one outstanding long race by a matter of seconds; this was a match against *Britannia* for the Brenton's Reef Challenge cup which *Genesta* had won on her visit here in 1885. This race started off The Needles at the west end of the Isle of Wight on September 13, 1893. I was very lucky to have Charlie Barr describe this race to me and he thought it was the most thrilling race he had ever been in. The course was from The Needles to and around the breakwater at Cherbourg and return, a distance, I suppose, of around a hundred miles. There was a fine breeze and quite a sea running. Two hours after the start the yachts had run twenty-five miles and were racing neck and neck and must have been a beautiful sight, but as the wind increased they both decided to house their topmasts which

Fig. 78. VIGILANT

must have been quite a stunt in the sea that was running. *Navahoe* led around the breakwater at Cherbourg, but the wind here was very strong in puffs and knocked them both almost flat at times. After rounding the break- water *Britannia* got a slight lead but they raced back across the Channel neck and neck, neither getting more than a hundred yards ahead of the other. At the finish they were abreast and at first *Britannia* was proclaimed winner

Fig. 79. VALKYRIE II

by two and one-half seconds, but as the mark boat had moved or dragged her anchor since the start and the line was not at right angles to the course favoring *Britannia* more than 2½ seconds the owner of *Navahoe* protested and the race was given to *Navahoe*.

While some used to say this race showed that *Navahoe* could challenge the best British yachts in open water, still the race for the Cape May Cup, which was three days later over the same course, showed that *Britannia* was a better drifter and beat *Navahoe* about an hour in this long, drawnout calm race. *Navahoe* won several important cups after she came back to this country but later was changed to a yawl and spent most of her life in Europe and for some years was owned in Germany where her shallow draft was an advantage. After *Navahoe* was slightly beaten by the big British cutters—(she was pitted against four of them so could usually be covered by one so another could win)—the hue and cry again sounded that the American cup defender could not have won if she had to cross the ocean. So two wealthy New Yorkers, George and Howard Gould, purchased *Vigilant* and sent her to England under the command of the seagoing captain, L. A. Jeffries. She made the crossing to Gourock, Scotland, in fifteen days and nine hours which was very good, considering the fact that she was under a reduced rig. On her return in 1895 under the command of Charlie Barr, she happened to also make a quick passage, 17 days and 19 hours, so that I believe this round trip is the fastest on record for a sailing vessel.

Vigilant's designer and her racing captain, Hank Haff, followed with the Goulds on their steam yacht *Atlanta*. They hurriedly prepared *Vigilant* and she entered her first race abroad on July 4, 1894. This race started in Holy Loch, a rather restricted part of the Clyde, and as there was quite a spectator fleet of large steam yachts the starting line was rather dangerous for the four large single stickers which started. There was a strong wind blowing and my father, who was handling *Vigilant,* had her shortened down to jib and mainsail and determined to make a late start. *Britannia* also did the same thing, either to avoid danger or to cover *Vigilant,* but at about the time of the starting gun a heavy rain squall came down the loch and shut off visibility. When it cleared up some *Britannia* and *Vigilant* squared away and boiled down toward the starting line. Right before them they could see *Valkyrie II* and *Satanita* locked in a death struggle for *Satanita* had collided with *Valkyrie II* cutting her down below the waterline. After they had been separated *Valkyrie II* fouled one of the nearby steam yachts and sank in fourteen fathoms of water, fortunately with only one fatality. *Britannia* and *Vigilant* continued the race, and on the first leg *Vigilant* beat *Britannia,* rounding the weather mark some two minutes ahead of her, but on the return to the finish in light wind *Britannia* passed her near the finish line to win by thirty-six seconds. Figure 80 shows how *Satanita*'s bow looked after the collision, and Figure 81 shows *Valkyrie II* after she was raised and floated.

Vigilant's designer had to return to America after this

Fig. 80. SATANITA'S bow after collision

Fig. 81. VALKYRIE II after being floated

race but *Vigilant* raced with rather indifferent success the rest of the season and won six firsts out of eighteen races. She had trouble with her centerboard and sails and, being one boat against three, did not have much of a chance. However, she often sailed faster than the British yachts only to lose out later because of lack of knowledge of local sailing conditions. Both *Navahoe* and *Vigilant* did prove that an American yacht could cross the ocean and show that they could do quite well under the disadvantage of racing against several competitors.

If all these races had been match races against one competitor the score might have been quite different. After *Vigilant* came back to this country she was used as a yacht for many years, first as a sloop and then as a yawl. She won many important prizes and finally was broken up in 1910 when many of her fittings and parts were used in the Cary Smith-designed schooner *Enchantress*.

In 1894, designer Herreshoff invented the cross-cut sail, and as none of the other sailmakers was willing to risk his reputation on such a radical departure in sail cutting, the Herreshoff company had to set up a sail loft and manufacture their own sails, and from this time on they furnished most all of their yachts with cross-cut sails. It is my belief that the cross-cut sails gave Mr. Herreshoff a great advantage over other designers until other sailmakers cut their sails in the same way.

16 *Dunraven's Last Try and the Great British Cutters*

In these days the challenges for the America's Cup came in quick succession. In the fall of 1894 Lord Dunraven challenged again with a new and larger yacht named *Valkyrie III*. But rather strange things were to take place, for Watson designed *Valkyrie III* wide like *Vigilant*, while Herreshoff designed the new cup boat, which was named *Defender,* rather narrow. So that year you might say the British had the sloop and we had the cutter. *Valkyrie III* was a very sporty looking yacht, and I think Dunraven thought he had the cup clinched this time. Figure 82 shows her in a trial spin before she came over. You can identify her in photographs for she had her martingale, or bobstay spreader, attached to the bowsprit some two feet forward of the stem head. After *Vigilant*'s indefinite showing in England the year before, designer Herreshoff was determined to produce a yacht that would win without question, so, after some dredging was done, the Herreshoff Company had ways laid which could launch a much deeper vessel than the *Vigilant*. Mr. Herreshoff then went to work unrestricted and produced a beautiful model for this new yacht. Her bottom was polished bronze, but her topsides, deck beams, and some of her deck framing were aluminum. *Defender* (Fig. 83) was not the first vessel to use aluminum in her construction, for the English Navy had a couple of aluminum torpedo boats around 1893. In the trial races of 1895 *Defender*'s principal competitor was *Vigilant,* and after the new yacht was straightened out she could beat *Viligant* quite handily, so this was another year when it was easy for the cup committee to select the fastest yacht.

The first race between *Valkyrie III* and *Defender* was on September 7. It was intended to be a windward and leeward race, but as the wind shifted it became a beat and reach. At the start the wind was about six miles an hour from the east with a little chop. Both yachts made a magnificent start with *Valkyrie* a few seconds ahead but with *Defender* on her weather quarter. In the first part of this race *Valkyrie* seemed to foot the faster and many thought she was beating *Defender,* but evidently *Defender* was pointing higher, for after a few tacks she was definitely ahead, and from then on steadily sailed away from *Valkyrie* and rounded the weather mark three minutes and twenty-three seconds ahead. The wind was about eight miles an hour by this time and I should think that *Valkyrie* could have done better on the fifteen-mile reach to the finish, but she gradually dropped behind so that *Defender* won on corrected time by over eight and one half minutes.

Lord Dunraven was extremely chagrined at the result of this first race and thought *Defender* had taken on ballast and increased her waterline length since she was measured, so he demanded a remeasurement, but when both yachts were remeasured no differences from their previous measurements were found. There is no doubt that *Defender* had several speed-giving qualities that gave her an advantage. They were as follows:

1. Crosscut sail.
2. A high percentage of lead ballast carried very low in her bulbed keel, made possible by her aluminum topsides and aluminum deck framing.

107

Fig. 82. VALKYRIE III on a trial run

3. Polished bronze bottom.
4. A very nice model which was narrower than the challenger and seemed to allow *Defender* to slip through a chop of a sea with little resistance.

The second race was on September 10 over a thirty-mile triangular course in a nice, true breeze, and it is very unfortunate that *Valkyrie* fouled *Defender* right at the start, for this might have been a fine, definite chance to compare the speed of the yachts. It seems that *Valkyrie III* (Fig. 84) was a few seconds ahead of time at the start and so to kill her way she was sailed a crooked course just ahead and to weather of *Defender*. On one of her swings *Valkyrie's* boom caught on *Defender's* starboard topmast shroud and broke it. *Valkyrie* continued right along in the race but *Defender* had to be brought up in the wind while her crew rigged a watch tackle on her broken shroud which of course took several minutes to accomplish. *Defender,* however, continued the race although she had set a protest flag, and in spite of being crippled on one tack, and being unable to carry her jib topsail, she did so well when sailing with the wind over her well side that she gained on *Valkyrie*. Thus the challenger won the race by only forty-seven seconds corrected time, which of course was much less than *Defender's* delay at the start. In other words, *Defender* sailed over the course in the least time, if we subtract the time for repairs, though she was unable to carry her jib topsail when on the starboard tack.

As this foul took place right under the eyes of the race committee and was a clear case of a weather yacht coming down on and fouling a yacht on her lee, the race was given to *Defender*. C. Oliver Iselin, the managing owner of *Defender,* very sportingly offered to resail the race, but Dunraven would not accept the offer. Instead, he seemed to blame the New York Yacht Club for the accident on the grounds that they did not properly patrol the race course. Of course there was much justification for his grievance, as I will describe below, but the general public by this time was disgusted at the challenger's sportsmanship, and the press did not do anything to help the matter. The cause of the foul was somewhat like this: just before starting time the large steamer *Yorktown* blundered right into the position the yachts would be in in making a start on the starboard tack. *Valkyrie* went to windward of *Yorktown* which brought her too soon near the starting line while *Defender* went to leeward with her time and distance about right. Thus *Valkyrie* had to kill her way by both letting out her main sheet and making a quick change of course, but in this swing *Valkyrie's* long main boom swept across part of *Defender's* deck and caught on her weather or starboard topmast shroud and broke it.

I suppose that if *Valkyrie* had been ten feet farther to windward, or had her boom more aboard, both yachts would have made a fine start, but the *Yorktown* had interfered with both yachts and probably was one reason *Valkyrie* was a few seconds early at the start. In these races some of the faster steam yachts of the New York

Yacht Club were supposed to patrol the course, but they were not very successful in that respect, principally because the spectator fleet did not acknowledge their authority and it would be difficult for a light, fragile yacht to assert her authority over a large steamer, for on the water in most cases might is right. However, after these races the New York Yacht Club called on the Navy and Coast Guard to patrol the courses.

In the meantime Lord Dunraven had written a rather bitter letter to the cup committee complaining about the crowding of *Valkyrie III* by the excursion fleet, and even refused to sail the third race unless the course was better patrolled. He even suggested postponing the race and sailing it on an unannounced date to get rid of the crowding fleet of excursion steamers. The Cup Committee discussed the matter with Dunraven, but while they were powerless to keep the fleet at a distance, they were of the opinion that the crowding did not affect the challenger more than it did the defender. In this latter opinion they were somewhat wrong, for the wide *Valkyrie III* had a marked tendency to hobbyhorse in light weather and a chop, while the narrow, sharp-bowed *Defender* would slip along almost unaffected by the churned up water of the excursion fleet.

On September 12 both yachts were at the starting line on time, *Defender* with a new topmast to replace the one sprung in the previous race. The wind was light and *Defender* had set her largest club topsail, but, strange to say, the challenger hung around the starting line with no topsail, jib topsail or fore staysail set. There was a nice light breeze at the time and the excursion fleet had kept well out of the way. The course was signaled fifteen miles to windward and return. There was every prospect for a good, fair race but the challenger did not set her light sails. Right after the start *Valkyrie III* pulled down her racing pennant and hoisted the yacht club flag and headed back to her anchorage. *Defender* sailed over the course in four hours and forty-three minutes which was very good speed considering the light wind, and thus the cup races of 1895 ended very uninterestingly.

The American press at that time was very outspoken and antagonistic in matters which pertained to American honor, and in a year or two were to be one of the causes of the Spanish war. The press handled Lord Dunraven rather unmercifully but it must be remembered that this country had not then become of age diplomatically so the ridiculous controversies about the challenger's several protests were kept up during the next winter, but I am sure that today the New York Yacht Club would handle such a matter far more amicably. It is my opinion that Lord Dunraven saw in the first race that *Defender* was a much faster boat than *Valkyrie III,* and he was so sorely disappointed and mentally upset that he was not responsible for his actions, so I drop the matter at that though much could be written on the subject which would prove almost nothing. However, where there was such an apparent difference in the speed of the yachts it might be interesting to look more closely at some of their char-

110

acteristics. Their dimensions were:

	Valkyrie III	Defender
L.O.A.	129′	123′
L.W.L.	88′ 10″	88′ 5″
Beam	26′ 10″	23′
Draft	20′	19′
Measured sail area	13,028 sq. ft.	12,602 sq. ft.

While there was not much difference in their rating, for Valkyrie only allowed Defender twenty-nine seconds over a thirty-mile course, there seemed to be quite a difference in their action. The narrow Defender, with her high percentage of ballast, had little head-on resistance but could carry her sail well. She heeled easily at first and let her sails sleep, or draw properly, while her rather sharp bow allowed her to slip through a chop with little interference to speed. Defender was the first cup defender to have crosscut sails, and this no doubt helped her quite a lot. All of her spar and deck fittings were very light, neat and scientific. Among other things she had wire rope anchor cables which coiled on a drum that fitted over the capstan so that, after the anchor was up, drum, cable and all could be hoisted off the capstan and lowered into her hold near the top of her lead keel. On the whole she was a very scientific creation for a yacht before the Spanish-American War.

Valkyrie III also was a super creation and if anyone thinks they did not have sporting yachts in the Gay Nineties they will show their ignorance for in those days art and science went hand in hand quite contentedly, and in Scotland skilled shipyard labor was paid only about a pound a week and they had such titans as Watson and the Fifes to lead them. Valkyrie III's rig was undoubtedly a masterpiece and one of its peculiarities was that she had three sets of backstays, one to hold the mast aft at the gaff jaws; one to take the strain of the jib, and the usual topmast backstay which must have taken considerable strain when a balloon jib of several thousand square feet was set. The principal trouble with Valkyrie III probably was that she was both wide and deep and had rather a shallow body which gave her a large amount of wetted surface. Now, when you consider that in yachts of this size surface resistance is more than half of the total head-on resistance, you can see one of the disadvantages Valkyrie sailed under. It is too bad these yachts did not have a race in a breeze when the increase in speed would have made surface resistance less than wave resistance, but perhaps even then the Defender's high percentage of ballast and crosscut sails would still have given her the advantage.

I have written some of the above to emphasize the advantages Defender had over Valkyrie III, and believe Lord Dunraven saw this in the first race, for he was a very keen man. So I believe the real cause of the disagreeable controversy of 1895 was the difference in speed of the competitors, and I can partly understand Dunraven's great disappointment after trying so hard and at such expense to create a winner, so I have always felt somewhat sympathetic toward him. On the other hand there is no valid reason why England's daughter, New England, should not produce as fast a sailing vessel as the mother country did. Perhaps in the future England or Scotland will have some sons as talented as the Fifes and Watson and the English Nicholsons, and if at that time we have run out of talent the cup will go back to the country of its origin and stay there a long time.

Aluminum Plating

I do not know what became of Valkyrie III after her return to England but Defender was very foolishly laid up in the water near Mr. Iselin's summer home at New Rochelle where there was a protected cove with draft enough for her deep keel. Here she lay during the Spanish War and until she was prepared for the trial races of 1899. So she was more or less afloat for over three years with her mast stepped. Defender's plating above water was aluminum, but below the waterline it was bronze. It was not known then that these metals did not get along well when close to salt water, but the action of these large surfaces with bare bronze submerged in the salt water was considerable and caused Defender's aluminum plating to start to disintegrate even under the paint. The aluminum seemed to suffer most under her long overhanging stern and several aluminum rivets actually fell out. I speak of these things now because aluminum acquired a bad reputation in its infancy from its use on Defender, but we know today that when aluminum is kept insulated from the more noble metals, and if well painted or occasionally polished, it has its use as a nautical material. I have on my drawing board a lacquered cup that was made out of part of Defender's plating, and although it must now be sixty-five years old it looks nearly as good as new. But I have known other trinkets made from the waste of her plating that turned back to their original clay in less than ten years.

However, the modern aluminum alloys are a different matter and in the future these aluminums will probably be the principal materials for yacht construction, large and small, for aluminum has some very desirable qualities, not the least of which is that it has increased in price less than the other structural materials, so that by the year 2000 small vessels plated with aluminum and painted with some of the modern hard neutral paints may very well become standard. I hope the patient reader will excuse me for dwelling so long on aluminum but a knowledge of the past is most helpful in making advances, and few people seem to know that aluminum was used in large quantities on a cup defender some sixty-eight years ago if the defender Defender was plated up in 1894.

It was in 1895 that the American fin keeler Niagara went to England to race in the popular 20-rater class. She was owned by Howard Gould who was one of the brothers who had owned Vigilant when she was racing in England the year before. The captain of Niagara was

Fig. 83. Shows DEFENDER in 1895

John Barr of whom I have spoken before as having been captain of the Scottish challenger *Thistle,* so he knew the British waters and ways of racing. During the season *Niagara* won forty-one prizes out of fifty-three starts, and I believe won a pennant in every race but one, which is probably an all-time record for a yacht racing in foreign waters, and most remarkable for a single alien racing in a large class where, unless she could get a good start, her chances were small.

Britannia—*Two Kings and Five Hundred Races*

Now I will say something about the larger English yachts for these were the greatest years of yacht racing. Figure 85 shows the wonderful *Britannia* which was probably the handsomest all around good yacht ever built. Her beauty perhaps was somewhat after the style of Juno, and she could carry her sail so well that in a breeze she went to windward like a steamer—in fact in

Fig. 84. VALKYRIE III on the railway

Fig. 85. Shows the BRITANNIA

a wind and sea the average steam yacht of the time could not keep up with her. *Britannia* was raced many more years than any of the larger yachts, having been owned by two kings. Altogether she competed in some five hundred and thirty-nine races during the twenty-one seasons she was in commission, and in her first years she accumulated a considerable amount of valuable trophies and racing money. This picture was taken May 17, 1895, by the famous photographer West of Southampton and the plate is now in possession of the present great visual recorder of yachting, Beken and Son. Mr. Beken told me recently that he still occasionally sells prints from this fine plate. It might interest the modern photographer to know that this is a contact print taken from a plate about twelve inches by fifteen and one quarter inches, and how Mr. West handled such a large camera from a small boat in a sea and wind is a mystery to me indeed.

Britannia appears to have a working topsail set over a reefed mainsail, and the wind is no doubt blowing about thirty miles per hour. I have seen her racing on The Solent in even heavier wind and considerably more sea when she would pitch her bowsprit into each coming sea and then, as she passed the crest, throw her bow out of the water way back to the mast step, and this was a sight to be remembered always. It was befitting that the crowds along the esplanade at Cowes cheered themselves hoarse at the spectacle of their king forging to windward like a steamer. English yacht racing is often quite different from ours in that it was close to shore where the general public can watch it, and so a very great many people in that country were keenly interested in the sport. Even small boys on the streets of Southampton, Cowes, or Southsea could recognize most of the yachts at a distance, while a large percentage of our boys could not tell a racing yacht from a haystack, and they care less for they can seldom see them racing. So there is much to be said for inshore courses, although on account of the tides and shoals it is more of a competition of piloting and seamanship than a test of the relative speeds of the yachts. The British gentlemen like it that way and have always tried to let the less fortunate share their pleasure, so the yacht owner in England on the whole was more popular than in this country.

In this fine picture of *Britannia* you can see her competitor half a mile astern; she was the then brand new *Ailsa* designed by William Fife. *Ailsa* has her topmast housed and at least one reef in the mainsail. In the background there is a fleet of Thames barges, but nowadays it would be unusual to see one under sail on The Solent. *Ailsa* was considered by many to be the sweetest lined yacht of her time and if I described *Britannia* as handsome after the Juno style, I will call *Ailsa* (Fig. 86) beautiful after the style of Venus, for she was lovely and dainty. She was somewhat smaller than *Britannia* but perhaps the only yacht which gave *Britannia* consistent competition in those days.

These two yachts raced in the Mediterranean early in the spring of 1895 when *Ailsa* got the best of it, but after *Britannia* had returned to her home waters she was nearly invincible. Figure 87 shows them on March 7, 1895, off Cannes. *Ailsa*'s new sails have not yet stretched out but they will grow perhaps three feet on the head and five feet on the foot while the stretch of the mainsail and club topsail will allow the club to overlap the gaff as it does on *Britannia* whose sails are fully stretched. However, this picture gives you a chance to compare these great beauties and appreciate the work of those great Scottish artists, Fife and Watson. *Ailsa* later was painted white and rerigged as a yawl. She came to this country about the turn of the century and every sailor who had an eye for shape fell in love with her.

You should look at these pictures carefully and with reverence for there will never be such beauties again until the net income of the yacht owner is as much more than the shipyard worker's as it was in 1895. Even then the world at that time will have to produce an artist equal to Watson or Fife, and that is not at all likely to happen for the skill of designing large yachts has gone for the lack of practice at it.

Figure 88 shows *Santanita*, designed by J. M. Soper in 1893, which was the longest on the waterline of the large English single stickers. She showed great bursts of speed on a reach in strong winds, and though she won several notable races she often lost out on time allowance. Figure 89 shows *Meteor II* that G. L. Watson designed for H. I. M. Wilhelm II in 1896. Before this the Kaiser had been using the old cup challenger *Thistle* whose name had been changed to *Meteor*. *Meteor II* was very much like *Britannia*, perhaps one foot longer on the waterline, one foot more beam, and appears to have less freeboard. She raced quite a little with the big English cutters and several times beat *Britannia*, although she usually finished near the middle of the class. She probably was a better boat than *Britannia* but perhaps not sailed as well. From 1893 to something like 1897, there were often four or five of these large cutters racing in England, but somewhere around that time Prince Edward sold *Britannia* and the interest in first-class cutter racing died out. Edward, as king, bought *Britannia* back and raced her with time allowance against all sorts of yachts for several years. We in this country seldom have had large sloop racing except in cup boat years, and *Vigilant* was rerigged as a yawl and *Colonia* as a schooner and both sailed year after year. On the whole we have preferred schooners in the larger classes.

Germany did little yachting before Kaiser Wilhelm's time though for centuries there were talented naval architects there who produced the plans for commercial and naval vessels as carefully and scientifically as anywhere else. It is said that the Kaiser inherited his love of yachting from his English mother, but as there were few, if any, good yacht yards in Germany before 1890 most of the large German yachts were bought in England or the United States. The *Hamburg*, ex *Rainbow*, designed by G. L. Watson in 1898; 116 feet on the waterline, was said to be a fast, good seaboat. She came in second in the Kaiser's transatlantic race of 1905. The Kaiser also encouraged an interest in a small yacht class that was called the Sonder or Special Class which had a simple measurement which, as I remember it, consisted of length on the waterline, the beam and draft added together which could not exceed a certain amount like thirty-one feet, and there was a limit on the sail area. These boats became very popular in Germany, the United States and Spain, and there were several international races for these countries for several years. Germany began to develop boat yards that did very fine work indeed, and of course as the reader knows, Germany has since then developed into one of the principal yacht building countries.

Fig. 86. AILSA

Fig. 87. Shows BRITANNIA and AILSA off Cannes. BRITANNIA competed in 539 races

Fig. 88. SATANITA designed by J. M. Soper

Fig. 89. METEOR II designed in 1896

17 Skimming Dishes and the First Lipton Challenge

England and America were to continue with their length-and-sail area measurement rules for several years, roughly between 1880 and 1905. Prior to this the length of hull taken at some point was an important factor in the rating, and, as most measurement rules both here and abroad up to the present time use waterline length to control other factors like displacement in their multiple standard rules, sailing yachts have been all too short on the waterline for best performance. Between 1895 and 1905, there was a mania for building sailboats with long overhang to gain proper sailing length, and these yachts were as freakish in hull form as our present yachts are in sail plan, for some of these boats were twice as long on deck as they were on the measured waterline, while some of our present boats carry more than twice the measured sail area.

The reader may wonder why the yacht clubs continued so long with L.W.L. as the principal hull measurement after *Gloriana* in 1891. Well, the principal reason for it was that the eminent William Froude of England, who was looked upon as the leading scientist in the study of hull resistance, gave the world his Law of Comparison in about 1876. One of Froude's mathematical formulae was that the speed of vessels of like shape and proportion was in mathematical proportion to her L.W.L., and so many people believed this throughout the world that they seemed to think there was no other hull measurement than L.W.L. necessary to rate a boat. They seem to have overlooked Froude's words "of like shape and proportion."

These words are not quoted exactly from Froude for he would have taken half a page to make this statement,

but the meaning is what I believe Froude inferred. However, almost all mathematical laws for gauging the speed of a vessel are very inaccurate, and perhaps that is fortunate for otherwise we could all beat one another on paper without the benefit of getting out on the water. All the yachting countries built long overhang yachts during the Gay Nineties with the American yachts in the small classes, the worst freaks of all. As a rule they were called skimming dishes and often went very fast for short distances reaching, under perfect conditions, when their speed was perhaps twice what Froude's law called for. I must say that many of these freaks were good shapes for planing, and often planed in strong breezes when the spinnaker was set although their average speed was less than our later boats that had less wetted surface as compared to their sail area.

Perhaps the most extreme of the racing skimming dishes was *Outlook,* designed by W. Starling Burgess in 1902. She was the only yacht that I remember that was over twice as long on deck as on the waterline. Her principal dimensions were L.O.A. 51' 5"; L.W.L. 21'; beam 16'; draft of hull less than 9"; and sail area 1,800 square feet. *Outlook* was built over a complicated steel girder frame which, though it was very light, held her ends from sagging and resisted the twisting strains that were great in the yachts of this class. *Outlook* was built to defend the Quincy Challenge Cup which she did successfully, and perhaps she was the most famous yacht that Starling Burgess designed before he went into the aeroplane business before World War I.

Another extreme craft of the time was *Dominion,* (Fig.

90) the Canadian defender of the Seawanhaka Cup of 1898. *Dominion*, besides being nearly twice as long overall as on the measured waterline, was a catamaran; that is, her hull was so shaped that the port and starboard sides were semicircular bulges while amidships the hull was arched up to about three inches above the water, so that she was very similar to some of the rigid catamarans made today. She was designed by G. Herrick Duggan who raced on her, and for several years Mr. Duggan created boats of this class that beat anything the New Yorkers or the Seawanhaka Yacht Club could build. Figure 91 shows a larger sloop with long overhanging ends. The Canadians had been building some of the world's fastest light small sailboats for years. Although these light skimming dishes went fast at times their average speed over a course was seldom over six miles an hour. In other words, no faster than a sensible boat of the same sail area but with longer waterline.

It is noteworthy that the Seawanhaka Yacht Club, which had been formed to promote wholesome sailboats for amateur sailing and had at first promoted the narrow cutters in this country, was now putting most of its energy into racing craft that were about eight feet wide with hulls drawing some six inches of water. Some of these craft had hulls that weighed under five hundred pounds although their length on deck was over thirty feet. This was another generation of Seawanhakans from the cutter cranks, and they brought the American centerboard back to stay for use on small craft. Most of us who were boys during the happy nineties were much carried away with the skimming dishes. I suppose one of the reasons was that before the fast motor boat, the automobile and the aeroplane these skimming dishes gave quite often an impressive sensation of speed, and we were willing to overlook their low average speed.

It is interesting that larger sloops, schooners, yawls and

Fig. 90. DOMINION

catboats should imitate these skimming dishes and adopt wide, shallow hulls with long overhanging ends. Figure 136 shows a larger sloop. When *The Rudder* of 1898 brought out its "How to Build a Racer for $50.00," we boys were very excited about the racing catboat *Lark* (Fig. 92), and I think there must have been several hundred of them built.

Of course the larger yachts, and the schooners in particular, remained quite sensible between the Spanish War and 1900, and the upper classes took a great interest in this racing because it made an interesting spectacle for guests on the many fine steam yachts of the time. Also there were then in this country few other sporting events of note for league baseball and organized horse racing had not come in, while golf and tennis were just being introduced to society at Newport.

First Lipton Challenge

This brings us up to the first of the Lipton challenges. In August, 1898, the New York Yacht Club received a cable from the secretary of the Royal Ulster Yacht Club of Belfast, Ireland, saying that that club desired to challenge for the America's Cup on behalf of Sir Thomas Lipton. The Royal Ultster Yacht Club sent a committee to make the final arrangements and this committee consisted of their vice-commodore, secretary, and a member; also William Fife, Jr., the Scottish naval architect, who

Fig. 91. A larger sloop with long overhanging ends

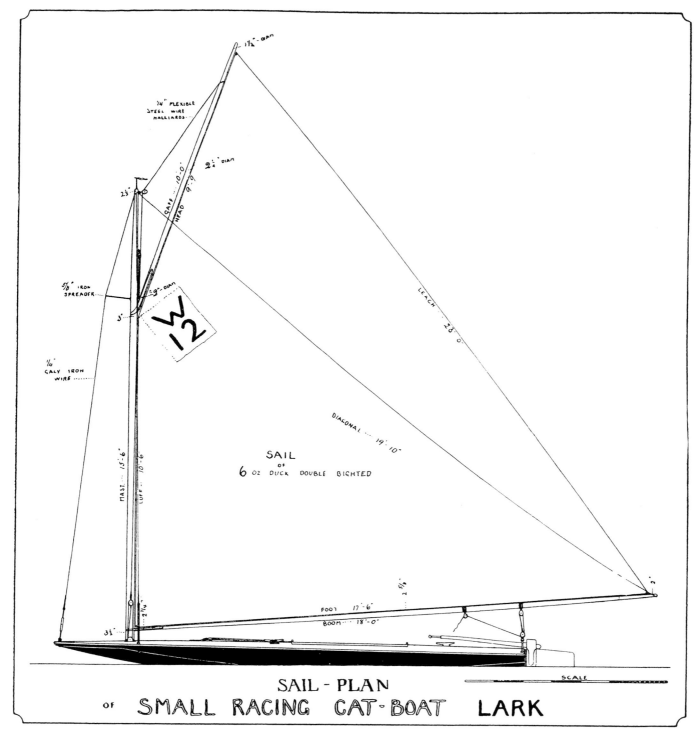

Fig. 92. Racing catboat LARK

was to design the challenger that would be named *Sham-rock*. The meeting with the New York Yacht Club was so amicable that the club accepted the challenge the same day that the signed challenge was handed to them, thus showing that the Irish gentlemen of that time were most agreeable, for no match for the Cup had ever been arranged so easily and pleasantly.

Thomas Johnstone Lipton was born in Glasgow, Scotland, of Irish parents in 1850. He got his first job as errand boy when he was ten years old, and worked at various trades until he reached sixteen years, when he had

saved enough money to pay his steerage passage to America. His adventures here included working on a tobacco plantation in Virginia, a rice plantation in South Carolina, driving horse cars in New Orleans, and finally working as a grocery clerk in a New York store. These experiences seemed to give him a keen understanding of human nature. After he returned to Glasgow he worked for a while in the little store that his father ran, but on his twenty-first birthday he opened a store of his own, and with his great ability and energy he soon opened a chain of stores throughout the Empire, and, as the concern expanded, he owned and ran tea, coffee, and cocoa plantations in Ceylon. He also had packing houses in Chicago and Omaha, and owning a huge international food company he became very wealthy by the time he was fifty.

Up to that time his mind had been entirely on business, but in his later years he became very charitable. At the time of Queen Victoria's Jubilee he gave twenty-five thousand pounds to the poor of London. Later he opened soup kitchens and hospitals for the poor of the city, so in gratitude London honored him with the high title of Lieutenant of the City of London. He was knighted in 1898 and was made a baronet in 1901, perhaps partly for his large contributions to the India famine relief fund.

By this time King Edward had given him some of his patronage and it is my opinion that Lipton challenged for the cup mostly to please the king and not so much to advertise the tea company. Although Lipton owned the fine steam yacht *Erin* (Fig. 93) he had not been concerned with racing sailboats until he decided to challenge, but then Sir Thomas, as he was fondly called, joined the Royal Ulster Yacht Club and presented the club with a thousand guinea cup, which was the first of the Lipton cups he gave throughout the world for yacht racing.

His next move, according to W. P. Stephens, was to buy a yachting cap. I think Sir Thomas was a very remarkable character for it was not so easy to rise financially and socially in England then as it was over here. Some modern writers have belittled Sir Thomas, partly because he became rather canny in his old age, but I believe this was because he could not get used to the loss in the value of the pound after World War I.

At the time of Lipton's first challenge J. P. Morgan was Commodore of the New York Yacht Club and the owner of the fine new steam yacht *Corsair,* which had recently been designed for him by J. Beavor-Webb to take the place of his previous *Corsair* that had been turned over to the United States Navy at the time of the Spanish War. Mr. Morgan had just presented the New York Yacht Club with the site in New York City of the present clubhouse at 37 West 44th Street. In spite of this and of recently having had *Corsair* built, he was willing to finance the new cup boat to be named *Columbia.* Mr. Morgan started life quite differently from Thomas Lipton, having been born into wealth and having been partially educated in England, Switzerland and Germany, an ideal education for an international banker. He joined his father in the firm of J. S. Morgan which had recently taken over the interests of the George Peabody international banking house which had enjoyed much respect and prosperity for many years.

J. P. in his youth had the opportunity to meet and to know many of the world's leading financiers. From what I have heard about him I should imagine that he had been one of the world's best judges of character. With his remarkable memory he could thus choose the most reliable person to accomplish business transactions, and could generally pick the proper man to be the leader of the various heavy industries whose financial arrangements were handled by his house. When he reorganized some of the railroads that had been running in competition on parallel lines and arranged them so they served their own districts it is said he added much to the nation's economy. When he reorganized the United States Steel Company so that the various rolling mills could specialize on one or a few products instead of competing with one another in the varied lines of merchandise that they most all were producing, he may have increased the nation's economy a billion dollars in a few years for, not only was the manufacturing of steel much accelerated, but the storing and marketing of steel was simplified. Mr. Morgan was a very religious man and in his later life the church was one of his great interests.

I have written about these national heroes so the readers of this generation may partly understand why there was so much interest in the cup races of 1899, and I must add that in those days successful men were honored and looked up to while the present-day tendency is to belittle and vilify the capable.

At first, Sir Thomas talked of having *Shamrock* built at Queenstown to be an all-Irish product excepting for the design, but Lipton usually let his designers work things out to their own liking so it was arranged to have her built by the famous torpedo boat builders, Thorneycroft & Company, in England, as they had perhaps built the lightest vessels for their strength in Europe. *Shamrock* (Figures 94, 95) was too large a vessel for designer Fife's yard, and the Fifes specialized in wood construction. *Shamrock's* construction was said to be very light and scientific, as might be expected by the combined talents of the designer and builder. She was like the previous defender, *Defender*, in being bronze plated below water but plated with an aluminum alloy on the topsides, and it was said that this metal stood up ever so much better than the pure aluminum of *Defender*.

There is no doubt that *Shamrock* was a super-creation as far as construction was concerned, and her rigged model at the New York Yacht Club shows that she had speed giving qualities in the hull with little to be criticized today excepting that her wetted surface may have been a little excessive. But when we look at her sail plan it does not appear as modern as *Columbia's* which was narrower or shorter fore and aft for its height, and *Shamrock* still used up-and-down cut sails some of the time. Both challenger and defender that year had hollow steel main masts, booms and gaffs. *Shamrock's* topsides were painted green so she appears black in most photographs. This was the first year a challenger was allowed to be towed over, or permission granted to tow in light weather, thus deviating somewhat from both the word and spirit of the deed of gift. *Shamrock* was completed rather late so did not have time for more than a couple of trial races in which I believe she did not beat the seven-year-old *Britannia* consistently.

As for *Columbia,* (Fig. 96) J. P. Morgan gave her designer a free hand and did not interfere with the design whatsoever. He invited C. Oliver Iselin to manage her and join him as part owner, and Mr. Iselin chose young

Charlie Barr as her captain which caused much public criticism, for Captain Barr was a Scotsman who had only taken out American papers a few years previous to 1899. To somewhat make up for this *Columbia* shipped a crew of mostly Americans, but in later years, when American sailors became scarce, Charlie Barr preferred a Scandinavian crew which, as he said, would obey orders promptly without stopping to think about the matter.

Mr. Herreshoff designed *Columbia* very much as an enlarged *Defender* with longer overhangs. She was very much of the same construction but used steel, which is lighter than bronze, for her upper plating and deck framing. She had a soft pine deck like *Defender* and was the last of the Herreshoff defenders to have a wooden deck. It was a nice job of building as her builders by this time were fully practiced in this class of work, and I believe she never showed structural weakness in her hull though she was to defend the cup twice without alterations. *Columbia,* however, had all the usual trouble in straightening out her rig, and once carried away her steel mast.

In the trial races of that year the only competitors were *Defender* and *Columbia*. *Defender* was in charge of W. Butler Duncan, Jr., a very able amateur yachtsman of an old yachting family, and while *Defender* also had a hollow steel mast which was much lighter than her previous wooden one, she was no match for *Columbia*. The two yachts raced throughout the season with *Columbia* proving the fastest under practically all conditions. The official trial races were held in the first part of September, but as *Columbia* won the first two so decisively the cup committee gave her the honor of defending the cup. There is no doubt that *Columbia* went to the starting line well tuned up and with her crew well trained after their summer's racing.

First Scheduled Race

The first race against *Shamrock* was scheduled for October 3, and at the time of the start there was the largest fleet of spectator steam yachts and large excursion steamers that had ever appeared at the cup races, for the general public took a very great interest in the competing yachts that were owned by such notables as Sir Thomas and J. P. Morgan. I note that Lipton was the most popular person who ever challenged for the cup although Mrs. Henn perhaps was the best liked of all challengers by the yachtsmen, for she paid for *Galatea* and sailed over and back on her. Neither J. P. nor Sir Thomas sailed on their racers, watching the races from their steam yachts. Lipton's *Erin* of 1,027 tons was about the handsomest English steam yacht of her time, while Mr. Morgan's *Corsair* of 1,136 tons was certainly the best American built large yacht of her time.

Fig. 93. ERIN

The New York Yacht Club had anticipated this large spectator fleet and called upon the government to patrol the course, so the Coast Guard ordered several of its revenue cutters to this duty and the Navy sent a flotilla of torpedo boats under the command of the then Captain Robley D. Evans, "Fighting Bob" of Spanish American War fame, and these ships kept the whole fleet well off the race course. (In speaking of the large spectator fleet I mean tonnage and not number of individual craft.) At these races there were numerous vessels of over a thousand tons and only very few of them under one hundred tons; there may have been one hundred vessels whose average tonnage was five hundred tons making an aggregate of some fifty thousand tons. The spectator fleet of the cup races of 1958 may have numbered five hundred. With the average tonnage of ten their aggregate tonnage would be only five thousand tons for most of them were small, unseaworthy craft that the old navy sailor would call a fleet of spit kids. (A spit kid was a small, open wooden vessel or tub used in the old Navy for a spittoon, for in those days most all hands chewed tobacco.) This shows what harm the income tax has done to yachting.

But we must get back to the race. It was intended to be a windward and leeward race of fifteen miles to a leg with a time limit of five and one half hours. There was a light northeast breeze so the yachts were given a leeward start with the course down the Jersey shore. *Shamrock* (Fig. 97) got the start by almost three quarters of a minute, or almost enough to have her air free, but it was a very fluky day and *Columbia* (Fig. 98) managed to get a draft of air which took her by *Shamrock* about an hour after the start, so she rounded the leeward mark two minutes in the lead, and this seems strange for at that time I think Ratsey was making better spinnakers than Herreshoff. However, on the way home the wind petered out so that the yachts could not finish within the time limit. After this attempted race there followed a very unusual spell of fog and calm for nearly two weeks in which several attempts to finish a race within the time limit were made. The crews of the competitors were under considerable nervous tension during this time and the spectator fleet dwindled to about half its original size. The height of *Shamrock*'s sail plan appears much less than its length, but *Columbia*'s is about the same height as length. We know today that the high, narrow sail plan is much the better.

Second Race

After October 12 the race committee had the yachts sail every week day, but it was not until October 16 that a race was completed and that is quite late in the season. In the meantime the press, to use up some of the space allotted for the races in the newspapers, began knocking Charlie Barr and the crew of *Columbia*, and it is of interest that in a few years he was to be one of their heroes. The race of October 16 was started in a moderate east wind, light fog and chop of a sea. It was a windward and leeward race with the first leg to the eastward. Although *Shamrock* got the start by a few seconds the chop of a sea seemed to bother her some while *Columbia*, with her moderately sharp bow, seemed to be going well so that before long she was dead to windward of the challenger where she stayed the rest of the leg and rounded the outer mark over nine minutes ahead of her. On the run home *Columbia* gained a few seconds more and won the race by ten minutes and eight seconds corrected time.

The next day the wind was still east but the fog had cleared away leaving quite a lop of a sea. This time the race was a triangle of thirty miles with the first leg to windward. There was quite a lot of jockeying at this start, and Captain Hogarth of *Shamrock* proved to be as good as Charlie Barr for they went over the starting line lapped with *Shamrock* two seconds ahead, but *Columbia* to weather. The two yachts sailed very evenly indeed in the first part of the race and, though the wind was only moderate, about half an hour after the start *Shamrock*'s topmast broke at the cap iron letting her club topsail and all its gear go to leeward. According to an agreement in these cup races, if one of the competitors was crippled the other was to continue the race which *Columbia* was forced to do, but not being in competition she lowered her jib topsail in spite of which she covered the triangular course at a little under ten knots.

Third Race

The next day, the 19th, *Shamrock* made some changes, taking on about four tons of ballast and was remeasured, with the result that she now had to give *Columbia* a small amount of time allowance while before this *Shamrock* rated the least. After a new topmast was rigged she was ready to race, so, on the 20th, they competed again. It was a rather cold day with a brisk north wind of perhaps twenty knots; the course was a windward and leeward one with the first leg off the wind. At that time they were using what is called a two-gun start in which the actual time that each individual yacht took to cover the course was used to determine the winner. Under these conditions Captain Barr decided to make a late start for in running off the wind this gives a yacht a chance to blanket her competitor and sometimes pass her, thus making the best time over the course. So *Columbia* started about a minute after *Shamrock*. On the run to leeward *Columbia* had a great deal of trouble carrying her spinnaker which seemed to balloon up very high at times and caused her long spinnaker boom to bend alarmingly while *Shamrock*'s spinnaker behaved much better. *Shamrock* had a working topsail set at the start, and *Columbia* set hers later on and began to gain on the challenger. Shortly before reaching the leeward mark *Columbia* sailed by *Shamrock* and took in her topsail; she luffed sharply around the mark and got her sheets in quickly while *Shamrock* did not get flattened down for some time. Captain Barr luffed *Columbia* again to take up on his main halliards and after that

Fig. 94. SHAMROCK after topmast broke

Columbia settled down to one of the most magnificent thrashes to windward that has ever been seen with the larger yachts.

Columbia both outpointed and outfooted *Shamrock* although the latter was tried under working topsail, no topsail, and finally a club topsail which only made her heel excessively without sailing faster. All the time on the windward leg *Columbia* had her working topsail hoisted ready to break out, but she was doing so well they kept her under her three lowers. Captain Barr and *Columbia*'s designer sailed her so well on this last leg that she won with corrected time by six minutes, thirty-four seconds. She probably could have won by a larger margin, but after she got well ahead of *Shamrock,* she simply played safe so she would not strain her spars and gear for she had proved to be a stiffer vessel than the challenger. She had her topsail ready to break out if more speed were necessary. This magnificent thrash to windward vindicated Charlie Barr from the blame the press had been putting on him throughout the season. Thus ended the races of 1899. But it may be of interest to some readers to look at the speed-giving qualities of the two yachts.

Shamrock		*Columbia*
128'	Length overall	131'
87.69'	Length waterline	89.66'
25'	Beam	24'
20.25'	Draft	19.75'
13,492 sq. ft.	Measured sail area	13,135 sq. ft.

Figures 95 and 96 show *Shamrock* and *Columbia* in dry dock at Erie Basin being measured, and you can see that *Shamrock*'s keel has considerable wetted surface for it is both deep and long. This may have been one of her defects for *Columbia*'s keel was big enough to allow her to outpoint *Shamrock*.

There was a great deal said at the time about the light scientific hull of *Shamrock* that was constructed by builders who made a specialty of torpedo boats, but the facts of the case look different. She was four feet three inches deeper than *Columbia*, and that is a great deal; she was a foot and a half wider than *Columbia*; she appears to have a lower center of sail plan although *Columbia* was ad-

mittedly the stiffer yacht. These things indicate that *Columbia* had the lightest hull and highest percentage of ballast. The press then and since has overlooked the fact that the designer and builder of *Columbia* was also a torpedo boot designer. *Dupont* made a speed of thirty-one miles on her trial trip; she exceeded this speed for quite a long run when in service during the Spanish-American War. She was in active service over twenty years and is reported never to have had a major overhaul of her engines in this time. I wonder if any English torpedo boat of that time could equal this record. I believe most steam torpedo boats throughout the world were designed by several people in the following manner—one worked

Fig. 95. SHAMROCK in dry dock

Fig. 96. COLUMBIA in dry dock

up the general arrangement, or outboard plan; one specialized on her lines; a staff of men worked up the construction plan; other separate staffs worked up the design of the boilers and engines even if they were made by another company. But *Dupont* and several other torpedo boats were designed completely by the designer of *Columbia*.

According to the photographs of these two yachts, and I have several of them before me as I write this, *Columbia* had much the best sails. Figure 97 shows *Shamrock* with a cross-cut mainsail, but she generally used an up-and-down cut one. All the sails in this picture have tight leaches and appear to have no battens. *Columbia*'s de-

signer had an advantage over all designers of the time, both English and American, in having his own yacht yard and sail loft so that every piece and part of *Columbia* was made under his supervision. Thus there was no weak link in the chain. This combination was the principal reason why New England was to continue beating Old England for several years to come.

There are not many alive who can name these men, but the one in blue farthest forward I think is the English representative; the next one partly in the hatch is Butler Duncan who managed *Defender* in the trial races of that year. Next come Mr. and Mrs. Iselin, and I believe Mrs. Iselin is the only one alive today. Next aft is the designer of *Columbia* with a jacket over a white sweater. Partly in front of him is Charlie Barr at the steering wheel. The next two gentlemen who are wearing blue jackets and white trousers are Mr. Thorne and Mr. S. Newberry Kane. The gentleman farthest aft with his hand on the topmast backstay tackle is E. D. Morgan who was to be managing owner of *Columbia* the next season that she raced. It is noteworthy that *Columbia* has a racing reef rove off ready to flatten her mainsail if necessary.

Fig. 97. SHAMROCK with crosscut mainsail

Fig. 98. COLUMBIA

18 *Preparations for the 1901 Challenge*

In the last few years of the nineteenth century the British yachts were more sensible than ours. This was partly because their rating rules used other hull measurements besides L.W.L. One of the important measurements that prevented the scow type of hull from being used was the so-called girth difference rule. The girth difference was taken by two girth measurements from rail to rail; one measurement was called the chain girth and was the distance a tight tape would take from rail to rail around the keel of the boat, bridging all hollows. The other girth measurement was the distance a tape would take when held against the yacht's skin from rail to rail. This was called the skin girth and the difference between these measurements was used as an important factor in the rule and made a deep hulled yacht with high, narrow garboards rate very high. This rule had been used by two or three European countries before England adopted it, and was originated by Alfred Benzon of Copenhagen, and it continued to be a factor in most all English and European rules until some of the later rules requiring a certain displacement for the L.W.L. made this girth difference rule unnecessary.

The Yacht Racing Association rule of about that time was what some people have called an addition rule. The formula was

$$\frac{L + B + 3/4G + 4^d + 1/2\sqrt{SAILAREA}}{2 \cdot 1}$$

In this L is LWL, B is beam, G is chain girth, d is girth difference. This rule, and the somewhat similar earlier

130

rules, produced fine looking craft above water, but the chain girth rule eventually produced yachts with a great deal of drag to the bottom of the keel, i.e., the keel was deep at the rudder but rose up on quite an angle forward of this to make the chain girth measurement less. Therefore some of these fine looking yachts were difficult and dangerous to dock, and all but impossible to lay-to in a wind and sea. On the whole, however, the British sailing yachts between 1890 and 1900 were the best looking in the world. Figure 99 is the fine G. L. Watson designed eighty-three rater *Bona*. Figure 100, the fifty-two footer *Senga* designed by W. Fife, Jr. Figure 101 shows the thirty footer *Sorais II* with which Mrs. Allen won so many prizes. These are only a very few of the many outstanding sailing yachts used in England and Scotland at that time, and I would like to impress on the reader's mind that the British had ever so many more fine sailing craft than we did right up to World War I.

The New York Yacht Club seventy footers came out in 1900 and were the largest yachts in a one-design class we ever have had. There were four of them named *Mineola*, *Rainbow*, *Virginia*, and *Yankee*. They were raced very hard in their first season with many of their races in the rough water off Newport. While this class was called seventy footers their rated length was seventy-six and five tenths feet, their waterline length was sixty-nine feet, and measured sail area 7,000 square feet, and the press of the time considered them the fastest craft of their size in existence. On one windy day off Newport one of these yachts sailed over a thirty mile triangular course with an

Fig. 99. 83-Rater BONA

eleven mile beat to windward in two hours and forty-five minutes. While yachts of this size often got up to twelve knots on a reach, it is very difficult to maintain an average speed of ten knots if one leg of the course is to windward. One of the reasons these yachts were sailed so hard their first year was that two of them had English captains and crew while two of them had a mixed crew of Scandinavians and Yankees and these latter yachts were handled by an amateur.

As this was a year between cup races you can imagine the great rivalry there was between two large one-design racers sailed by English captains and crew against the other two which were handled and somewhat manned by Americans. At the end of the season *Mineola,* owned by August Belmont and sailed by Captain Wringe (who had been the second captain of *Shamrock* the previous year), stood highest in points, but as *Mineola* was the first of the seventies to go into commission Captain Wringe had a better chance to tune her up and train his crew. However after *Yankee,* sailed by Herman Duryea, one of our best amateur helmsmen, came out she was gaining on *Mineola* so that many thought her the fastest or best sailed of the seventies at the end of the season.

The seventy footers (Fig. 102) on the whole had great influence on American yachting for their flat-ended model with its long overhangs gave such trouble that their hulls had to be somewhat rebuilt and braced during the first winter after the races, and thus was the principal cause of the New York Yacht Club adopting a new measurement rule—the Universal Rule—which very much handicapped models with long, flat overhanging ends. Also Mr. Belmont, after his success with *Mineola,* decided to get up a syndicate to build a trial cup boat for the following season. At the time, August Belmont was one of New York's leading bankers and had financed several successful undertakings like building the rapid transit tunnels under New York City.

It seems now appropriate to say a few words about yachting in general near the turn of the twentieth century.

Both in England and here the total tonnage of the steam yachts was perhaps the greatest of any time, and, while many of our largest steam yachts were built in Scotland, there were several yachts of over 1,500 tons on both sides of the Atlantic and, if the average tonnage of our outboard motor boat is 500 pounds, then one of these yachts would equal six thousand of the outboards. While some of these very large yachts later became the royal yachts of various countries, or became government yachts like our *Mayflower,* still I doubt if the aggregate tonnage of the later smaller yachts was ever larger than it was in 1900 and for a few years after.

At this time, while we still raced some of the fine, wholesome, large schooners, most of our small and medium-size yachts had become freaks with short waterlines and long overhangs somewhat like the smaller craft that were in vogue. They were rather poor sea boats and quite unfit for cruising. Some of the reasons for this were first, the importance of waterline measurement; second,

Fig. 100. 52-Rater SENGA

there were few long outside races excepting the runs of the New York Yacht Club; third, many of the owners of racing yachts also had steam yachts on which they lived so the poor accommodations of the racers was of little consequence.

However, there were two good, wholesome American schooners built near the turn of the century: they were *Yampa* and *Endymion* (Fig. 103). *Yampa* was a very fine

Fig. 101. 30-Footer SORAIS II

Fig. 102. N.Y.Y.C. 70-footer

handsome, able vessel that lasted a long time. Her designer, A. Cary Smith, said she was developed from the experience her owner, Chester W. Chapin, had acquired in cruising in two other Smith-designed schooners that Chapin had built, one of which was the famous *Iroquois*. Mr. Chapin had had much experience with the sea and owned some fine Long Island Sound steamers which Cary Smith had designed for him. *Yampa* in model was an enlarged *Iroquois*—one hundred and ten feet long on the waterline with a beam of twenty-seven feet. This designer had originally been one of the most active in introducing the cutter in this country, but by the time he designed *Yampa* he made the statement, "It may be said that a poorer sea boat than a narrow cutter is hard to find." After he began to design what might be called vessels of the compromise type—i.e., halfway between the narrow cutter and the wide, shallow sloop—he became our leading schooner designer between about 1895 and 1905.

Yampa made several winter cruises and rode out or drove through some heavy gales and I think acquired the name of the best American schooner of her time. On one occasion in a strong beam wind and sea she logged 284 nautical miles in twenty-four hours. The captain of *Yampa* at this time was Captain Eldridge who had served his time in the last of the China Clippers, and maybe Opium Clippers, and in his time was known as China Josh. Perhaps part of *Yampa*'s good name came from Captain Eldridge's skillful handling when in heavy weather. *Yampa* was sold to His Imperial Majesty Wilhelm II in 1898 and renamed *Iduna*. Before this the Kaiser had been using cutters and his *Meteor II* even after she had been changed to a yawl, but he liked *Yampa* so much that he ordered a new and larger schooner from Cary Smith's designs that was built by the Fore River Ship Building Company near Boston and launched with quite a ceremony being christened *Meteor III* by Miss Alice Roosevelt, the daughter of the then president, Theodore Roosevelt. This *Meteor* was a large vessel of 361 tons.

After she arrived in Germany in the summer of 1902, *Yampa* was turned over to the Empress and continued to be raced under her colors until something like 1910, proving to be one of the best all-around sailing yachts of her time though not very well known in this country. *Endymion* was designed by Clinton H. Crane in 1899 when the late Mr. Crane was quite young, and it is remarkable that he produced such a fine vessel for much of his previous experience had been in designing light skimming dishes. But this design, like many of his later ones, proves that he was one of the most versatile American designers of his time, most all of the other designers, excepting Mr. Herreshoff, rather specialized in certain types.

Perhaps Mr. Crane's ability to design successful yachts of varying types came partly from his training at the University of Glasgow. *Endymion* was designed for George Lord Day who had previously owned the fine seagoing schooner *Fleur De Lis* which Edward Burgess had designed in 1890. *Endymion* was a composite vessel built by George Lawley with principal dimensions of L.O.A. 137'; L.W.L. 100'; beam 24'; draft 14'; gross tonnage 144. *Endymion*'s first cruise started in early February, 1900, when she ran to Bermuda in very heavy weather and had to take in most of her sails while those that were not taken in blew out of the bolt ropes so that she had to scud under bare poles. She steered and behaved remarkably well under these varying conditions and proved to be a very able ship. She was well shaken down by June, 1900, and sailed from Sandy Hook to The Needles off the Isle of Wight in thirteen days and eight hours which was to remain the best record for a sailing yacht until 1904. The two best days' runs on this crossing were 266 and 262 nautical miles.

This brings us up to the next challenge for the Ameri-

Fig. 103. Sail plan of ENDYMION

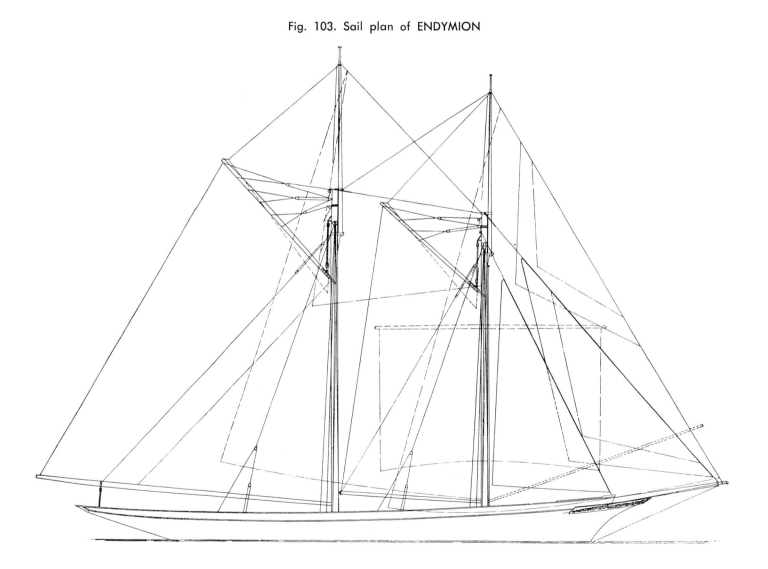

Fig. 104. DENNY'S tank

ca's Cup for Sir Thomas challenged again in October, 1900, for a series of races to be sailed in 1901. This time he chose G. L. (George Lennox) Watson as the designer of the new challenger that was named *Shamrock II*. Mr. Watson was probably the world's all time greatest yacht designer for, not only had he designed more of the larger sailing yachts than anyone, but he had designed by far the greatest tonnage of steam yachts. I class him as the greatest of designers for the fact that his yachts were almost invariably beautiful. One of Watson's greatest ambitions was to win the America's Cup and if he had lived longer he might very well have done so, but he died at the age of fifty-three. He had already designed the cup challengers *Thistle, Valkyrie I* and *Valkyrie II*.

Shamrock II was built at the yard of William Denny and Brothers at Dumbarton which is some sixteen miles below Glasgow on the north bank of the Clyde. Denny's shipyard was a large concern which had taken over the control of two or three nearby yards. Their engine works, established in 1850, employed a thousand men; the forge shop three hundred men; the foundry two hundred and fifty men; the shipyard employed two thousand five hun-

dred men and covered forty acres of land. The Dennys had the first privately owned test tank that was built about 1880 although there were several other government tanks in Europe before this, and it is said that the great naval architect, F. H. Chapman, experimented somewhat with tanks in the seventeen sixties, and our straight forward thinker, Benjamin Franklin, suggested towing models of the same weight by a cord which was activated by a weight falling into a pit and timing the length of the run. Except for digging the pit this would be far the simplest and most accurate arrangement I have heard of.

Our large tank in the Washington Navy Yard was completed in 1901. The building is 500 feet long and fifty feet wide; the water surface about 470 feet long by forty-three feet wide and fourteen feet deep. At the time our Washington tank was built it was by far the largest one in the world. At first the test models were from ten to fourteen feet long, made of paraffin, but later wooden models twenty feet long were used as standard to gain greater accuracy. In the Washington tank the carriage which spans the pool is so heavy that it takes some time to bring it up to speed and stop it at the end of the run.

The Denny tank and its ingeniously simple apparatus was designed by Professor William Froude, son of the eminent Froude who worked out the Laws of Comparison still used in tank tests and who had a tank in about 1870, spoken of in another place. Figure 104 shows the Denny tank at Dumbarton at the time *Shamrock II* was designed.

One or two years previous to this the Dennys had built the fine steam yacht *Lysistrata* from G. L. Watson's design, and Mr. Watson was so much impressed by the tank testing of *Lysistrata* that he decided to make an exhaustive test of models for the challenger of 1901. It has been written that in designing *Shamrock II* Mr. Watson tested no less than eleven models for that yacht and made sixty alterations to these models before the final form was adopted. Apparently Watson used a great deal of time in tank testing, which he later thought was a waste of time, and when he returned to Scotland after the slight defeat of *Shamrock II* and was asked why he was beaten he said, "Because Herreshoff did not have a test tank." As a matter of fact Watson had designed more tonnage of large racing sailboats than the American designer, and if he had kept as much data, or had as good a memory as Herreshoff, he should have been in less need of help from the tank than Herreshoff. However, Herreshoff had his own yacht yard and sail loft and kept thinking of new and original improvements in hulls, spars and rigging. But we will see as things turned out that we nearly lost the cup in 1901.

In model *Shamrock II* was long overall with quite flat ends; she had a pronounced sheer with a low freeboard amidships, perhaps to save weight. She was rather full forward above water and the end of her bow was snubbed off right under the bowsprit, otherwise she would have had a long overhang forward and I have no doubt that such a model went better in the test tank than in light wind and choppy sea. *Shamrock I* had been rather full aft but *Shamrock II* had rather straight lines aft and terminated in a small transom, and I should say her center of displacement was farther forward than usual. On the whole both *Shamrock II* and *Valkyrie III* were not as handsome as most Watson yachts.

Some of the features of *Shamrock II* construction were a steel deck with a thin covering of wood to give a better foothold. She was plated with a light bronze composition called immadium. Her plating below water was flush, that is the plates were not lapped at the seams. At the joints of the plating there were intercostal butt straps of nickel steel which held the edges of the plates together and allowed them to be caulked. *Shamrock II* had steel mast, boom and gaff of rather larger diameter than usual. Her topmast telescoped, or housed inside her mainmast, as it had on *Columbia* in the previous races, and the other American ninety-footers of that year—*Constitution* and *Independence*—used the same arrangement. She was steered by a tiller about fifteen or more feet long for the British then thought a long tiller used with a tiller tackle was best for quick maneuvering. *Shamrock II* was too deep for the water right off Denny's yard so she was launched between two large wooden cofferdams or caissons so that her draft at the time of launching was about one third of her designed draft. In the trial races she was not much faster than her older sister, and one day carried her whole rig out. By strange coincidence this was the day King Edward was aboard and the incident happened somewhat as follows.

On May 22, His Majesty the King was to be Sir Thomas Lipton's guest aboard *Erin* to watch the races. It was a perfect day with a fine easterly sailing breeze, but just before the start the King, good yachtsman that he was, decided that he would rather sail on *Shamrock II* than watch her, so *Erin*'s steam launch was hurriedly lowered away and His Majesty, Sir Thomas, and one or two other gentlemen disembarked from *Erin* and soon were embarked aboard *Shamrock II*. By the time the starting signal was given the wind had increased considerably and both yachts had their lee rails awash as they stood off close hauled. Although this was just the kind of sailing the King enjoyed, the whole rig of *Shamrock II* collapsed and fell to leeward, and it is a miracle that no one was injured. When Captain Wringe of *Shamrock I* saw what had happened he immediately put up his helm and bore away so that he would be in a position to luff up beside *Shamrock II,* but in doing this *Shamrock I*'s gaff collapsed making her almost as unmanageable as her younger sister. The crew of *Shamrock II* was unable to haul her spars and rigging aboard (I suppose the hollow steel spars were full of water), so after the rig was detached or cleared from the vessel it was well buoyed and allowed to sink so it could be recovered. Both disabled yachts were then towed to Hythe.

While the writers of the time seem to think that there was some mystery in the accident, the photographs clearly show that the martingale, or bobstay spreader, broke and this let the bowsprit spring up and break; this in turn left the topmast head unsupported, as well as the head of the mainmast above the forestay, so that the leverage of the topmast which was stepped inside the mainmast made the latter collapse a little below the forestay and lower shrouds. Thus the unsupported mast buckled again just above deck and allowed everything to go to leeward. At the time of the accident the upper end of the martingale seemed to be rigged to bear against the bowsprit, as Watson had rigged it on *Valkyrie III,* but in later photos of *Shamrock II* the martingale bears against the bow. If it had been rigged this way originally the dismasting might not have occurred for the martingale can be much shorter. Both *Shamrock I* and *II* were very fast yachts with sheets slightly started, and Figure 105 illustrates them in a trial race when the length of their waves indicates that they are traveling fourteen knots or more, but, of course, none of the short waterline yachts ever made high average speed over a course that had windward work in it. After the dismasting of *Shamrock II* Lipton requested a postponement of the races for one month and that gave us a long summer of sailing the big cup boats which was to our advantage.

Fig. 105. SHAMROCK I and II in trial race

Two New Contenders

In America that year two new cup contenders were built —one named *Independence* owned by the stock manipulator Thomas W. Lawson who made quite a name by making a million dollars in one day. However, when he tried to join the New York Yacht Club, he was blackballed perhaps because some of the New Yorkers did not like his way of doing business. However, Lawson thought he could force his way into the club by building a cup boat that would beat any craft that the club owned and then he would be voted in, for one of the conditions of the final races was that the defender must be owned by a member of the defending club. This was the year that the New York Yacht Club's new clubhouse was completed so there was quite a strong feeling of pride in the club, and perhaps a member had to have stronger qualifications to be elected then.

Independence was designed by B. B. Crowninshield who belonged to an old shipping family of Salem and was familiarly known as Bodie. He had been very successful in designing racing sailboats of the scow or skimming dish type and had designed larger vessels both for the fishing industry and commerce. He is the only one who has designed a seven masted schooner. In 1874, Bodie's parents moved to Marblehead and from then on he gained much experience in sailing and racing. After attending private schools he finished his education at Massachusetts Institute of Technology and Harvard, graduating from the latter in 1890. His first business ventures were in the West, but after a few years his love of the water became so strong that he returned to Boston and, having some capital to work with, opened a yacht designing and brokerage office in that city, specializing in the skimming dish type of sailboat that was then popular. He became very successful so that by 1900 he had altogether the largest yacht designing and brokerage firm in Massachusetts, and his company published a large annual catalog listing yachts for sale and showing many of his later designs.

Mr. Crowninshield had several able men working for him so, although he had not designed any of the larger racing yachts, he produced a design for the new cup boat that was better than would be expected with this lack of experience. The new yacht was named *Independence* and all Massachusetts thought she would as easily beat all the New York owners' boats as General Paine had with *Puritan, Mayflower* and *Volunteer,* and this feeling was so strong that fifty years later you would occasionally meet Bostonians who thought *Independence* was the fastest cup boat of 1901. But Mr. Crowninshield was to have all the troubles that are usual with a large racer whose hull was built by one concern, and spars, rigging, fittings and sails by other separate companies.

In spite of this *Independence* was sailing early in June. I must say that when I saw the picture of the *Independence* I thought my father's cup boats would be beaten by *Independence,* but things turned out quite differently for she had structural trouble and leaked badly; she did not steer well, and her very flat model had so much wetted surface that she was very dull in light weather.

The other new cup boat of 1901 was *Constitution* built for a syndicate of New York Yacht Club members headed by August Belmont. She was designed by Mr. Herreshoff and managed by William Butler Duncan who had run *Defender* when she was the trial boat for *Columbia* in 1899. Mr. Duncan was a very capable amateur yachtsman who was a graduate of Annapolis, but perhaps a better sea man than a racer. In model and sail plan *Constitution* was an enlarged *Columbia* but her construction was quite novel for she was the first vessel built on what is called longitudinal framing over widely spaced web frames, a construction that has the advantages of,

1, greater strength for its weight,
2, plating can be laid flush with one of the longitudinal frames making a continuous butt strap at the seams,
3, local strains, such as the mast step, et cetera, can be taken care of by the location of the web frames,
4, this type of framing, when properly designed, is the cheapest.

For these very reasons many of the world's fastest steamers, as well as most all large aeroplane bodies, are made that way today. *Constitution* also had the first of the two-speed self-releasing worm gear winches that her designer had developed to handle wire rope, and which were to be used on the next five cup defenders and several other trial cup boats. Altogether *Constitution* was quite an improvement on *Columbia* as she proved in the season of 1903, but the cup committee chose *Columbia* to defend the cup in 1901 for quite good reasons as we shall see.

Almost every one had thought the old *Columbia* would only be a trial boat that year, but with the large yachts helmsmanship and management can be of more importance than improvements in design. In the year 1901, Mr. E. D. Morgan had bought out Mr. Iselin's share in *Columbia* so in that year she was owned by J. P. Morgan and E. D. Morgan, both very wealthy men who were not related. E. D. Morgan's father had been governor of New York during the Civil War and had become wealthy partly through his ownership in both sail and steamships so the son, E. D., had such an income that he could take a great deal of time off, and he had owned many fine yachts large and small. He is sometimes spoken of as the number one yachtsman of all time. He had been part owner and in the afterguard of three previous cup defenders and was probably nearly as good a manager of this sort of craft as General Paine. The joke of this season was that these two wealthy men were to defend the cup at less expense than it ever had been done before or since. The Morgans were prompt in securing Charlie Barr, *Columbia*'s previous skipper, to sail her through the year. Captain Barr got together many of the old crew of *Columbia* who had been trained on her and who had laid her up so that she, you might say, was in racing trim at the beginning of the season while things on *Constitution* were quite different.

The captain of *Constitution* was a middle age, full bearded man who had served most of his time in schooners. He was no match for Charlie Barr, either in handling a sloop of this size or in choosing and training a crew. *Constitution*'s manager, Mr. Duncan, had insisted on an all American crew which had always proved to be a disadvantage for it is best to pick a man for his ability rather than nationality. *Constitution* was rigged with a pair of swinging spreaders each side; the upper spreaders which spread the topmast shrouds were about twelve feet long while her lower spreaders, which were about ten feet long, spread the masthead shrouds. These latter spreaders were pivoted on the main mast well below the gaff jaw or saddle, and I speak of them now partly because *Constitution* can only be distinguished from *Columbia* in some photographs by her two pairs of spreaders. These spreaders were made of locust, one of the strongest woods for its size, but in spite of this on one of her trial trips off Newport her starboard spreader that spread her masthead shrouds broke which allowed her mast to buckle near where the lower shrouds were attached. In this case the collapse was rather gradual and this allowed most of the crew to jump clear of the falling wreckage, so fortunately no one was badly hurt but the second mate Nelson was knocked overboard but soon picked up. As a result of this accident *Constitution* could not be on hand in the first half dozen races that she was scheduled to compete in, but, worst of all, this accident made her crew jumpy all season and particularly scared of the swinging spreaders.

Trial Races of 1901

The first trial race between *Columbia* and *Constitution* was a windward and leeward one of fifteen nautical miles to a leg. On the first leg *Constitution* pulled the clew out of her jib and before a new jib was set *Columbia* had a good lead, rounding the weather mark two minutes before her younger sister. On the run home there must have been a fine breeze and smooth sea for it is recorded that *Constitution* made this leg in a little over one hour and six minutes, or at the speed of thirteen and seven-tenths knots, and that is a very high speed to hold for fifteen nautical miles when running. In fact *Columbia* covered the whole course in forty-eight less seconds and won easily with time allowance.

In the next race *Columbia* broke down and *Constitution* sportingly dropped out. The breakdown was similar to *Shamrock II*'s the same year for it was her bobstay spreader, or martingale, which gave out. In the case of *Columbia* the martingale only bent and she lowered sail before other parts began to collapse. I do not know the details of this accident but suppose *Columbia*'s rig was saved by the quick work of Charlie Barr.

Independence did not compete in these two races because, as I said before, one of the rules of the New York Yacht Club was that a boat competing in these races had to be owned by a member of that club, or sailed under the colors of a member of the club, but Lawson would not consent to the latter. However, the Newport Yacht Racing Association arranged races for all three yachts and the first of these took place on July 6. It was a windward and leeward race of fifteen miles to a leg in a light easterly breeze with an old sea rolling in. At the weather mark *Constitution* was two minutes and thirteen seconds ahead of *Columbia,* and *Independence* rounded the mark an hour later. On that day the wind shifted and *Constitution* did well to windward reaching and running, beating *Columbia* over ten minutes corrected time while *Independence* withdrew. If I remember correctly Charles Francis Adams sailed *Independence* in this race, and it was reported that when she was towed into harbor toward dusk he jumped ship near the north end of the harbor and caught the night train for Boston. About twenty-five years later I was talking to him about some of the yachts he had sailed, and he said *Independence* felt like an ice wagon. Just exactly what he meant I do not know, nor dared to ask. However, he was about the only Bostonian I

have met that did not think *Independence* was fast.

The race of July 8 was over a triangular course of ten nautical miles to a leg; the wind was light from the southwest with the average ground swell to be expected off Newport. This time *Constitution* beat *Columbia* something like twenty-eight minutes corrected time with *Independence* well over an hour behind.

In the last race of this series *Independence* steered by Captain Haff did very well and kept well up with the other two yachts on part of the windward leg. There was enough wind this day so she sailed somewhat on her long leeward side and lifted her flat bow a little out of water, but unfortunately she carried her topmast away, consequently *Columbia* won, beating *Constitution* some two minutes, and *Independence* by nearly eight minutes and twenty-five seconds. This race at once revived an interest in *Independence* for the Bostonians all said that if she had not carried away her topmast she would have won. However, the series of races arranged for *Independence* by the

Fig. 106. The three big American sloops of 1901

Newport Yacht Racing Association were now over and she had shown that she was only fast in strong winds and that her hull could not stand a sea and wind without leaking seriously. Her average speed certainly was slow for a yacht of that size.

Figure 106 shows the three big American sloops of 1901 at the start of one of those races. As far as I can remember this was the only large racing yacht B. B. Crowninshield designed and he did well considering his lack of experience. Perhaps if he had made less of a freak he would have done much better.

This left Columbia and Constitution the rest of the summer to fight it out, but soon after this on the New York Yacht Club cruise in the run from New London to Newport Constitution struck bottom heavily off Race Rock and was taken to the builders and hauled out, but her keel structure was so strong that it was not materially injured. This again made her crew jumpy. During the summer both yachts were at their builder's yard several times for minor changes among which Constitution's mast head was lengthened and Columbia's boom was lengthened, and they both had numerous new sails and sail alterations so the Herreshoff sail loft had all the work it could properly handle.

In the middle of the summer both yachts required new main sails, but as only one could be made in time the Herreshoff brothers, J. B. and N. G., had an embarrassing decision to make for they did not want to turn down their old friend, E. D. Morgan of Columbia, but naturally wanted to do all they could to help their latest creation, Constitution, so the mainsail was made for Constitution and this had three important consequences as follows,

1. The manager of Constitution, Mr. Duncan, insisted that the sail be made of heavier duck which made her logy in light wind the rest of the season.
2. When Columbia was chosen for the honor of defending the cup the second time her sails were pretty well stretched and played out, and this nearly caused us to lose the cup that year as we shall see later.
3. Columbia's influential owners thought that there should be another sail loft in this country that could cut large sails when wanted, so they encouraged Ratsey to open a branch of their famous English concern in America.

While Constitution was considered the fastest of the two during the first of the season, toward the last of it Columbia was winning most races. The reason for this, of course, was the perfect management of Columbia and the way she was handled by clever Captain Barr. He was considered by the press of the time to be reckless in some of his starts, but I believe he always had Columbia under perfect control for by the end of the second year he sailed her he knew exactly how she would swing or turn under all conditions. However, he might be criticized for one little trick and that was that a few minutes before the start he usually managed to head Columbia directly toward Constitution for a moment and rather close aboard so by the latter part of the season Constitution's captain and crew were so unnerved that they were content to follow Columbia over the starting line.

The races between these two yachts were very close with the smaller Columbia sometimes winning by a few seconds corrected time. The whole yachting fraternity was greatly worked up and the general sentiment seems to have been in favor of the older yacht. Perhaps this was somewhat on account of the popularity of E. D. Morgan, and also perhaps it is human nature to side with the smaller boat.

It may be of interest to some readers to know that tacking to leeward was first tried successfully in one of these races. It happened that designer Herreshoff was aboard Constitution in this race, and after Columbia had beaten them to windward, he saw no sense in following the leader in the spinnaker run to the finish, so he persuaded Constitution's after guard to run to leeward in a series of jibes under the balloon jib. He gave them the courses to steer and told them how to trim the sails. In a little while they had the lead and came in an easy winner much to the dismay of Charlie Barr and the wonder of E. D. Morgan. Mr. Herreshoff had worked out the proper angles in tacking to leeward years before, first in iceboats and later in catamarans, and from this time on in the larger classes, particularly the schooners, it was somewhat customary for a yacht that was behind on a run to try tacking to leeward. I believe though that it has seldom been successful in smaller yachts than the New York Yacht Club fifty footers, for the smaller yachts are not fast enough to bring the wind over their beam when running wind on the quarter. Strangely enough some of Captain Nat's later schooners which had led at the windward mark were beaten home in this manner.

During the summer Constitution and Columbia met in twenty races, each won nine of them and in the two races that were called off for lack of wind Columbia was ahead. In the latter part of the season Columbia won quite regularly mostly because the two yachts were so evenly matched the way they were sailed that whoever got the start won, so the Cup Committee chose Columbia to meet Shamrock II in the fall. This caused quite a little criticism from the general public who thought the two-year-old Columbia would be no match for the new challenger. The final races were the closest match races ever held with the larger yachts, and if Columbia had not been the smaller vessel and received a small handicap the races would have been even closer.

19 *1901 Cup Races*

Although *Shamrock II* was a larger vessel than *Columbia* in several ways and carried about 800 square feet more sail area, Watson had designed her so skillfully that she had to allow *Columbia* only forty-three seconds on a thirty mile course. The first race was scheduled for September 26, but the wind was so light that the race was postponed when it turned out that neither yacht could complete the course in the time limit of five and one half hours, and, although *Columbia* was ahead, the weather had been so fluky that this proved nothing except that in light weather and a choppy sea her rather sharp bow was better than *Shamrock*'s bow which, you might say, was nearly as flat as that of *Independence*.

They tried again on September 28 in a rather light easterly wind with a moderate ground swell; the course was a windward and leeward one. After a close start they had a remarkable race to the windward mark with *Columbia* trying three or four times to cross *Shamrock*'s bow as they cross tacked, but each time *Columbia* just could not do it. Once at least she tacked ship close enough ahead of *Shamrock* to give her back wind. It was said that both yachts were handled perfectly and both had fine looking sails. The two captains of *Shamrock* were Sycamore and Wringe, both of whom had sailed challengers in cup races before and were probably as good men in this size of yacht as Barr, and Ratsey now had almost caught up to Herreshoff in the art of cutting crosscut sails.

Shamrock seemed to hold a very slight lead most of the time to windward and rounded the weather mark with a lead of forty-one seconds. By this time the wind had a speed of eight or nine knots and everyone who was familiar with the smaller skimming dishes expected *Shamrock* to run away from *Columbia* in the run to leeward, but in this size of ship the narrower, comparatively sharp-bowed *Columbia* surprised many by not only catching up with,

but moreover by passing *Shamrock* just before the finish and crossed the line thirty-five seconds ahead of her so that with her handicap *Columbia* won by one minute twenty seconds corrected time.

After this exciting close race many people were of the opinion that *Shamrock* would win out for she was a notably fast reacher, but the race of October first was called off for lack of wind after both yachts had led for a while in going to windward, and again *Shamrock* had rounded the weather mark first. A more successful attempt to sail the second race was made on October 3. This time there was a fine northwest breeze of ten or twelve knots at the start, and much stronger wind in puffs later. It was a triangular course and I guess Charlie Barr thought he had rather poor chances under these conditions if he were interfered with by what was supposed to be the fastest yacht on a reach, so, after luffing *Shamrock II* over the line before time, so that she would have to recross the mark and lose time, he waited until nearly the time of the second gun and started with good way on so that under these conditions he had a chance to win with *Columbia*'s handicap without actually catching up with *Shamrock II*.

The first two legs were reaches, and *Shamrock* did not prove to be the fourteen-knot reacher she had been reported to be for *Columbia* actually caught up on her slightly at about a twelve-knot speed. At the second mark *Shamrock* flattened down rather gradually, but when *Columbia* rounded Captain Barr shot her to windward long enough to get her sheets way in at once. This day *Shamrock* had a lighter and somewhat draftier mainsail probably for the reaches of a triangular course, but now that they were hard on the wind in a good breeze *Columbia* pointed highest and finally, after several tacks, got the weather gauge which she held until the finish, ultimately winning by three minutes thirty-five seconds corrected time. This beat to windward in a dry wind of some force was nearly too much for *Columbia*'s old sails for they had stretched out considerably and the head of the mainsail was now longer than the gaff.

It was getting late in the season so in order to get the races over before cold weather the final race was held the next day, October 4. Very early that morning Captain Barr and the sailmaker, Mr. Hathaway from the Herreshoff sail loft, attempted to shorten the head rope of *Columbia*'s mainsail by running a small rope along its heart, but this was not enough so they had to make a small bight or fold in the head of the sail near the throat and

took in her spinnaker. Perhaps she experienced a little side wind and thought she would do well under her large, fine ballooner. *Columbia* carried both ballooner and spinnaker close to the mark and so made quite a gain, but in taking in both of her light sails at once the luff of her spinnaker caught in one of the snap hooks of her balloon jib and caused a slight delay, but she got straightened out and close hauled for the beat home in less than a minute behind *Shamrock II*.

The wind at the start was about ten knots from the north-northwest, but at the leeward mark the wind had materially dropped. When each yacht made a tack to the west it turned out that the wind coming off the Jersey

Fig. 107. The start of the final race between COLUMBIA and SHAMROCK II in 1901

make shift to race that way. It was another dry day with clear sky and a light breeze more nearly from the north— a beautiful fall day. Both yachts were on hand promptly and the start of this last race was made at 11:00 A.M. for a leeward and windward course. Both yachts hung back, not wanting to be blanketed by the other in the downwind start, but when the two minutes of a two gun start had nearly expired they went over the line at practically the same time and soon after spread out sideways so that neither would easily be blanketed by the other.

Some people say this was for the spectators the most interesting race ever run, for the yachts changed positions often with each being ahead four or five times, but in the run to leeward *Shamrock II* proved to be the faster and in the latter part of the run had quite a lead. About fifteen minutes before rounding the leeward mark, however, she

shore had more westerly in it together with a little more velocity so that both yachts, one after the other, as she stood to the westward got in the lead, and when in that position tacked eastward to obey the law of a leading yacht keeping between her adversary and the finish. So, first one and then the other lost its lead. This finally got on the nerves of the crew and helmsman of *Shamrock* and everyone agrees that Captain Barr, with his iron nerves, sailed *Columbia* best in the last few miles of the race. Perhaps all of my readers cannot understand what tension the helmsman of one of these large yachts is under in a long beat to windward in light airs, and if your competitor has passed you two or three times it is enough to break anyone's nerve. Having raced with Charlie Barr, I can well imagine how he was enjoying it and could have continued the game for hours without losing any of his finesse.

Fig. 108. The two yachts nearing the finish line

Now I should like to show you some pictures of this race taken from the committee boat. Figure 107 shows the start of the final race. Figure 108, the two yachts nearing the finish. Figure 109, *Columbia* and *Shamrock II* tacking to cross the finish line. The two yachts were very even at the last tack, but *Columbia* turned quickest and filled her sails first, thus gaining a few seconds just before the finish so that *Shamrock* only beat her two seconds over the line boat to boat, but as *Shamrock* allowed *Columbia* forty-three seconds, *Columbia* won on corrected time by forty-one seconds. This is said to be the closest finish ever witnessed in the larger classes over a long course.

In all the cup races of 1901, three times over a thirty nautical mile course, *Columbia* only beat *Shamrock II* three minutes twenty-seven seconds in the ninety nautical

miles. In describing the previous challengers I have tried to bring out their defects as seen with modern eyes, but as G. L. Watson did so well with the design of *Shamrock II*, I hesitate to criticize; however, she seems to have had so low freeboard amidships that she put the lee rail under at a slight angle of heel. She also had too big and too long a keel which made her turn slowly and probably gave her unnecessary wetted surface. We have shown *Columbia* in dry dock in a previous chapter. *Shamrock II* certainly looks like an out-and-out thoroughbred and why she did not go faster on reaches I cannot say, but modern knowledge tells us that *Columbia* was a good model for average speed, and perhaps if her sails had not been old, dead and over-stretched she would have done better. Thus ended the cup races for another two years.

Designers Criticized

Near the turn of the century, Thomas Fleming Day, the founder and editor of *The Rudder,* devoted much space in knocking the types of yachts the designers of that time were developing, and at times used rather harsh words. If he had attacked the rule makers or the rules themselves he would have been quite justified, but if the designers' reputations depended on designing winners under a rule where waterline length counted so much in rating they could do nothing else than design flat skimming dishes that were miserable cruisers and poor sea boats. So Mr. Day decided to create a type of boat that would be easy to build and a good sea boat as well. With the help of C. D. Mower and others *The Rudder* magazine produced the famous *Sea Bird* design which came out in 1901, and

Figure 110 shows the original *Sea Bird* on one of her first cruises. Day was so much carried away with this design that *The Rudder* gave it much space during the next few years, consequently a great many *Sea Birds* were built in many parts of the world and at least one of them has made a world encircling cruise. While you occasionally see a *Sea Bird* today, it is doubtful if they have appeal for the experienced yachtsman. Day himself was a boatsman at heart and not a yachtsman or racer, and, while I have no doubt the *Sea Bird* appealed to the average reader of *The Rudder,* she was too much of a swing away from what the yachtsman then wanted. As for designing a boat that is easy to build, that is a very difficult matter, for if you end up with something that is heavy, slow, wet and homely you haven't accomplished much. There were several designers during this time who

Fig. 109. The two yachts tacking to cross the finish line

Fig. 110. The original SEA BIRD

had produced good, wholesome boats when the owner would allow them to do so, and *Cock Robin II,* Figure 111, was one of them. But Tom Day did not recognize nor encourage construction of these good yachts. On the contrary, he began to knock the yachts and yachtsmen as well as the designers.

This gave an opportunity to start the magazine called *Yachting* which has been very successful because it never has objections against yachts that are in vogue or says harsh words about the yachtsmen. We have had three or four other magazines of an aquatic nature but most of them devoted much space to rowing and boating and

seemed to go out of existence when the many rowing clubs ended in the first years of the twentieth century. England's fine old magazine, *The Yachtsman,* was started the year after *The Rudder* (1891), and all during these nearly seventy years has been the most accurate recorder of racing and yachting. At present most every European country that skirts the water has its yachting magazine while England has four or five, Australia at least two, Brazil one, and at the present time there are perhaps seven United States of America yachting and boating magazines, all you might say without a knock.

The Search for New Measuring Rules

Soon after 1900, the defects of the Seawanhaka rating rule became so glaring that the New York Yacht Club decided to do something about it for the American yachts and boats were becoming nothing but wide, flat scows of short waterline length and large sail area. Mr. Day had tried knocking the yacht designers as a means of producing a more wholesome type of yacht, but the New York Yacht Club saw that a new measurement rule was the only practical means of accomplishing this, so on February 13, 1902, the New York Yacht Club appointed a committee of its members to make a thorough investigation of the matter. No yacht designer or builder was purposely put on the committee but the first move of the committee was to send letters to the most prominent yacht designers of the United States, Canada, Australia, France, Germany, England, Denmark, Norway and Sweden, asking for suggestions in forming a new measurement rule that would produce a more wholesome type of yacht. The

Fig. 111. COCK ROBIN II

148

response to these letters was voluminous and thus the committee had the help of the leading designers of the world. The consensus of opinion of all this universal thought was that length, sail area and displacement should all be factors in the rule, and while all these factors had been used before in various ways, the difficulty of making a simple formula that properly proportioned the speed giving qualities of length and sail area against the retarding force of displacement was a puzzle.

The Herreshoff Rule

When the committee consulted N. G. Herreshoff, the yacht designer, he suggested multiplying the length by the square root of the sail area and dividing this sum by the cube root of the displacement. This formula gave equal weight to the three factors but its resulting figure was much greater than the yacht's waterline length, and as the yacht club tables for allowance which Mr. Herreshoff also originated were for a rating of approximately a yacht's length on the waterline a constant was used with this formula so that the rule finally adopted by the club was eighteen per cent of the product of length, multiplied by the square root of sail area, divided by the cube root of displacement. At the same time Mr. Herreshoff suggested measuring the yacht's length not on the center line but at a line parallel with the center, halfway out to the yacht's greatest beam, as he thought this measurement gave a better approximation of a heeled yacht's sailing length.

This measurement that is usually called the quarter beam measurement was very effective in preventing yachts from having full ends, for the actual waterline could be fifteen per cent more that the quarter beam measurement without penalty. This rule at first was called The Herreshoff Rule, but as many other minor details were added to it, and as the basis of the rule came from the almost universal letters the New York Yacht Club had received in answer to its inquiries of 1902, the rule was later called the Universal Rule and, although the New York Yacht Club did not officially adopt the rule until 1905, by 1908 almost all American yacht clubs were adopting it so it did become universal over here at least.

Lipton Again Challenges

In the meantime, Sir Thomas Lipton again challenged for the America's Cup, but as the club's official rule was still the length and sail area rule of the past the cup boats of this series carried the largest sail areas ever set on one mast. On October 7, 1902, Sir Thomas sent a pleasant personal letter to the New York Yacht Club apologizing for his persistency in trying to win the cup and again challenged for a set of races in August, 1903. This time Lipton switched back to William Fife, the designer of his first *Shamrock,* and Fife produced an all-around good boat that was very similar in model to the unsuccessful *Constitution* but perhaps had more sheer and less free-

board amidships. Her whole rig was conservative excepting the large sail area. Needless to say the new yacht was named *Shamrock III.* She was plated with nickel steel coated with white enamel and had an aluminum deck covered with canvas. She was the first of the single masted challengers to be steered with a wheel, but I imagine her sail area was too great to be handled well with a tiller unless it had been extremely long. *Shamrock III* was built by Denny at Dumbarton, as the previous *Shamrock* was but this time Mr. Fife only used their test tank a little in developing her model, depending more on his experience with full size yachts. He seemed to realize better than Watson that the tank tests were more suitable for power vessels than for sail.

Shamrock III

Shamrock III was completed in good season and launched in March, being christened by the Countess of Shaftesbury whose husband was Commodore of the Royal Ulster Yacht Club, the club through which all of Lipton's challenges came. This *Shamrock,* like the previous one, was launched between two cofferdams or camels to take her into water of sufficient depth. This launching was quite a party with a full band playing Scotch and Irish music; the builders gave a large luncheon for about three hundred people in their notable model room, followed by several fine speeches delivered by the most prominent persons present.

The new *Shamrock* had an advantage over the previous two in having more time to get tuned up and as usual there were reports of the new challenger's great speed for she seemed to beat *Shamrock I* quite easily. (By the way, *Shamrock II* stayed here after her races and was stored near Erie Basin until she was broken up somewhere around 1905.) However, *Shamrock III* had the misfortune to carry away her mast in a manner about like this: On April 17 there was a stiff off-shore breeze at Weymouth with occasional heavy puffs coming down from the higher land. It was a cold day which usually makes the wind noticeably heavier when it strikes in puffs, but Captain Wringe seemed determined to give the yacht a hard test so he carried a club topsail. On the first leg to windward both *Shamrocks* heeled considerably at times in the puffs, but when *Shamrock III,* which was in the lead, was swung off to round the mark she was knocked over by a hard streak in the wind which put her lee rail so far under that water came nearly up to her hatches. With this great strain her weather turnbuckles gave way and her whole rig went to leeward with the mast buckling about seven feet above deck.

She righted so suddenly that all those who were not lying down were knocked down, and Sir Thomas, who was in the companionway was knocked down to the cabin sole with a sailor falling on top of him. There were few casualties from this accident, as is usual when a rig goes clear to leeward, but the steward was knocked overboard and, as he could not swim, sank before one of the

Fig. 112. SHAMROCK III under sail

mast headsmen who jumped to save him could reach him. Two or three of the crew were slightly hurt, but her rig was almost ruined and I believe nothing but her main boom could be used again. This was because the dismasting occurred in comparatively shallow water, so when her topmast fouled bottom the upper part of her mainmast buckled in two more places while her gaff and topmast were damaged. After the wreckage was cleared away *Shamrock III* was towed to Southampton and docked for a Lloyds survey. She was then towed to the Clyde where a duplicate rig was very quickly made and she was under way again by May 7. Figure 112 shows her sailing at about that time.

We will now take a look at the New York Yacht Club's preparation to defend the Cup. Soon after the challenge for 1903 was received a syndicate of very wealthy members of the New York Yacht Club gave N. G. Herreshoff an order for a new Cup candidate for the honor of defending the Cup, and I use these words because Mr. Herreshoff never called his yachts "Cup defenders" until they had performed that feat. Mr. C. Oliver Iselin was appointed manager of the new craft that was named *Reliance*, (Fig. 113) and he at once secured Charlie Barr as captain and helmsman. This made a very strong combination for it would be the fifth time that one of designer Herreshoff's yachts had defended the Cup; it would be the fourth time that Mr. Iselin was manager of a defender, and the third time that Charlie Barr was captain of one of these craft. And these are the principal reasons that *Reliance* went through the season as practically unbeaten.

Reliance

At the beginning, Mr. Iselin tried to persuade *Reliance*'s designer to make her an out-and-out scow for the scows were then nearly unbeatable in the smaller classes, but Mr. Herreshoff would not do this for he thought that in the larger classes a scow was slow in light weather. He compromised by making a model that was as long overall as a scow but had nicely modeled, fine ends. I remember very well watching my father cut this model which he did in about two evenings, proceeding very rapidly with the work as if there were no question in his mind as to the exact shape to do the work best. This is in great contrast to the other designers of that period, or since, who generally spent much time in developing several sets of lines and never quite deciding which was best. As *Reliance* (Fig. 114) was ordered early, and as her shape problem was settled so rapidly, this left plenty of time for the designer to spend an unusual number of hours on the construction and details. I will mention some of her features:

1. Longitudinal framing, like *Constitution,* which allowed a saving in weight, together with flush seam plating which I have described before.
2. Her rudder, which was lightly plated up over a frame, was arranged so that it could easily be changed from heavy to light, according to how the yacht steered. This was accomplished by having a small hole at the bottom of the rudder that let in water and made the rudder heavier if the yacht were carrying a strong weather helm, but if the yacht had a tendency to head off, then air was forced down her hollow rudder stock with a foot pump, forcing some of the water in the lower part of the rudder to escape, hence making the rudder lighter. With this arrangement the helm of *Reliance* could be adjusted to the weather or to the individual liking of the helmsman. Of course there was also a rudder indicator which told the actual angle at which the rudder was sailing. The steering gear consisted of two wheels so that four men could give their power if necessary, and there were two foot brakes near where the helmsman stood when either to windward or leeward of the helm. These brakes were to prove a great relief to the helmsman and, although Charlie Barr was a small, light, man, he usually could steer *Reliance* through a long hard race without relief, in spite of her sail area being the greatest ever hung from a single mast.
3. Two-speed self-releasing winches for wire rope. Although Mr. Herreshoff had designed the first of these winches for *Constitution,* he improved some models and used more of them on *Reliance,* so I believe she had six of these winches below deck—two for the jib sheets; two for the forestaysail sheets; two for the lower backstays. These winches were one of the finest things Mr. Herreshoff ever designed for he was more of an engineer than an artist. They were mounted on ball bearings, used worm gears and multiple disk clutches before the automobile industry was organized. The winches handled wire ropes which were led below deck; the high speed handle or wheel quickly took in the slack, then the slow speed worm gear handle was brought into play which not only had power enough for hard winds but, with its use, fine adjustments could be made. To release the wire or sheet one of the handles was revolved in the opposite direction which released the multiple disk clutch and allowed the rope or sheet to run out quite freely but still be under instant control. It was these underdeck winches that enabled *Reliance* to be so quickly maneuvered around the marks that the press, who knew nothing about the matter, invariably said the defender had a smarter and better crew than the challenger, but I doubt if there ever were any better Jack Tars than the English crews of the various challengers.
4. *Reliance* had a double-end tapered main sheet which was quite large or strong in its middle section for the strains of sailing close hauled, but the ends were tapered to a small diameter for sailing off the wind, and this to quite an extent allows the sheet to stay up and not drag in the water which often happened before the wire forward boom guy could be connected to a whip which was taken to the anchor capstan. While a tapered main sheet was not a new thing the ingenious arrangement for handling it was, for on *Reliance* both ends of the main sheet were led well forward, perhaps seventy-five feet ahead of the traveler, so that all hands and the steward could haul in on it. Where the sheet ends went below forward there was a series of V-shaped pulleys that could handle any of the sizes of the tapered sheets, and these pulleys were arranged with ratchets and brakes that held any amount of sheet that was taken in without belaying, for the slack of the sheet ends led below and wound up on light drums. With this arrangement the long sheet could quickly be hauled in or slacked out without the danger of tangling.
5. The topmast housing mechanism was also very ingenious for when it was completely lowered away its heel went down to slightly below the waterline. The wooden topmast was cylindrical, or of parallel diameter, and thus could run well supported the full length of the mainmast because the mast diaphragms had lightening holes slightly larger than the topmast. The topmast was hoisted by a wire rope which wound on a drum at the foot of the mast, and this drum was actuated by gearing and an endless rope that ran over a large flanged pulley, allowing several men to haul on this mechanism at once. When the topmast was down, its cone and all of its rigging stayed securely socketed in the mast head, but when the topmast went aloft it automatically picked up its cone and the rigging and traveled up until a series of small ratchets automatically fell in place around the topmast's steel ferrule, so no one had to go aloft to secure it. Much of this description may sound like some of Jules Verne's writings, but it is accurate and few people of the time understood much of *Reliance*'s advanced engineering. Perhaps no one but her designer and Captain Barr understood all of it, and her designer died long before the general public could appreciate such things.

At the time *Reliance* was designed her designer was fifty-four years old and perhaps at the peak of his genius. Even then she would not have been possible if Mr. Herreshoff had not had his own very complete yacht building establishment and sail loft manned by a picked crew whom he had trained to be particularly skillful workmen. *Reliance* cost $175,000.00, but it is very doubtful if she could be duplicated for one million today for there was a lot of manual work on her—such as beautiful forgings and hand finished castings that it would be nearly impossible to find people to make now. *Reliance* went on her first trial trip on April 25, 1903.

Racing between the three great sloops, *Columbia, Constitution* and *Reliance* started early that year giving much time for training. The first race was on May 21. After the yachts got straightened out they finished their races in tiresome monotony with *Reliance* first, *Constitution* second, and *Columbia* last, no matter what the weather was, showing clearly that *Constitution* was a better boat than *Columbia*. They had one heavy weather race off Newport in quite a sea near the first of July when all three yachts were under their three lowers. They should not have raced that day for *Constitution*'s gaff collapsed and *Columbia* had two or three men swept overboard when she ran her bow under on the reach. Fortunately all but one man was picked up by the skillful handling of *Columbia* and her racing rowboat but E. D. Morgan, her owner-manager, was so disheartened by the accident that he raced her half-heartedly the rest of the season. I must

mention that sailors were often lost on the big racers of those times, and I have been on New York Yacht Club runs more than once when two or three men were lost from the larger racers which generally happened when taking in the big balloon jibs.

The year 1903 was perhaps the greatest in the annals of American yachting. The New York Yacht Club cruise was earlier than usual so as to be over before the International Cup races. The rendezvous of the Squadron was at Glen Cove on July 16. This was in the thrilling days when gun salutes were still popular, and I well remember when Commodore Bourne's beautiful flag ship *Delaware* came in and fired her gun as the anchor was let fall and the salute was answered by the gun fire of nearly a hundred yachts. Some of the finest steam yachts I have ever seen were on the cruise that year and they made an impressive sight backed up by the wooded hills of Glen Cove, while the sound of bo'suns calls was accompanied by the shrill tones of the whistles on the many steam launches that were running from yacht to yacht. This flotilla included beautiful yachts that had steamed over from England to go on the cruise and be present at

Fig. 113. RELIANCE on her first trial trip

the Cup races. To give the modern reader an idea of the number and size of the racing sailboats of that cruise I will enumerate them:

90 FOOTERS
Reliance
Constitution
Columbia

B-CLASS SCHOONERS
Ingomar
Emerald
Ariel
Corona
Chanticleer

C-CLASS SCHOONERS
Elmina
Esperanza
Latona
Katrina
Quickstep
Quisetta
Seneca
Valmore

G-CLASS YAWLS
Vigilant   (ex Cup defender)

H-CLASS SLOOPS
Neola
Weetamoe

I-CLASS SLOOPS
Queen Mab
Eelin
Isolde
Isolita
Aspirant
Effort
Senta
Khama
Mimosa II

J-CLASS SLOOPS
Challenge
Hebe

Besides these there were two special classes for schooners and one special class for sloops.

If two or three of our modern 12-meter boats had been out there when this squadron came along the Twelves would have been blanketed, run over, and sunk. A sailor man of that time would think a Twelve a queer piece of kid that had more resemblance to a bloated whale than a yacht, and he would never believe that the time would come when it would be smart to have a boat that was homely, slow and no good for cruising.

That year on the run from Morris Cove to New London, there was a beam wind all the way, and toward the end of it, when the breeze strengthened, *Reliance* ran away from the whole fleet with the exception of one or two of the fastest steamers. On that day the first five yachts to finish, regardless of class, were *Reliance, Constitution, Vigilant, Columbia,* and the new schooner *Ingomar,* all designed by the same man and all between eighty and ninety feet on the waterline. New London harbor was filled up that year for, besides the naval craft that are generally present there, the two square-rigged training ships *Annapolis* and *Hartford* were also present. The Eastern Yacht Club on its annual cruise had arranged to join the New York Yacht Club at New London, so, besides other notable yachts, this added the old Cup boats *Puritan* and *Volunteer* to the squadron, so perhaps this cruise saw more Cup boats together than any other year.

Owl and Game Cock Races

In those days the Owl and Game Cock races were still important features of the cruise for the small gasoline launch had not been developed and the steam launch and naphtha launch had perhaps only just taken the place of the four-oared cutter on the larger yachts, but in the early history of the New York Yacht Club these rowing races with different sizes of yachts' tenders were looked upon as important, and part of a fine yacht's best equipment were rowing boats. At the time I was in my 'teens and thought the most exciting part of a New York Yacht Club cruise were the Owl and Game Cock races. They generally were held in a suitable place in the middle of the anchored squadron on some morning when the fleet was to remain at anchor. As I remember the course was only about an eighth of a mile straight away. First the dinghies with one man had their run, and in this class for several years dinghies designed by the designer of *Reliance* won.

20 1903—

the Giants Race

There were strong, skillful rowers among the sailors of the fleet in those days and besides the natural rivalry between the yachts, the men who won received a good cash prize which undoubtedly was donated by the Commodore. I don't think other yacht clubs here or abroad had these races for the professional crewmen and I do not know the true origin of the name but I was told, when young, that the custom started on an early New York Yacht Club cruise when the rowing boats of the yachts *Owl* and *Gamecock* had a race for a wager. If so, it must be an old custom for I think the *Gamecock* was one of the original yachts of the New York fleet. It is too bad that this custom was given up for, although today the tender might have to be rowed by amateurs, it is very important that a racing yacht should have a good, light rowing boat and several men who can handle it, for nothing will ever take the place of a light, fast rowboat in case of an accident. But it is nearly as hard today to find a good rowing boat as to find a man who can row one.

1903 was also the year the large steam yachts *Kanawha* and *Noma* raced off Newport during the New York Yacht Club cruise.

Reliance *an Early Choice*

Now to get back to the Cup boats. The three large yachts raced all summer without serious accidents, but *Constitution* carried away her topmast in one of the races on the Sound while *Reliance* withdrew from one race because her topmast settled a little in the lower ferrule which

was quite easily remedied. She did not break her topmast as Herbert Stone has written in the book *The America's Cup Races*. That such a large and delicate machine as *Reliance* went through the season without any serious trouble was great credit to Captain Barr and Mr. Iselin, and I must say it would be impossible today to find a crew and after guard that could perform this feat, for you must know that the length of *Reliance* from her head stay to the end of her boom was about 202 feet; her measured sail area was over 16,000 square feet, while a twelve meter boat's measured sail area is something like 1,800. *Reliance* carried sixty-four men aboard in the races. The result of the trial races and the New York Yacht Club cruise showed that *Reliance* was about ten minutes faster than *Columbia* in light weather, and about three minutes faster in a strong breeze over a thirty-mile course, so it was easy for the committee to choose her as the defender quite early in the season.

Shamrock III *an Even Bet*

This time *Shamrock III* came over early so there would be time to tune her up before the final races, but instead of putting into commission *Shamrock II* (Fig. 115) which was here, it was decided to bring over *Shamrock I*. After fitting out for the crossing they left Gourock on May 28 with *Shamrock III* in tow of *Erin*, and *Shamrock I* in tow of the seagoing tug *Cruiser*. Each of the *Shamrocks* had forty-one men aboard so that with the crews of *Erin* and

153

Fig. 114. RELIANCE

Cruiser Sir Thomas had quite a crew to feed and pay. They made the crossing one hour short of sixteen days. In the trial races here between the two *Shamrocks* the new challenger was said to be considerably faster than the older one so betting on the coming race at times was quite even. When the yachts were measured it was found that the racing length of *Shamrock III* (Fig. 116) was 104.37 feet, and *Reliance* 108.41 feet, so *Reliance* had to allow *Shamrock III* only one minute and fifty-seven seconds over a thirty-mile course. Though *Reliance* looked quite a bit larger I would like to mention that from the time she was launched *Shamrock III* had the singular peculiarity of looking smaller than she really was.

The final races of 1903 were a long-drawn-out affair because of bad weather, fog and calms with all the while quite a sea running off Sandy Hook. I was there on my father's steam yacht *Roamer* which stayed anchored back of the Hook in all but the last race, for my father was on *Reliance,* so I shall have to give you an account taken from the writing of the time flavored perhaps with a local feeling, for I was too young to realize the seriousness of the affair. The first attempt at a race was made on August 20 over a thirty-mile windward and leeward course. *Shamrock III* went over the line first, but Barr had more way on *Reliance* so it was a close start. However, the wind was light and the head sea bothered both yachts so

much that they made slow progress. About forty minutes after the start a rain squall came up but as it passed away there was a slight change in its direction which favored the defender. It took *Reliance* over four and one half hours to get to the weather mark while *Shamrock III,* which was a long way behind, gave up as she saw the race could not be finished within the time limit.

First Completed Race

The next race, or the first one finished, was on August 22, the fifty-second anniversary of the day the schooner *America* had originally won the cup. The course was again a windward and leeward one but this time there was a good breeze and quite a ground swell running. *Shamrock* again got the start by some four seconds and at first seemed to slip along best for *Reliance*'s long overhanging bow seemed to pound quite badly. Both yachts had medium size club topsails set, and after a while both took in their jib topsails for it was reported that the wind now was up to sixteen knots. The sea was more from ahead when on the starboard tack. After a while Barr took a long port tack which took him toward the Jersey shore. *Shamrock* soon followed suit and, as they got in smoother water and less wind, they both hoisted jib topsails again. Before this *Shamrock* had been leading, but somehow when crossing tacks Barr managed to place *Reliance* so she gave the challenger back wind. After that the sea diminished perceptibly and *Reliance,* finding this to her liking, began to foot faster. About this time there was a shift of wind which seemed to favor the defender and required both yachts to tack again to make the mark. *Reliance* rounded the weather mark three and one quarter minutes ahead of the challenger and got her light sails set and drawing very quickly, while *Shamrock* had trouble getting her light sails drawing. It seems that her balloon jib was hoisted with a turn in it and had to be lowered away and rehoisted. By this time *Reliance* had a good lead and increased it on the run, so that she won this first race by seven minutes three seconds corrected time.

The next race was on August 25 over a triangular course with the first leg nearly to windward. The heavy ground swell during the previous race had almost disappeared which was much appreciated by the spectator fleet. The wind was moderate to light at the start and both yachts had their largest club topsails set. *Shamrock* had a new Ratsey mainsail made from Egyptian cotton and its Jersey cream color was in contrast to the white American cotton of the defender's sails. Barr took *Reliance* over the line quite promptly after the starting gun, but Wringe preferred to hold *Shamrock* back for the second gun two minutes later. Both yachts stood over toward the Jersey shore on a long tack with apparently no difference in their speed. *Reliance* tacked ship when it seemed she could make the weather mark, but *Shamrock* stood on a little farther and as it turned out overstood the mark. As the yachts neared the weather mark the wind shifted more toward the westward so that the last of that tack became a close reach in which *Reliance* made a perceptible gain, and of course the sailing *Shamrock* had done in overstanding the mark was all wasted time. In spite of this *Shamrock* rounded the weather mark after *Reliance* almost exactly the same amount of time that she had started after her, showing that *Shamrock* might have sailed the weather leg of the course fastest if she had not overstood. The first part of the second leg was a close reach and *Reliance* carried her large jib topsail over her jib and reaching forestaysail. When *Shamrock* rounded she broke out a balloon jib and took in her other head sails, and under these sails made a slight gain until the defender shifted to her ballooner. At this time *Shamrock* may have been ahead if we include her time allowance and late start time, but soon the wind shifted more toward the west, so both yachts set their spinnakers. Under these conditions *Reliance* made a gain, but the wind hauled back more into the south, so the spinnakers were taken in. *Reliance* was a notably fast yacht on a reach and must have made good speed on this part of the last leg for as she neared the finish line she ran into very light wind while *Shamrock* was rapidly overhauling her.

This was a very tense and exciting time for everyone, crew and spectators alike, for it looked as if *Shamrock* would finish within her time allowance. However, the challenger, as she got closer, also ran into the light weather

and slowed down. After *Reliance* finished there was a breathtaking pause for it looked at first as if *Shamrock III* might win on time allowance, but for some reason she went rather slowly. When it is calm at a finish the time factor becomes more important than the distance between the yachts would indicate, so *Reliance* won the race by one minute nineteen seconds corrected time, but the spectator fleet saluted *Shamrock* as she crossed the line quite as enthusiastically as they had the winner, for she certainly had sailed a fine race and with a little luck could have won. This fine performance of the challenger made betting quite even again.

Bad Weather Dogs Series

From August 25 to September 3 several attempts were made to finish a race and for several days the whole fleet was storm bound. It was a very disagreeable spell of weather with rain, fog, gale and calm which nearly drove the contestants frantic as they lay anchored back of the gloomy Hook listening to the fog whistles. The last race was sailed in misty weather, for the spell of foul weather had not properly cleared off. There was quite a chop of a sea from the recent easterly winds, but on the morning of the third of September there was a light southwest wind, not enough to start with until noontime when it freshened a bit. Then the signal was given for a course fifteen miles to the south and return.

At the start the wind was light, five or six miles an hour, and both yachts decided to start on the second gun. *Reliance* went over the line with a few seconds' lead with both yachts on the starboard tack, but both yachts soon tacked ship to stand toward the Jersey shore with a strong lee bow tide. *Shamrock* was sailed rap full and seemed to foot well while *Reliance* seemed to point perceptibly higher and began to work out to windward. Half an hour after the start the wind increased to a good sailing breeze and the defender gained steadily on every tack from here to the weather mark which she rounded some eleven minutes ahead of the challenger. After rounding the outer mark and running home with spinnakers and balloon jibs set, both yachts rolled considerably in the sea that was coming in from the southeast, and in about half an hour after rounding the mark a very thick fog also came in from the southeast.

The fog entirely enveloped the yachts so they could not see each other or be seen by the spectator fleet. *Shamrock*'s compass must have been improperly corrected for from here on she ran considerably to the eastward of the course while *Reliance* loomed up out of the fog like a huge phantom headed straight for the finish line. The Regatta Committee had anchored the tug *Navigator* close to the lightship so they could see it in the fog which made it necessary for the defender to make a small change in her course to cross the now shortened finish line, when she broke out large American flags from her topmast head and spreader ends. After being in tow by her tug, *The Guiding Star,* and stowing her sails, a fourth ensign was set from a staff aft and she was saluted by every passing craft. In the meantime an anxious watch was being kept for *Shamrock;* as time slipped by it was feared she had had some accident in the fog, but at about six o'clock, half an hour after the defender had finished, the fog lifted and *Shamrock III* appeared some distance off to the northeast with her light sails down, when her tug, *The Cruiser,* took her in tow and brought her in to her anchorage under the Hook. Thus ended the long drawn out series of cup races of 1903.

Relative Merits

While I do not feel qualified to criticize the design of either the challenger or the defender, even after the benefit of fifty-six years of world progress, I do think though the

forward end of *Shamrock III*'s lead keel was remarkably blunt, and if it is true that a small over-curved part of a vessel's under body will have a tendency to retard the whole vessel to a speed appropriate for the over-curved part, then if she had had a better shaped lead she might have won the second race. While the model in the New York Yacht Club may not show this bulbous keel exactly, it seems to me that her hull above the keel is nicely shaped for an average speed of nine knots. The upper part of her sharp narrow keel may be correct for its depth in the water for a speed of twenty knots, while I should think the forward lower part of her keel would begin to cause undue resistance at speeds of over six knots. When the *Reliance* was in dry dock, I think, that it would be hard for anyone to say what part of her under body gave more resistance than another part, but, of course, her flat bow caused

Fig. 115. SHAMROCK III

Fig. 116. RELIANCE

much resistance in the choppy water in which the final cup races were sailed.

In connection with the shape of bows and models in general, it might be of interest to the reader that the designer of *Reliance* to his dying day thought *Constitution* was the best modeled ninety-footer he had designed, and, although I believe *Reliance* had several mechanical advantages over *Constitution,* still it was Mr. Herreshoff's opinion that if the crew and after guard of those two yachts had been shifted *Constitution* would have won. The *Reliance* had two bobstays—the reason for this was that there was not then available a suitable wire rope that was strong enough for the strains that sixteen thousand square feet of sail would throw on a single wire.

We should speak about the sails for they push a vessel along even more than the hull's various resistances hold her back, that is until the drive and resistance become equal when we reach the sailboat's very variable limit of average speed. While the sails are willing to go as fast as they do on an ice boat, the boat in the water has for centuries been one of the most interesting things that God has let man race, and the racing at the low speeds often takes the greatest skill. Well, the sails of *Shamrock III* show that Ratsey had now nearly caught up to Herreshoff in the art of cutting crosscut sails, and in the many photographs of the two yachts that I have there is little to choose between them in the set of the sails. Nevertheless Ratsey had much the best material to work with, for the English sail cloth was more carefully woven than ours, and when made from Egyptian cotton it had a smooth silky surface that had less surface resistance and was almost airtight. Egyptian cotton sails also seem to have more vim or life than sails made from American cotton, so *Shamrock III* and *Reliance* were probably equal in driving power except in the difference in sail area. Their dimensions were as follows:

	Shamrock III	*Reliance*
L.W.L.	89.78	89.66
L.O.A.	134.42	143.69
Beam	23.	25.
Draft	19.	20.
Length of spinnaker boom	81.40	83.75
Forward point of measurement to end of main boom	187.54	201.76
Measured sail area	14,154	16,159
Rating	104	108

Some of the figures compare with the cup boats of 1958 as follows:

	12-Meter	*Reliance*
Length from farthest point forward to farthest point aft, about	71 ft	201 ft.
Sail Area	1,800	16,000 or nearly nine times as much.

Reliance's sail area was also well over twice as much as the "J" boats of the 1930's.

We should say something about William Fife, Jr., the designer of *Shamrock I* and *III*. Mr. Fife belonged to an ancient Scottish family that made a specialty of building fast sailboats. I believe he was the third generation which had shown marked ability in producing fast boats. He had served some time in other shipyards to become experienced in the various new construction methods of the time, returning to the family yacht yard at Fairlie on the Clyde. This Mr. Fife had designed some very fast sailboats which included *Clara, Minerva, Ailsa,* and scores of others, and altogether I believe the Fife family built fine wooden vessels for some hundred and fifty years. William Fife was succeeded by his sister's son who took the name of Fife and continued to produce as fine yachts as the previous generations. The Fife's had the advantage of having their own yard, and it is my opinion that they built the best constructed medium-size racing sailboats. However, their yard was not equipped abroad for building metal vessels so that the *Shamrocks* were built in the nearby shipyard of the Dennys of Dumbarton.

21 *The Kaiser's Cup Race*

I must not forget to mention the first Atlantic crossing of a power boat which took place in 1902, and, although at the time it was not looked upon as a yachting event, it was nevertheless an important and heroic feat that I find few people remember today because the crossing for some reason or other was not advertised. The little ship that made the crossing was named *Abiel Abbot Low,* and Figure 117 shows her before the start. She was 38' long and 9' wide with 3' 8" draft. *Abiel Abbot Low* was built to demonstrate the reliability of the engine then manufactured by the New York Kerosene Engine Company which built her in their shop at College Point. She was built under the supervision of Captain William C. Newman who took her over with only his sixteen-year-old son as crew. She had a ten horsepower engine and tank capacity of eight hundred gallons of kerosene and two hundred and fifty gallons of fresh water. She carried food

Fig. 117. ABIEL ABBOT LOW

for a sixty day passage. On the voyage the motor used four hundred and forty gallons (440) at the rate of four-fifths of a gallon an hour, which would be very economical even today for a vessel of that weight, but I imagine her average speed under power on the trip was only about five knots.

On the crossing they had very bad weather with a series of gales and had to lay-to the sea anchor so much that that contrivance required mending several times. The boy generally steered all day and Captain Newman all night. In the first part of the trip the boy had a hard time but as he became accustomed to the life at sea he acquired more endurance and it was Mr. Newman in the latter part of the voyage who was seriously exhausted and sick while the whole vessel and their clothes, bedding and food became saturated with kerosene from leaky tanks. They had left College Point, N. Y., on the ninth of July, 1902, and they arrived at Falmouth, England, on August 14, making a thirty-six day crossing in which much time was used up in laying-to the sea anchor.

At about the turn of the century a remarkable character named Morton F. Plant became prominent in American yachting. He had made a large fortune in the management and ownership of railroads and steamship lines, and while in the prime of life decided to sell out these properties which had grown to a considerable size. It was said he received forty million dollars for his transportation facilities, and in those days, when things in general and yachts in particular, were so very much cheaper, you could do a great deal with a million dollars. Mr. Plant's particular hobby was yachting and between something like 1901 and 1911 he had a great many fine yachts built which ranged from fifteen foot open sailboats to the 647 ton steam yacht *Iolanda.* Mr. Plant owned yachts of almost every type including early gasoline launches and high speed

159

steam yachts, but several of his sailing yachts were for their size the best in the world. Among these were the schooner *Ingomar*, sloop *Nellie* (afterward named *Iskhoodah, Butterfly, Ediana, Maraquita*), which has never been surpassed for a smart cruising boat; the sloop *Shimna* and the schooner *Elena*. He often had several of his yachts moored off his beautiful home at Eastern Point in Groton, where there were some partly sheltered anchorages inside of shoals.

Ingomar *Sweeps Germany*

Mr. Plant was commodore of the Larchmont Yacht Club in 1904 and I suppose he thought he should do something of note in yachting so he decided to take his eighty-six foot waterline steel schooner *Ingomar* to Europe to see what she could do against the large sailing yachts there. She had been built as a centerboard schooner in 1903 but for racing abroad it was decided to remove her centerboard and add a slab of lead to the bottom of her keel which made her a very stiff vessel. For captain Mr. Plant secured Charlie Barr who had been helmsman of *Reliance* the year before. Captain Barr cast off his moorings promptly at 9 A.M. April 30, from Bristol, Rhode Island, where *Ingomar* had been built and refitted for this European invasion. As usual Captain Barr had an uneventful crossing and in the racing in Europe won twelve firsts, four seconds, and a third out of twenty-two races, and it is said the *Ingomar* would have made a clean sweep of her races in Europe except that in Germany the larger schooners did not respect the right of way rules and interfered with *Ingomar* in the first part of the races until Charlie Barr was forced to run into one of them. After they saw that they could not fool with him he won most of the races.

The wind was unusually strong in the races in Germany and, after *Ingomar* got clear of the fleet, she usually sailed away from the larger German schooners. She was an unusually stiff yacht and did not reef in these races while the German yachts generally had a reef or two taken in.

And England

In the races in England *Ingomar* soon proved that she could beat all the English schooners when racing under the rating that was derived from measurement, so during the rest of the summer they rated the yachts in this class by an arbitrary rule derived from the previous performance of the yacht's speed and finally rated *Ingomar* so high that she had little chance of winning. When all things were considered she was one of the most successful large American yachts which had campaigned in Europe, and Mr. Plant, his guests and Captain Barr had a very enjoyable time for they usually beat all comers boat-to-boat.

Kaiser Wilhelm took great interest in *Ingomar* and visited her twice, looking her over very carefully. He tried to order a large schooner from the designer of *Ingomar*, but after the first preliminaries and some disagreement about

Fig. 118. INGOMAR

dimensions, Mr. Herreshoff refused the commission. Figure 118 shows *Ingomar* sailing. She was one of the last large yachts built under the old New York Yacht Club rule, or a length and sail area rule; she therefore had rather a flat bow to acquire shorter waterline length, and in the races in Germany she was driven so hard that she actually dented or bent in her plating between the frames in her forward overhang. All of the later large schooners built under the Universal Rule had sharper bows and were more wholesome vessels.

One of the American designers who produced some remarkably handsome, medium-size sloops at the end of the length and sail area measurement era was William Gardner. Mr. Gardner was born at Oswego, New York, on Lake Ontario in 1859. A graduate of Cornell University, soon after 1880 he started to work at the Roach Shipyard at Chester, Pennsylvania, where he worked first as a fitter —(he laid out the shapes of the plates and other metal members of the ship being built)—and later worked in the foundry, mold loft and drafting room, thus acquiring a very practical education that gave him an advantage over most designers of his time. Later on he was working for the Government and was sent to England to study at the Royal Naval College at Greenwich, then the most advanced institution of its kind. While there Mr. Gardner took advantage of the opportunity to visit many of the shipyards of England and Scotland and became acquainted with the leading naval architects including Fife and Watson.

On the whole, Mr. Gardner was probably the best educated yacht designer we have ever had. You might say he represented a later generation than A. Cary Smith (1837), Edward Burgess and Mr. N. G. Herreshoff who were born in 1848, and, while none of these three gentlemen attended a school of naval architecture, each of them had some natural talent that more than made up for their lack in nautical education. Cary Smith started life as a marine artist. Edward Burgess had an absorbing love of yachts, while N. G. Herreshoff had a strong determination to do things in the best possible way which he often succeeded in doing. In later years Mr. Gardner had to compete with Clinton Crane and Starling Burgess and it is quite likely that he would have been at the very top of the profession for a while if, when studying in England, he had not acquired the habit of depending on stimulants which probably reduced his ability in his later years. Mr. Gardner opened a designing office in New York City in 1888 and became at once very successful for he was a popular man. He designed a great many nice looking, well built yachts, both sail and steam, until about 1930 when he retired because of failing eyesight.

Between 1900 and 1905, Mr. Gardner designed some outstanding medium size sloops, one of which was *Aspirant* of 40' WL, built for Addison and Wilmer Hanan, who were about the best amateur helmsmen of their time. *Aspirant* won the Astor Cup in 1904, and Figure 119 shows her sailing. Then there were the two Gardner sloops, *Neola* and *Weetamoe*, which were 85' OA, 51' WL, and carried 5,000 square feet of sail. They were probably the smallest bronze sailing yachts ever built. Designed in 1902 they were the last expensive yachts built under the old New York Yacht Club rule of WL and SA, and I speak of them now partly because they were the

Fig. 120. WEETAMOE

only yachts I now remember that were rebuilt or remodeled to make them rate reasonably under the new Universal Rule of the New York Yacht Club. Before rebuilding, these yachts had long flat overhangs at both ends, but after rebuilding they had sharper bows with five feet longer waterline. They were handsome yachts and continued racing for some years under the new rule. Figure 120 shows *Weetamoe*.

Trans-Atlantic Race for the Kaiser's Cup

The next important event in yachting was the Trans-Atlantic Race for the elaborate trophy presented by Kaiser Wilhelm II who was much interested in the large schooner yachts and had for some years given prizes for such races as the one from Dover to Heligoland. This race was from Sandy Hook Lightship to The Needles off the Isle of Wight in England, and started May 17, 1905. While for various reasons you do not hear much about this race nowadays, it stirred more general interest in yachting at the time than any contest ever held. The reason for it was that all of the competing yachts were large, fine vessels and the eleven competitors carried British, American and German flags. In those days there were a great many sailormen who served in the sailing merchant marine in the winter and made up the crews of the larger yachts in the summer.

During the six months before the race this contest was the most constant subject of conversation of sailormen, and one of the competitors, the ship-rigged *Valhalla*, greatly excited their imagination. Some of the Nordic sailors would swear by Oden and all that was nautically holy that if the *"Walhalla,"* as they called her, got a strong following breeze and sea she would sail away from the fore-and-afters. "Ya, and by Yesus, if she carry a westerly gale

Fig. 119. ASPIRANT

way across she will show them de way into port with a day to spare." And these sailormen were probably right for, although there was not a westerly gale in the race, *Valhalla* came in third. However, the other square riggers in the race did not do particularly well, and one of them came in a bad last which rather dampened some of the square rigger enthusiasts, still we must remember that these square riggers were all steam auxiliaries and probably had large propeller apertures, etc. The yachts in the race and their time of crossing were as follows:

Am. Schr.	*Atlantic*	Wilson Marshall	12 dys.		4 hrs.		1 min.	
Ger.	"	*Hamburg*	A. Tietjens	13	"	2	"	6	"
Brit.	"	*Valhalla*	Earl of Crawford	14	"	2	"	33	"
Am.	"	*Endymion*	Geo. Lauder, Jr.	14	"	4	"	19	"
Am.	"	*Hildegarde*	Edward R. Coleman	14	"	4	"	33	"
Brit. Bktn.	*Sunbeam*	Lord Brassey	14	"	6	"	23	"
Am. Schr.	*Fleurs de Lys*	Lewis A. Stimson	14	"	9	"	33	"
Am. Ywl.	*Ailsa*	Henry S. Redmond	14	"	11	"	10	"
Am. Schr.	*Utowana*	Allison V. Armour	14	"	11	"	51	"
Am.	"	*Thistle*	Robert E. Tod	14	"	19	"	29	"
Am. Bark.	*Apache*	Edmund Randolph	18	"	17	"	3	"

Here are some details about the ones I remember in the order listed above.

Atlantic was a fine three-masted steel schooner designed by William Gardner and built in 1903. She was an auxiliary with a good size steam power plant. She won both the Cape May and Brenton's Reef cups in 1904. She was built for Wilson Marshall and when he decided to enter her in the Kaiser's ocean race he at once engaged Captain Charlie Barr to sail her and prepare her for the race. Before this she had a large quantity of inside ballast but at large expense this was taken out and cast into an outside keel that was secured below her original steel keel plate. This was said to have greatly improved her, but she was too low freeboard amidships and had high bulwarks so that when driven hard she carried tons of water on deck which ran fore and aft as she pitched, and Charlie Barr told me he had to wear hip boots at the steering wheel when she heeled much. She was 187 feet long over all, 137' WL; 29' beam, 303 tons, and was undoubtedly a fast sailor in medium beam breezes but very dull to windward in light airs, and hard to get up to a high speed length ratio when her rail was under, so Charlie Barr did remarkably well with her. However, *Atlantic* was a handsome vessel that lasted a long time. Figure 121.

Fig. 121. ATLANTIC 3-masted steel schooner

The schooner *Hamburg,* the Germany entry, had originally been built as *Rainbow* in Glasgow in 1898. She was a composite vessel designed by G. L. Watson and was 128' long between perpendiculars (probably more than 140' OA); 115' LWL; 24' beam; and, though not designed for racing, she had a large sail area of 12,600 square feet. She had made some records over long English courses and probably was the fastest large two-masted schooner in Europe.

The ship-rigged auxiliary *Valhalla,* owned by the Earl of Crawford, was one of the finest and handsomest yachts in the world. She was built of steel by Ramage & Ferguson at Leith in 1892, and had been designed by W. C. Storey. Her dimensions were—length between perpendiculars 239'; beam 37'; 1,270 tons. All things considered *Valhalla* did very well in this race and if she had had an old-fashion clipper ship captain and crew, and strong westerly winds, she might well have been the winner. Of course her great length was a speed-giving quality.

The next of these great yachts was the composite two-masted schooner *Endymion* which was built by George Lawley in 1899. She was designed by the late Clinton Crane when he was a young man, and her dimensions were LOA 137'; LWL 100'; beam 24'; draft 14'. She was a fine vessel and her photograph and sail plan have been previously shown. At the time of this race *Endymion* held the Transatlantic record for a sailing yacht, but in this race across the ocean she only came in fourteen minutes ahead of the schooner *Hildegarde*.

Hildegarde was a two-masted steel schooner built by Harlan & Hollingsworth Company of Wilmington, Delaware, in 1897, and designed by the author's first cousin, A. S. Chesebrough. She was 135' OA; 103' WL; 26' beam; 17' draft, and of 185 gross tons. She was a heavy seagoing vessel that had proved to be quite slow in coastal races, but she was a strong, comfortable craft with high bulwarks and certainly did well in this race. She is shown in Figure 122.

The next to finish was the famous barkentine *Sunbeam,* owned by the right honorable Lord Brassey, K.C.B., and perhaps the most famous cruising yacht the world has ever known. She had made many Atlantic crossings and this probably was a help to her crew and afterguard, but both *Sunbeam* and Lord Brassey, who was sixty-nine years old, had some years on them by that time. *Sunbeam* was a composite vessel built by Bowdler, Chaffer & Co., of Seacomb, Cheshire, England, in 1874. She was an auxiliary barkentine, 159' long between perpendiculars; 154' WL, 27' beam; 14' draft, 532 tons Thames measurement. She was designed by St. Clare Byrne, and an illustration of her was given in the section about steam yachts.

The next competitor was the American schooner *Fleur de Lys* and before the race she was perhaps the most talked about of any of these racers. This was because she was to be fitted out and manned by a Gloucester crew, and around 1900 Gloucester sailors were considered about the hardest driving mariners in the world. Also *Fleur de Lys* had been designed by Edward Burgess who developed

Fig. 122. HILDEGARDE 2-masted steel schooner

the first fast Gloucester schooner when iced, or fresh, fishing came into use so she was often spoken of, or thought of, as representing Gloucester, and this seemed to please the newspaper reporters of the time. She was a wood keel schooner built by J. McDonald at Bath, Maine, in 1890; LOA 105'; LWL 86'; beam 22'; draft 13'. She was a heavy-built vessel intended for ocean cruising and somewhat smaller than the leaders in the race. Eight of the competitors came in on their fourteenth day out though there was great difference in their waterline length.

Next was the beautiful yawl *Ailsa* which we have shown and spoken of before when she was cutter-rigged and painted black and owned in England, but still she was very handsome painted white under a yawl rig and American flag. In her day *Ailsa* won some long distance coastal races and I assume that was the reason why she was entered in this contest, but she was rather unsuited for deep sea work having low bulwarks, large sail area and comparatively light construction. She was built by A. & J. Ingels of Glasgow, Scotland, in 1895 and was designed by William Fife, Jr. She was 131' OA; 89' LWL; 25'5" beam; draft 17'. An account of *Ailsa*'s crossing was given in the 1905 Transactions of the Society of Naval Architects and Marine Engineers. I should say she experienced heavier weather and sea than the others. When only a few days out she broke her spinnaker boom and with her large mainsail and no spinnaker she was hard to steer off the wind in a following sea, so they took down her mainsail and sailed her with her trysail a great part of the way across the Atlantic. She also lay to with oil bags to windward some of the time. Her principal difficulty was her strong tendency to yaw with a sea on the quarter; however, she made some very good day's runs when they could

steer her, and ran 268 N.M. one day, covering 50 N.M. in one four-hour watch. Of course *Ailsa* was not a suitable boat for ocean racing, but if she had been fitted out and sailed by Captain Barr she might have come in a day sooner or made a very creditable showing.

Next came the American auxiliary three-masted steel schooner *Utowana* designed by J. Beavor-Webb and built by Neafie & Levy at Philadelphia in 1891. Her dimensions were LOA 190'; LWL 155'; beam 27.5'; draft 14.5', and 414 gross tons. She was what might be called a full powered auxiliary and not fast under sail alone.

Then there was the schooner *Thistle*, designed by H. C. Wintringham and built by Townsend & Downey, Shooters Island, N. Y., in 1901. She was 150' long OA; 110' LWL; 27.8' beam; and 14' draft. Her tonnage was 235. She should have done better in this race for her owner, Robert E. Tod, had had quite a lot of ocean sailing and racing, but she may not have had as favorable winds as the others. (See Figure 123).

The last one was the bark *Apache*, a steel auxiliary designed by R. C. Hanscom and built by the Bath Iron Works in 1898. Her general dimensions were LOA 198'; LWL 168'; beam 28'; draft 16.5'. She had a heavy boiler and machinery and probably never was a fast sailor, but an A-100 vessel when built.

Fig. 123. THISTLE

I have given the dimensions of the competitors in this race to show the reader what an important event the ocean race of 1905 was. Of course there were some strange stories circulating about the winner, *Atlantic,* and one of them was that when Charlie Barr got ready to drive her he first drove her owner to his stateroom and locked him in. But the version of this incident, as told to me by Captain Barr, was about as follows: "One night there was a good beam wind and *Atlantic* was reeling off the knots when the owner came aft to me at the wheel and requested me to take in some sail. I said to him, Sir, you hired me to try to win this race and that is what I am trying to do." After that he went to his stateroom. I suppose *Atlantic* had tons of water on deck and as it swished fore and aft it must have been a startling sight at night.

The Kaiser Is Miffed

After the race *Atlantic* visited German waters and one afternoon when anchored, I think at Kiel, a highly polished steam launch came out and made a circle around her. The launch was steered by a man of high rank in naval uniform including a boat cape, but the afterguard of *Atlantic* paced up and down her deck and paid no attention whatsoever to the steam launch. The next day *Atlantic* was ordered to leave port and Captain Barr was of the opinion that the man steering the launch had been Kaiser Wilhelm. Another story about the *Atlantic*'s visits along the coast of Europe was that just before the colors gun of the port was to be fired a man was hoisted to each of her mast heads in bo'suns chairs and when the gun was fired they were all three let down on the run almost as fast as if they were falling, and many people used to watch this startling sight each evening. I presume, that like most good captains in the Navy or Merchant Marine, Captain Barr allowed a little skylarking to keep his crew on their toes and in good spirits, and I suppose *Atlantic*'s crew felt cocky after making a transatlantic record and winning the greatest ocean race ever held.

The last yacht race that I remember that had several square riggers in it was the run for auxiliaries between Glen Cove and Newport sponsored by the New York Yacht Club in 1909. (Fig. 124). As for three-masted schooner yachts—why, there were several of them, perhaps a dozen or fifteen over here all together, and while I cannot remember them all and have no way to look them up, the ones that I do remember were—*Atlantic, Alcyone, Azara, Dauntless, Intrepid, Visitor, Karina, Shenandoah, Sea Call, Migrant,* and *Guinevere.* In England, between the World Wars and after the staysail rig came into use, Charles Nicholson designed and built large ones and Figure 125 shows one of them sailing. It has been reported that these vessels were capable of high speed in strong breezes, perhaps fifteen knots, but I do not have any record of twenty-four hour runs they made.

Fig. 124. RACE for auxiliaries 1909

Universal Rule Adopted

Perhaps the thing that affected American yachting most after the turn of the century was the New York Yacht Club's adoption of the so-called Universal Rule of measurement for under this rule our finest yachts were built. The first yacht of any size that I know of built under this

Fig. 125. Staysail rigged yacht

Fig. 126. DORIS

New York Thirties

The first one-design class built under the rule was the New York Yacht Club's Thirties. The Thirty is what they were rated, not their waterline length. Their general dimensions were LOA 43'6"; LWL about 29'; beam 8'10"; draft 6'3". Some people, and Lloyds Register, have thought these boats were 30' WL, but that is not so. They were called 30-footers because their rating was 30'. They cost $4,000.00, and I assume that several of them sold for higher figures during their long life. One of the reasons the Thirties were so cheap was that there were eighteen of them built at once. They were built in a carefully planned system of quantity production with four of them in the production line. After production settled down these boats took one month to produce, and were turned out at the rate of one a week. They even had a pattern for each plank, and, as the Herreshoff Company made all of the hardware and sails, there was no holdup in waiting for parts made by others. The builders also had the advantage of having built five or six other one-design classes. Although the Thirties were built cheaply they must have been built well for it is said some of them raced more races than any type of boat ever built, and I am told some of them are quite sound now at the age of fifty-seven years. They have probably given more pleasure and sport for the money than any yachts.

new rule was *Doris,* 57' WL which came out in 1905. (See Figure 126.) In that year some match races were sailed between *Doris* and the old *Gloriana* (Fig. 127), to see how the speed of the old and the new types compared, for they were of somewhat the same general size. It was found that there was not a great deal of difference in their speed although of course *Doris* rated least under the new rule, but as she was such a wholesome, roomy vessel a great deal of interest in the new rule was manifested, so in the next few years almost all sizeable American yacht clubs adopted this form of measurement, and the rule was to go on for about thirty years before power was brought to abandon it in favor of the International Rule and Cruising Club Rule. So we will take a look at some of these yachts.

It was found in their first year of racing that it never paid to reef in a race, and these little ships carried whole sail in heavy squalls and raced during storms. The Thirties went on many New York Yacht Club runs in their early years. They were very small vessels compared to the fleets before 1917. They were very much alike in dimension and speed, perhaps more so than any class ever built, and if I remember a-right after all these years, one of the best helmsmen on the Sound bought the one which came in last in their first year's racing and brought her in first at the end of the next year. This is not so strange for, although few people seem to realize it, slight variation in size and shape have much less influence on the speed of a vessel than such things as the condition of the yacht and her sails, while helmsmanship and tactics used in the race are of much greater importance. Thus in one-design classes the same few yachts win day after day with tiresome monotony, and the indifferent or second-class sailors should never compete in one-design classes but should always race in open classes where occasionally they have a chance to win if they have a yacht that is either generally superior or a one-weather boat that has an advantage under certain conditions. Figure 128 shows the Thirties racing on Long Island Sound.

In the few years before the income tax and after the Universal Rule had proved to produce desirable yachts in the larger classes, there was somewhat of a revival of interest in large racing schooners, particularly in class B, and two of the most successful of these craft were the two steel schooners *Elmina,* designed by Cary Smith for Frederic F. Brewster. The first *Elmina* was built by the Townsend

Fig. 127. Match race between DORIS and GLORIANA

Fig. 128. New York Thirties racing on Long Island sound

Company at Shooters Island in 1901 and was 68' LWL, while the second *Elmina* was built by George Lawley in 1905. Figure 129 shows her sailing. Her general dimensions were LOA 125'; LWL 87'; beam 25'; draft 15.5'. With these two schooners Mr. Brewster performed the remarkable feat of winning the Astor Cup seven times. Morton Plant is the only runner-up to this record with *Ingomar* and *Elena* winning four times, and, while Harold S. Vanderbilt won the cup three times, I believe no one else won an Astor Cup in the schooner class more than twice between 1899 and 1928.

Fig. 129. ELMINA

As for designers of Astor Cup winners in the schooner class between these dates, N. G. Herreshoff designed fourteen, A. Cary Smith nine, and William Gardner three. These three men designed all the Astor Cup winners in the schooner class up to 1928. On the whole we must consider Frederic Brewster one of our most successful schooner racers. The *Elminas* were all-around fine schooners; if they had any peculiarity it was the shape of their sections. While other yachts of their time had what is called wine glass sections amidship, the second *Elmina* in particular had what you might call rather V sections —that is the dead rise from the keel almost to the waterline was rather straight. In other words, *Elmina*'s underwater shape was similar to that of the Meyer form worked out in Germany several years later. I believe *Elmina*'s success can be credited mostly to her sails and captain, for Mr. Brewster experimented a lot with sails, and her captain was the famous Bill Dennis who specialized in schooner racing and was considered the best skipper on Long Island Sound for some years.

Another schooner that was one of the first large Universal Rule yachts was *Queen* built for J. Rogers Maxwell by the Herreshoff Manufacturing Company in 1906. Figure 130 illustrates her sailing later when she was named *Irolita*. She had the distinction of carrying the racing number of B 1 and may have been the first vessel in class B when the new classification in the New York Yacht Club was changed in 1906. *Queen* was a steel schooner 92' LWL, and it was said of her by people who were qualified to judge such matters that she was about the best constructed yacht ever built: her plating was as fair as the shell of an egg, without the least unfairness where the rivets pulled the plating up to the frames. In those days there was a great deal of skillful hand work on a vessel of this size, and her sails, spars and rigging were works of art. While her cabinet work was quite plain it was beautifully finished, mostly in hand rubbed butternut which is restful to the eyes. *Queen* had a fine main saloon with a large swinging table, and I have been on her in a race off Newport with the usual ground swell running when she forged along so steadily that the table was set almost as for a banquet with a large silver cup filled with American Beauty roses in its center. *Queen* was the best kept-up yacht that I was ever on, and I have been on a great many of the very best including *Britannia* when King George had her. I speak of *Queen* at some length because the art of yacht building was probably at its height when she was built and the average yacht yard workman's pay was around fifty cents an hour while a good sailor man was paid about $50.00 a month plus the cost of his food and clothes. If some of my readers had a piece or part of *Queen* in their hands to examine today I believe they would be amazed at the fine workmanship of the good yacht yards of fifty years ago. She was so badly damaged in the fire at City Island about 1914 that she had to be broken up.

Fig. 130. QUEEN

22 *1900 to 1920*

The Universal Rule Breeds

New Fleets

The first of the small open classes to become popular under the Universal Rule was the "Q" class. The *Little Rhody,* was among the first of them. She was designed by the late Professor George Owen of Massachusetts Institute of Technology who was one of the strongest advocates of the Universal Rule, and he was instrumental in having many of the smaller clubs and the Great Lakes' clubs adopt this rule. George Owen's father was a Providence, Rhode Island, man who owned fine yachts, and as a boy George sailed in Narragansett Bay and acquired a strong love of yacht design. After he had been graduated from both Brown University and M. I. T. he worked for a few years in the drafting room of the Herreshoff Manufacturing Company, so he acquired a fine education both theoretically and practically. Later, Mr. Owen was the one who got up the scantling rules to which most of the smaller Universal Rule boats were built, and he was one of the principal designers of the smaller Universal Rule boats between the time of *Little Rhody II* in 1907 and World War I.

At first, Universal Rule boats were not required to have deckhouses, so that some of the first "Q" and "P" boats were nearly as freakish racers as their predecessors, and it is noteworthy that *Little Rhody II* (Fig. 131) did quite

a lot of night racing and won one of the most important ocean races of the time. During the same year that she came out Herreshoff produced two boats for the "Q" class that were named *Dorothy Q* and *Eleanor.* They were of a model which everyone seemed to like, that fitted the new rule well, and it is no exaggeration to say that most of the later Universal Rule boats that were designed by Herreshoff, Gardner, Owen, and later by Starling Burgess, were of the *Eleanor* model.

The "P" class of thirty-one-foot rating was of much importance between 1907 and World War I. There were several reasons for this: first they were used for several years in the international races between Canada and the United States. The Manhasset Bay Challenge Cup and other important trophies were raced for in this class which made intersectional competition, particularly between Boston and New York, with the honors to the designers being very evenly distributed between Gardner, Owen and Herreshoff. Perhaps the other reasons for the "P's" popularity were that they were rather good looking, and had some cabin accommodations. Figure 132 shows the "P" boat *Joyant* which was particularly successful in this class. She caused considerable controversy because she was larger than her competitors and was sometimes called *The*

Fig. 131. LITTLE RHODY II

Giant. Under the Universal Rule at that time if a yacht were given large displacement she could have slightly more length and sail area, so in *Joyant* Mr. Hereshoff took a chance with a very potbellied boat which, although she could not under any circumstance be driven very fast, still seemed to do very well in the light, average winds of Long Island Sound. The photograph shows what a quarter wave *Joyant* made when up to a speed of over seven knots. After her success the New York Yacht Club added a clause to the rule limiting the credit that a yacht would get from large displacement. The clause reads:

"There shall be no limit on the actual displacement of yachts, but the cube root of the displacement, D, as used in the measurement formula, shall never exceed 20% of the L.W.L. plus 0.50."

Since that time all Universal Rule yachts have been designed right up to that proportion. The same year the builders of *Joyant* turned out a smaller "P" boat named *Corinthian* that was well sailed by Sherman Hoyt, and, although *Joyant* beat her slightly, today under the rule, with the credit from displacement limited, *Corinthian* would probably beat *Joyant*. *Joyant* was owned by William H. Childs who had a chain of famous restaurants in New York City and who was a great lover of the smaller racing sailboats, having owned *Joy*, *More Joy*, and *Joyous* besides *Joyant* of which we have spoken.

The largest one-design yachts that we had under the Universal Rule were *Aurora*, *Istalena* and *Winsome*. They came out in 1907 when Cornelius Vanderbilt was commodore of the New York Yacht Club. Mr. Vanderbilt owned *Aurora*, George M. Pynchon owned *Istalena*, and Harry F. Lippitt owned *Winsome*. These yachts were

composite construction with a L.O.A. 85' 3"; L.W.L. 62' 8"; beam 16' 7"; draft 11'. When they came out they rated 57', but their owners, all of whom had larger yachts under the old rule, thought that they would like to carry more sail, so at considerable expense the draft of these yachts was increased with more lead, and their sail area increased so that they then rated 65', and had less chance of winning

Fig. 132. "P" boat, JOYANT

races for their rating was increased more than their speed. However, they were nice looking craft and Figure 133 shows *Aurora* when quite new. Unfortunately she was destroyed in the fire at City Island together with *Queen* and other fine yachts. *Istalena* (Fig. 134) was acquired by E. W. Clark who had her changed to a schooner. *Winsome* was subsequently changed to a ketch and appeared like Figure 135. While both *Istalena* and *Aurora* had won Astor Cups, it is likely the smaller sloop *Avenger* took from them three or four Astor Cups, and a great many other prizes.

Avenger was one of our greatest prize winners of any time. Her story was something like this: Robert W. Emmons had owned the sloop *Humma* in 1906 when it was thought that she won the Astor Cup, and this cup had been awarded to him, but during the winter the great mathematician, Charles Lane Poor, reckoned the measurements and times of *Humma* and the Gardner-designed *Weetamoe* and showed that the Gardner boat really had won the race, so the New York Yacht Club took back the 1906 Astor Cup. This rather disturbed Mr. Emmons and he decided to avenge himself, so he ordered from Mr. Herreshoff a fast sloop to be named *Avenger*. She was designed and built right after the 57-footers the same winter and she too was a composite yacht but rated at the bottom of Class K, or, with a change of trim, could race in Class L.

Avenger's general dimensions were LOA 74' 9"; LWL 53'; beam 14' 6"; draft 9' 6" and, while she was not very different from the 57-footers in model, she did have all hollow spars except, of course, the bowsprit, while the 57's had rather heavy, solid Oregon pine masts.

Fig. 134. ISTALENA

Fig. 135. WINSOME

Fig. 133. AURORA

However, there were several reasons why *Avenger* did so well, and one of them was that two gun starts were still being used. At the first gun the three 57-footers (later 65-footers), went over the line together and did more or less luffing through the race, while *Avenger* made a later start all clear of the other yachts and could then concentrate on making the best time over the course. It is my opinion (and I raced on *Avenger* in many of the races of her first two years), that the thing that helped her most was a flat cut balloon jib that Mr. Emmons had made for her, and we carried this sail even close hauled sometimes in light weather. So I claim Mr. Emmons was the first to make practical use of what is now called a lapping jib, or Genoa jib. It is also interesting that Mr. Emmons told me he had used such a sail (we then called them flat-cut balloon jibs), on his Buzzards Bay Thirty in 1902. While I agree with the old saying that there is nothing new under the sun, and that English cutters have carried what is called a balloon forestaysail since about 1850, still I like to credit Bob Emmons with the first practical use of large jibs when close-hauled. I also remember that my father, who designed *Avenger* and followed her closely in the races, said rather crossly to me, "If you are not careful you will carry the topmast out of *Avenger*," but we generally had the jib set in stops so if it breezed up we could break it out and lower away this great jib topsail in its lee.

But to continue with large jibs, or lapping jibs—I was always interested in these from the time of *Avenger,* which is now over fifty years ago, and while working with Starling Burgess when designing two 6-Meter boats in the winter of 1920, I tried to persuade him to try slightly overlapping jibs, but he thought their back wind would reduce the efficiency of the mainsail, so it was not until I was running my own business in 1926 that I had an opportunity to design two lapping jibs that were for the "R" boats *Yankee* and *Mary*. These jibs were made by English Ratsey, and as soon as he got the plan he wrote me a letter in which he stated that he thought very well of these lapping jibs so had made some to send down to the Mediterranean for the 8-Meter boats that were to race there that winter. The first race when these jibs were carried was at Genoa which gave the name while our "R" boats did not get these overlapping jibs until the following summer.

Let us get back to *Avenger*. In 1908, there had been a financial panic of short duration and Mr. Emmons decided to sell her that summer, so he hired Charlie Barr to put her in commission and sail her in the New York Yacht Club cruise as the best way to sell her. I was a guest and the only amateur aboard *Avenger* while we were standing by at Newport for a few days before the Astor Cup race, when a nice looking, middle-age gentleman came out in his steam launch to look at *Avenger*. Captain Barr gave me the job of showing the gentleman around and I showed him all her parts so enthusiastically that the gentleman, who turned out to be Alexander S. Cochran, bought her on the spot and took her over, crew and

all, inviting me to be his guest for the next few days, so that I had the pleasure of being on *Avenger* when she was winning the three successive Astor Cups of 1907, 1908 and 1909. As she won this cup again in 1911 I believe that she has won the Astor Cup in the sloop class more times than any other vessel. Figure 136 shows her.

Charlie Barr was not much of a talker and never boasted but even when at the helm during a race, he could tell interesting anecdotes of past races and, as he had been captain of three or four much larger yachts that had won this cup, his conversation was very instructive. He had a remarkable memory and, as we sat in the cockpit at anchor, or if he were called into the cabin after supper, he told such interesting stories about racing *Ingomar* in Europe and driving *Atlantic* across the ocean that Mr. Cochran decided to have a large steel schooner built to go to Europe and that is how *Westward* came to be built.

Fig. 136. AVENGER

She was built by the Herreshoff Company and came out early in the season of 1910. She was a good, wholesome yacht built to Lloyd's rule and partly designed to fit the rules of measurement then in force in England and Europe that had girth measurements. After her trial trips she was given shorter gaffs, heavier and smaller sails, and sailed for Europe with her owner aboard. On her crossing they experienced some rather rough weather and head winds, which is usual early in the season, but *Westward* proved to be a very good sea boat and never took solid

Fig. 137. WESTWARD, close hauled

Fig. 138. WESTWARD, running free

water on deck during the crossing. Her general dimensions were LOA 136'; LWL 96'; beam 26' 8"; draft 17'. Figure 137 shows her close-hauled, and Figure 138 shows her running free. In this latter picture I think the yacht astern is the German schooner *Cicely* which was one of *Westward*'s principal competitors throughout the summer.

During the first half of the season *Westward* won nearly every race quite easily, and proved that no European schooner was a match for her under their International Rule of measurement, so the British officials decided to have her give the other yachts an arbitrary handicap derived from her previous performance, and they increased the handicap so much at the end of the season that she was allowing some of her competitors twice the amount that the difference in measurement called for. While this seems quite unfair, still the International Rule proved many times that it did not rate the larger yachts satisfactorily, so the British large yachts for several years were raced with an arbitrary handicap until they adopted our Universal Rule in 1931 for classes above 14½-meters.

Westward was undoubtedly the fastest schooner in the world in 1910 and Mr. Cochran and Charlie Barr had a great time racing in Germany and England but, unfortunately, the next winter, while she was laid up at Southampton, Captain Barr died suddenly of a heart attack. He was only in the middle of his life and his death was

a great shock and surprise to all interested in yachting. While there may have been some English captains who were as capable, all-around good men, it is generally thought that Captain Charlie Barr was the best professional captain and helmsman we have ever had.

Morton Plant had been so interested in *Westward*'s success abroad, which surpassed his successes in *Ingomar*, that he had the builders of *Westward* make him an almost duplicate schooner that was named *Elena*. (See Figure 139). The only difference between *Westward* and *Elena* was that the lead keel of *Elena* was deeper forward and not rounded off for the International Rule's girth measurement. She also had more sail area for she had more stability with her slightly lower lead. *Westward* was brought back to this country in the spring of 1911 by Chris Christiansen, the Norwegian who had been mate for Captain Barr on several yachts, and by this time Christiansen was well on his way toward being one of our best professionals. Mr. Plant had acquired Bill Dennis, the captain who had done so well with the schooners *Elmina*, to be in charge of *Elena*, and these two schooners raced very evenly during the summer.

The fine schooner *Enchantress* came out in 1911; she was designed by Cary Smith for William E. Iselin, who had for some years been racing the old *Vigilant* under a yawl rig. *Vigilant* was junked at the time and many of

Fig. 139. ELENA

her fittings were used on the new yacht. *Enchantress* was built by George Lawley and Sons and was 136' LOA; 100' LWL; 27' beam; 15' draft. Mr. Maxwell's *Queen,* although a somewhat smaller vessel, also often raced in this class which made the large schooners the principal interest in the year 1911, and I presume that the professional crews of these four schooners would outnumber all the professionals that have gone along on recent New York Yacht Club cruises. The Astor Cup in the schooner class was won by *Westward* in 1911, then she was sold to German owners. *Elena* won this cup in 1912 and 1913, and *Enchantress* won it in 1914, so this was about the last of the great schooner racing, for the income tax started in 1913, and World War I in 1914.

While *Westward* was in Germany she had a heavy interior put in her including large brass bedsteads and a grand piano, and so forth, which it is said slowed her up somewhat but Germany at this time was beginning to have capable yacht designers and, with *Westward* to work from, there was designed and built a larger version of her that could not be told from her in a photograph. This vessel must have been broken up in the war between 1914 and 1918. In 1914, *Westward* went to England for Cowes week, and at the outbreak of the war was laid up there and subsequently seized by the British government. After the war she was owned by T. B. F. Davis who sailed her with a Channel Island crew. Up to just before World War II *Westward* could beat all the later British yachts in a

Fig. 140. New York Yacht Club Fifties

good strong beam wind. She became one of the most popular British yachts after *Britannia* was retired, and as she only spent one year here she is often thought of as being English. *Elena* was laid up during the war and for a few years after during which time Mr. Plant died and she was bought by William B. Bell who entered her in the King of Spain's transatlantic race which she won, beating the much larger schooner *Atlantic* boat to boat.

New York Fifties

The New York Yacht Club Fifties came out in 1913, and perhaps this was the largest class of sizeable one-design yachts the world has ever seen. There were nine of them with the dimensions of 72′ LOA; 50′ LWL; 14.5′ beam; 9.75′ draft. (See Figure 140.) The Fifties raced very hotly the first few years and made some very close starts, and as I remember it there were few protests and no serious collisions. I raced on the one named *Barbara* many times; she was handled by Bob Emmons who had owned *Avenger* and was to be the manager of the next cup defender *Resolute*. One or another of the Fifties won the Astor Cup nine times under a sloop rig, and, as *Pleione* had won four Astor Cups under a schooner rig, this makes by far the greatest number of times these cups were won by vessels of the same model. In my opinion the Fifties were about the last high-grade, reasonably-priced yachts built. They were 72′ OA, and of late years there have been several yachts built with this same length on deck that cost fifteen times as much while the cost of clothes, food and real estate has only increased some three times. Some of the reasons for this great difference in cost of yachts now and in the year the Fifties were built (and that year happened to be the year the income tax started) are as follows:

1. The Fifties were designed and built completely—sails, spars, rigging, hull, and so forth, by one concern. The only things I can think of now that the builders did not make were the stoves, water-closets, and the larger rigging blocks.

2. Good plant management is the principal way of decreasing the cost of building yachts and, while this can only be learned by experience and the use of common sense, it is a fact that in those days there were two or three yacht yards that were well managed. One of the simple things of good management was to have all of the materials on hand before they were needed, and in those days the yacht yards carried an inventory of materials at least ten times as large as at present. This often allowed them to buy at considerable reduction in price.

3. The spirit, or enthusiasm and pride, of the workmen were important factors in building yachts quickly and well, and I do not know how this was arranged but, I do know that the workers were almost all paid different wages according to their accomplishments.

At present, almost all yachts are designed by one concern and assembled by another. This makes for never-ending complication and, as the designing concern is paid its commission based on the cost of the yacht, they seem to do little nowadays to simplify the construction. I have used the word "assemble" to describe what was once called "building a yacht" for today we even hear of yachts' keels being cast hundreds of miles away instead of the mold being set up on the stocks where the yacht is to be built, while the other parts of the yacht may be made by ten or more distant concerns. In the meantime, the art of yacht building, which has taken thousands of years to develop, is lost, and materials such as laminated wood and plastics are substituted in an effort to get around this lack of know-how, but the weight and cost of these materials is so much more than natural wood that the result is not very satisfactory.

As for the workers, they are paid alike and seem to try to make the job last as long as possible. Some of them who wouldn't know an adz if they stumbled over it, try pretty hard to master the new techniques and only time will tell if they will be successful. The modern worker hates all hand tools simply because he does not know how to sharpen or lubricate them, but I have known men who could swing a broad ax all day and every time the ax struck it would lop off a shaving you could cook a breakfast with. These men hewed so close to the line that to finish the job, be it straight, curved or rounded, it only took a few strokes with a well-sharpened plane whose sole was rubbed with paraffin. And that is how yachts were built in those times which is quite different from the present when workmen only want to work with materials they can finish with a power sander.

I have used all these words to try to explain why the New York Yacht Club Fifties cost only $17,000.00 while three or four modern yachts of the same length cost $250,000.00.

For crew the Fifties had a captain, two sailors and a steward but, even by their second year (and second year of the income tax) several of the owners complained about the cost of running them, and that was one of the reasons the New York Yacht Club Forties came into existence a few years later.

International Measurement Rule

We must now take a look at what was going on in the meantime in European yachting for, during the time we have been speaking of, the International Yacht Union was formed at a meeting in Paris in 1907, and at this meeting and subsequent ones in London the International Rule of Measurement was worked out. This rule is basically the English Yacht Racing Association Rule but uses the meter instead of the foot as the standard of measurement. The Y.R.A. measurement rule is descended from the Dixon Kemp Rule of 1888, and the R. E. Froude Rule of 1896, so, as our Universal Rule came into force between 1903 and 1905, it is actually older than the International Rule but, as it is only composed of modern thought, you might say its conception is more modern. The International Rule has gone through some changes and is sometimes spoken of as the first international rule of 1907, second rule of 1920, third of 1933, but as this rule did not seem to rate the larger yachts well the I. Y. R. U. in 1930 adopted our Universal Rule for classes over 14½-meter rating.

All yachts built to the International Rule must also be built to Lloyd's specifications and classifications and inspected during construction in order to get Lloyd's certificate of approval. As Lloyd's Rule calls for many impractical methods of construction the cost of yachts has been increased while unfortunately the strength and longevity of the vessel has been reduced so that many yachts built under these rules are prone to rot out in the main keel in a few years and require very expensive rebuilding. Nevertheless there have been many beautiful or handsome yachts built to the first International Rule, and Figures 141 and 142 show two of them of the period around 1910.

America's Cup Races of 1920

The next set of races for the America's Cup was not

Fig. 141. VANITIE, a yacht built to the first International rule

Fig. 142. NYAMA, another yacht built to the first International Rule

until 1920, a lapse of seventeen years since *Reliance* beat *Shamrock III*. During this time, however, Sir Thomas inquired of the New York Yacht Club several times under what conditions he could challenge. According to the deed of gift under which the cup was competed for, the club holding the cup must defend it under the rules of measurement that the club was then using, and by at least 1907 the N.Y.Y.C. had officially adopted the Universal Rule and was running all its regular regattas under this rule of measurement and, while the club had started to use the Universal Rule as early as 1903, it was not until about 1907 that the rule was sufficiently consolidated to make it practical for such an important event as the America's Cup races.

In 1907, Lipton sent over a conditional challenge, but the New York Yacht Club was so indefinite about the conditions under which they would accept a challenge that no agreement was reached. During the negotiations it was apparent that both sides favored much smaller and less expensive yachts than had raced for the cup the last time. During this period the author raced or sailed on the large schooners *Queen* and *Westward* and was aware of the fact that many of our racing men hoped that the next races for the cup would be in vessels of that type which could race in almost any weather, but the wiser ones were of the opinion that if large schooners were built expressly for challenging for and defending the cup, they would be as delicate freaks as the cup racing sloops. Also, the schooner *Westward* had just shown a clean set of heels to all European schooners, so apparently no challenger saw a good chance of winning in the schooner class.

After about five years of intermittent communication

between Sir Thomas and the New York Yacht Club, an agreement was made to race sloops of 75-foot waterline measured under the Universal Rule. This made a great reduction in size for cup boats for the older rule of waterline and sail area favored a short waterline vessel while the Universal Rule boats were of a model much longer on the waterline. The challenge was accepted in April, 1913, and this time Lipton went to Charles E. Nicholson for the design for, if I remember right, both Watson and the Fife who had designed Lipton's three previous challengers had died.

It is to assume Sir Thomas thought the youngest Fife had not had sufficient experience with the larger yachts for he shifted to the English designing and building firm of Camper and Nicholsons, Ltd., of Gosport, Hants. This yard was within sight of the world's greatest racing waters, The Solent, and they had been building yachts of various types for many years. At the time their designer was the famous Charles E. Nicholson, who had become noted for designing several of the most successful English yachts, and was to design the next four British challengers for the cup. Mr. Nicholson had not designed a yacht to the provisions of the Universal Rule, but thought some sort of a freak would have the best chance. This was before scantling restrictions (or construction regulations), were a part of the measurement requirements, so he tried to build a very light composite hull of most ingenious construction which used a great deal of laminated wood, and I think that her whole deck panel was made up of sheets of laminated wood. The new challenger was named *Shamrock IV* (Fig. 143) as might be expected. She was not very handsome, and Mr. Nicholson himself referred to her as The Ugly Duckling. Above water she was quite scow-shaped so that her lines were adapted to high speed, but below water her lines were as full as other Universal Rule boats, otherwise she would have rated very high. Altogether she had very high measurement rating for her waterline length of 75 feet. Her final rating was over 94 feet, but many Universal Rule boats of that time rated nearly the same as their waterline length and later ones rated considerably less than their waterline length.

The yachts built in 1914 for the honor of defending the cup were *Defiance, Vanitie* and *Resolute*. All were just under 75 feet waterline but varied quite a little in model. *Defiance* was designed by George Owen, professor in naval architecture at Massachusetts Institute of Technology who had worked some time in the Herreshoff yacht yard and had lately designed some very good medium-size racing yachts. She was built for a syndicate of New York Yacht Club members headed by George M. Pynchon and E. Walter Clark, both of whom had been owners of good size racing yachts.

Defiance was of composite construction with mahogany planking and, though her hull was considered a good design both in model and construction, her sail plan was probably her weakest point for she had her mast stepped well forward with a very small fore triangle which time has taught us is wrong, for this arrangement allows only a

178

small balloon jib and spinnaker. *Defiance*'s other great trouble was that she was built by six or seven concerns; one built the steel framing, another her woodwork, planking, deck, etcetera; the third company built her spars; the fourth her blocks and deck fittings; the fifth her rigging; the sixth her sails, etcetera. So she never really became thoroughly completed or tuned up.

Vanitie was designed by William Gardner who has been spoken of before and who received some of his training in Great Britain. He had had considerable experience in designing larger yachts including *Atlantic*, which still holds the record for an Atlantic crossing. At this time, Mr. Gardner was designing the large, three-masted schooner *Sea Call* for Alexander S. Cochran. Mr. Cochran was a very wealthy man and extremely interested in the larger yachts after his successful year of racing *Westward* in England and Germany, so he had Mr. Gardner also design for him a cup candidate. Both *Vanitie*, and *Sea Call* were built by the George Lawley and Sons Corporation of Boston at about the same time. *Sea Call* was plated with monel metal and *Vanitie* with manganese bronze, and it is said that the cost of these two yachts was the greatest sum that any one individual has paid in one year for sailboats either before or since 1913, or the beginning of the income tax.

In model, *Vanitie* was quite similar to the Universal Rule "P" boats which Mr. Gardner had recently designed, but perhaps had more overhang. She was considered a very handsome vessel by the yachtsmen of the time who were accustomed to the low-sided, long overhang yachts of a few years before, being always a great favorite with the general public. *Vanitie*, however, had two or three disadvantages, the first was that she rated rather high; second, her actual freeboard was too low but she had bulwarks along her top sides which carried considerable weight of water on deck at times. Her third defect was that she had none of the mechanical devices for handling sheets and backstays which had been developed for the last three cup boats, if we include the trial yacht *Constitution*. *Vanitie* was the result of a fine job of building and at her launching was polished bronze from rail cap to keel bottom and was usually spoken of as *The Golden Vanitie*, but it is the nature of the bronzes to turn color when exposed to salt water so that her topsides during the first year were a rather unattractive streaky brown with the slightest tinge of green. Her topsides were always painted after that.

The third contender for the cup was named *Resolute*. She was designed by N. G. Herreshoff who had had much experience with cup boats as *Resolute* was to be one of his yachts to defend the cup for the sixth time, while neither the designers of *Shamrock IV* nor *Defiance* nor *Vanitie* had designed an America's Cup boat. Mr. Herreshoff also had the great advantage of having his design almost completely built in his own yard, the only exception, I believe, being her larger blocks which were made by Merriman. Mr. Herreshoff was sixty years old when *Resolute* was built, and seventy-two years old the year she defended the cup. He also made the diplomatic mistake of designing *Resolute* to rate quite low which I will explain was a great handicap to her. The reason he did this was that there had been much talk about the expense of cup boats since the previous races in 1903 between the gigantic *Reliance* and *Shamrock III*, and he thought the best way to reduce cost was to design a small, low rating yacht, but Gardner with *Vanitie*, and Nicholson with *Shamrock IV* had designed large, high rating yachts for the 75-foot waterline limit of the challenge.

Resolute, as she came out was a nicely proportioned yacht with small sail area, but while the boat-to-boat finishes between her and *Vanitie* were often close, *Resolute*, as originally rigged, beat *Vanitie* quite easily with time allowance. The score of the three yachts at the end of the first season:

Resolute	15 firsts out of 18 starts	
Vanitie	5 " " " 20 "	
Defiance	0 " " " 10 "	

For the season of 1915 the afterguard of *Resolute* persuaded her designer to give her more sail area in order to increase her rating so *Vanitie* would allow her less, and under these conditions *Vanitie* made a gain and the score at the end of the second season was:

Resolute	12 firsts out of 16 starts
Vanitie	4 " " " 16 "

By this time World War I was raging in Europe and large yacht racing was stopped until about 1919. *Shamrock IV* had come over in the fall of 1914 and was laid up at City Island during the latter part of the war where all the experts who looked at her thought she would rate so high that she would have to allow *Resolute* nearly a quarter of an hour over the thirty-mile cup course of the time. So the cup defense committee and the afterguard of *Resolute* were again anxious to increase her rating for they thought the press and the general public would be very dissatisfied if she won out with time allowance while coming in last boat-to-boat. The designer of *Resolute*, who was then over seventy years of age, was really up against it for it is easy to increase the rating of a boat under the Universal Rule by increasing her sail area, but it is very difficult to increase her speed proportionately. However, the sail area was increased and a very light hollow wooden mast built for her. This mast was what is called a pole mast with the mainmast and topmast all in one, while her previous mast had been steel with a telescoping wooden topmast. Unfortunately, this new wood mast was carried out of *Resolute* in the first race of 1920.

It was off New Haven on May 22, and in the second time around the course a very heavy squall struck her. Her main sheet was slacked out without releasing the topmast and main backstays. This caused an uncalculated strain on the new wooden mast which broke in a thousand pieces under the terrific pressure. It was too bad, for it would have been interesting to see if *Resolute*'s lighter rig would have increased her speed in proportion to her increase in rating with more sail. This accident caused quite a delay in the racing, for *Resolute*'s two original steel masts and much of her rigging had to be changed to fit the new, larger sail plan.

Vanitie had been changed considerably above the waterline for the season of 1920. These improvements came about as follows: *Vanitie*'s owner, Mr. Cochran, had been failing in health so that he turned her over to the New York Yacht Club under the condition that she should be raced as a contender for the honor of defending the cup. Mr. George Nichols, who had been navigator on *Resolute* during the previous races, was chosen as her manager and he at once secured the services of his old friend, W. Starling Burgess, to improve *Vanitie*. Starling was a remarkable and lovable character, a son of Edward Burgess, who had designed the cup defenders *Puritan, Mayflower* and *Volunteer*. In his younger days he had been a yacht designer and builder, and then was one of the first builders of aircraft in this country. During World War I he was an officer in the Navy's air service and worked on the design of lighter-than-air craft.

Mr. Burgess thus had very good training with light structures. He drew up a new sail plan for *Vanitie* which was shorter and slightly higher than her previous one. He had her bulwarks cut down practically to deck level except at the bow where the bulwarks supported the bowsprit and other bow gear. The combined saving in weight of a lighter rig and deck, and the removal of bulwarks allowed *Vanitie* to take on quite a little inside ballast while, if I remember rightly, she rated slightly less or had less measured sail area in a more efficient rig.

Perhaps the greatest improvement though in *Vanitie* was that Mr. Nichols had persuaded the designer of *Resolute* to make for *Vanitie* a duplicate set of the *Resolute*'s sheet and backstay winches which neither Gardner nor Burgess apparently could design. *Vanitie* already had a duplicate set of all the blocks and components which Merriman had made for *Resolute*. Mr. Nichols also secured C. Sherman Hoyt to be his right hand man, and Mr. Hoyt had had experience in most all sizes of racing yachts and was one of our very best helmsmen. Starling Burgess also raced on *Vanitie* throughout the season and she was navigated by Charles J. Nourse who was to be navigator of two or three later cup boats, and the navigator of this sort of craft by this time was becoming very important, for few men can tell the helmsman at once where they are in tacking to windward in varying and changing winds, although in the past there were men like Charlie Barr who could tell by instinct just where they were under any conditions, and generally never referred to anything but the compass during a race, for all other matters were neatly stowed away in his head where in spite of wind, rain, and fog they were instantly available.

With all these changes *Vanitie* was greatly improved and during the trial races of 1920 the score was as follows:

Vanitie	4	firsts	7	seconds	1	other	12	total
Resolute	7	"	4	"	1	"	12	"

The score of the racing during their first three seasons under their gaff sail plans was:

Resolute	34	firsts
Vanitie	13	"

It is my opinion that if they had continued racing as they were originally designed *Resolute* would always have had a 3 to 1 advantage over *Vanitie,* for when the "J" boats of the 1930's came out both *Vanitie* and *Resolute* were quite out of the running principally because they both were too short on the waterline and had too much sail area.

Quite early in the season the cup committee chose *Resolute* to defend the cup and that gave her a chance to get things straightened out, for she was sailing under parts of two different rigs after her wooden mast was carried away. In the meantime some changes were made in the sail plan of *Shamrock IV* so that her rating was somewhat reduced and, as *Resolute*'s rating had been increased, the challenger did not have to allow the defender as much as had been contemplated. Sir Thomas had brought over his 23-meter International Rule *Shamrock* as a trial horse and these two *Shamrocks* were having practice spins and races off Sandy Hook while *Resolute* and *Vanitie* were racing off Newport.

The coming races were to be the first America's Cup races in which the yachts were steered by amateur helmsmen, and Sir William P. Burton, skipper of *Shamrock IV,* and Charles F. Adams, helmsman of *Resolute,* had a meeting (I think at Mr. Adams' request), to talk over each other's interpretations of the New York Yacht Club's racing rules for they differed in some cases from the Yacht Racing Association Rule. Sir William had raced for many years under the Yacht Racing Association Rule and it is probable that as the result of this meeting there was no misunderstanding on either side, and even the press could not find fault with the way both yachts were handled. This must have been great satisfaction to these two talented gentlemen. I should mention that Lady Burton took the time for Sir William in these races for he had become used to her performing this important function in his racing for several years. So, if we include Lord Dunraven's daughters, Lady Burton was the fifth woman to race on a cup boat. The professional sailing master of *Shamrock IV* was Captain Albert Turner.

First Race

The first of the final races was on July 15 which was a month or more earlier than many of the previous cup races. They started at noontime in a very light, fluky southerly breeze to sail over a windward and leeward course of thirty miles. At the time a thunderstorm was making up over the Jersey shore and the sky was very dark toward the southwest almost in the direction the yachts were sailing. Both of the yachts seemed to foot at about the same speed but *Resolute* pointed perceptibly higher. Some people said she was sheeted in too flat for the light

180

weather, a fault which Mr. Adams was inclined to with *Resolute*. However, in a half hour or so the defender was said to be a quarter mile to windward of the challenger. The wind then became very light but *Resolute* seemed to carry her way very well and worked up to a lead of perhaps half a mile. Then the thunderstorm struck with a heavy deluge of rain and resounding thunder but not much wind. After the rain squall a light breeze came from the southwest and the challenger took a tack close under the Jersey shore and stood in so far that she had to pay off to clear the buoy off Shrewsbury Rocks.

Resolute's Accident

In the meantime, *Resolute* was pointing high enough to make the mark with a lead of perhaps half a mile. During this time *Shamrock IV* had tacked ship several times and once or twice *Resolute* tacked to keep between the mark and her adversary, but she was too far ahead to affect the challenger's wind. In this part of the race the challenger appeared to sail very fast and at one time nearly had her rail under. As they were nearing the weather mark *Resolute*'s mainsail began to sag at the throat and finally the forward end of the gaff came almost all the way down. She continued for a while under her headsails and the triangular after part of her mainsail, rounding the weather mark some four and a half minutes ahead of the challenger, then dropped out of the race and headed for her anchorage under her jib.

Neither the crew nor the afterguard of *Resolute* were very mechanically bright and they had done a very foolish thing. After the rain squall they had felt they should slack the throat halliard for, as they thought, the luff rope would shrink and bring an unnatural strain on things, but *Resolute* had a wire luff rope and wire halliard, neither of which would shrink from the rain. One end of her halliard came down to a worm gear winch below deck; this winch was used to make slight adjustments in the sail when under way, and usually had a number of turns of the halliard around its drum so that the very end of the wire halliard was not strongly clamped to the winch. Now, with this below-deck arrangement on *Resolute* it had been the custom to tap on the deck a certain number of times as the signal to haul in, slack out, or belay, and the thoughtless Swede who worked the crank had got the order to slack out, but on deck they forgot to give him the order to belay, so he kept slacking out until he came to the bitter end when the halliard went up the mast and the throat came down.

At the time, the crew of *Resolute* was criticized for not continuing the race under balloon jib and spinnaker and trying to re-reave the throat halliard, for in sailing down wind a large yacht will sail quite fast under light sails only, and in no other cup race had a defender failed to finish. The challenger sailed the home stretch without setting her light sails and near the finish took in her topsail, for another thunderstorm was developing, and that is how

Shamrock IV won her first race in this unusual series of races.

An attempt was made to sail the next race on July 17, but when the time limit had expired they were little over two-thirds of the way around the course with the challenger some two miles astern.

Second Race

On July 20, *Shamrock IV* sailed a remarkable race. It was a triangular course with little windward work for the wind shifted at times to make it a reach most of the way around. Soon after the start the challenger had trouble in setting her balloon jib and finally tore it. In its place some sort of a reaching jib was set from her topmast at a point higher up than her working jib was set, and with this sail under her jib topsail she went very fast. She laid a course quite a little to weather of where *Resolute* was sailing with her regular balloon jib set, and sailed by the defender. Perhaps this sail combination of the challenger would not have been so good later in this leg if the wind had not shifted to more ahead; but it did shift so that *Resolute* had to take in her ballooner while the challenger was to weather of her and could make the mark sailing at an angle which must have just suited the reaching jib and jib topsail combination. To make things even worse for the defender she ran into a calm streak before reaching the first mark. At this point *Shamrock IV* is said to have been half a mile ahead.

At the first mark the challenger had a lead of four minutes, thirty-two seconds. It was a close reach to the next mark in light to moderate breeze, and this was about the only condition under which the challenger was fast, and she opened up her lead, it is said, to nearly a mile. The wind then changed to more ahead and freshened and the challenger, which had a good lead, got it about five minutes before the defender and romped toward the finish line to beat *Resolute* boat-to-boat ten minutes and five seconds. After subtracting the seven minutes thirty-nine seconds the challenger allowed the defender, she had beaten her two minutes and twenty-six seconds, thus making the challenger two up, and she received the great ovation that she deserved, for evidently Sir William had sailed a perfect race.

Third Race

The next race of July 21 caused a great deal of interest, for if *Shamrock IV* should win the cup would go to England. This race was particularly interesting for the spectators as the yachts boat-to-boat made the same time over the course and were never far apart. The course was fifteen miles to weather and return, the start being postponed until one in the afternoon. The wind was very light but increasing and it finally got up to a good sailing breeze so that both yachts covered the course in a little over four hours. Although the challenger got the start by nineteen seconds and footed faster than *Resolute*, the defender pointed higher and made less leeway so she was soon to windward of *Shamrock IV* who tacked many times in an effort to get her wind free, but *Resolute*, with her fast working sheet and backstay winches, seemed to get her sails trimmed so much faster that she gained perceptibly when both yachts tacked.

It is said that *Shamrock IV* came about eighteen times in the beat to windward. When they rounded *Resolute* had a lead of one minute and forty-seven seconds which was a pretty poor showing for her and something must have been quite wrong. On the way home the wind increased so that running under spinnaker the challenger passed the defender near the finish line making next to the closest finish boat-to-boat of the cup races, although in the races of 1901 *Shamrock II* and *Columbia* were actually lapped as they crossed the finish line in one race. However, in this race *Resolute*, with her big handicap, won quite easily making the score now one to two in favor of the challenger.

Fourth Race

The next race was to be a triangular one which was favorable to *Shamrock IV*, so in the intervening time she was hurried off to dry dock to have her bottom polished, and her crew felt quite confident that they would win the coming race. The start of this triangular fourth race was again postponed until one in the afternoon when the southwest afternoon breeze began strongly to develop. Both yachts tried hard to get the start in this important race and Sir William succeeded in taking the challenger over with a lead of twenty-three seconds. On the first leg, which was nearly to windward, the crew of *Shamrock IV* tried to make her head as high as the defender and she lost way so that the press thought she had got in a light spot, but somehow or other *Resolute* kept forging ahead until after a few miles the defender had the weather berth. When they reached the windward, or first, mark the wind was ten or more knots and as *Resolute* only had a lead of two minutes and ten seconds the spectators thought it was not enough to keep her ahead on the next two legs of the course which were reaches and expected to favor the challenger. There was a strong breeze by that time and both yachts covered this ten mile leg of the course at a rate of twelve knots or more, but *Shamrock IV* only gained a little on the defender for at the second mark the defender had a lead of one minute and twenty-seven seconds.

On the last leg there was a squall making up and as it approached *Shamrock IV* took in both her topsail and jib topsail while *Resolute* seemed to think she could luff through it with only her jib topsail down. When the squall struck there was little wind in it but a heavy shower which killed the nice breeze that was blowing before, and the wind now came out very light from the northwest. In this fluky air the challenger caught up to and apparently got ahead of the defender, but the wind swung back to the south whereupon *Resolute* set a ballooner and tacked to

leeward and thus picked up a breeze or, as the sailor would say, "made her own wind," going at a good rate toward the finish line which she crossed three minutes and fourteen seconds ahead of *Shamrock IV*. The yachts were now both two up.

Fifth Race

The fifth race was to be sailed the next day, but there was a smoky southwester developing and I should think the regatta committee should have stayed in port and not attempted a race, but the committee boat and the two racers went to the starting line, *Resolute* under jib and mainsail, and *Shamrock IV* under reefed mainsail, working topsail and jib. Shortly before starting time the regatta committee called the race off much to the relief of both yacht crews for there was a near panic aboard the challenger, caused as follows: *Shamrock IV* was built with some deep web frames in her bow, I suppose to stand the heavy pounding that her flat bow might receive in a choppy sea. Well, at the time we speak of a sail hatch was off in the forward deck and in maneuvering around before the intended start she had stuck her nose under slightly a couple of times so that quite a little water was gathered in the deep bay under the hatch. When one of the hands went forward he sang out "She is leaking forward." When one sings out something like this at such a time it is apt to cause a near panic, but they must have laughed at themselves later when they found out she was not leaking at all.

Heavy Weather Poor for Racing

Undoubtedly the crew of *Resolute* was mostly glad to call off the race because they thought the challenger could beat them under the existing conditions. However, the press made quite a feature of this called-off race and there was sarcastic criticism of both yachts. But I would like to say that there are three or four good reasons why yachts of the modern cup boat type should not race in heavy weather. First, if one side or the other had built a racer that could stand heavy weather she would be entirely outclassed in most of the weather they had had before this day; in fact they would be such poor drifters that a great many days they could not have covered the course within the time limit. Second, yachts of this type without bulwarks are apt to lose a man or two overboard if raced in heavy weather. Third, it is too hard on nice racing sails and all the above-deck gear, and thus is wastefully expensive. Fourth, while a heavy weather race is a good test of seamanship it is not much of a test of nice helmsmanship and racing tactics, and thus does not prove much.

Heavy weather races should be for ocean racing yachts. Also in races like those for the Astor and Kings Cups, where there is considerable difference in sizes of the competitors, the allowance rules are not satisfactory in light or heavy weather, for the larger yachts are almost certain to win in strong winds, and the smaller ones quite likely to win in light going if the wind does not become too calm after the larger ones have finished.

While I know that the New York Yacht Club has tried varying the rating according to the wind it is always more satisfactory if the races can be held in average wind velocities. It is certainly time that a rule for seagoing racing yachts was made, and some of its features should be that the racers should be required to have bulwarks and a much lower mast height limit than is allowed to the non-ocean racers. Also, if they are to be considered seagoing vessels, ocean racers never should be allowed light sails that might get them into trouble in a squall.

The last race of July 27 was in very light weather and someone had persuaded the designer of *Resolute* to sail on her although he was seventy-two years old. This race was a windward and leeward one in which the start was postponed until two-fifteen because of lack of wind. The starting line was in a calm streak with a light northwest wind inshore, and it was a matter of waiting until the usual afternoon southwest wind came in with strength enough for a start. Both yachts held back for the two minute handicap gun and crossed the line at two-seventeen. The challenger seemed to slip along quite as well as the defender, but the latter somehow appeared to be working windward of her so that after a while, with their cross tacking, Adams brought *Resolute* about almost dead to windward of the challenger. From then on the challenger gradually dropped back so that at the weather mark she was four minutes and seven seconds behind. After rounding the weather mark neither yacht laid a course toward the finish line for *Resolute* tacked to leeward with a balloon jib set probably

because Mr. Herreshoff could give them the proper courses to take as he had been working on the problems of tacking to leeward for many years.

At first *Shamrock* followed suit under her ballooner but it evidently occurred to her afterguard that she must adopt other tactics in order to pass the defender and also make up the seven minutes she had to allow her. So she set her spinnaker and took up a course to the westward of a line to the finish hoping to pick up more wind on that side, but as *Resolute* was tacking downwind it was easy for her to occasionally keep between her competitor and the finish line. *Resolute* evidently made quite a gain in tacking to leeward for the yachts certainly seemed to be far apart near the finish, but as they were now going at a good clip she only beat *Shamrock IV* about twenty minutes corrected time. It must have been a great satisfaction to *Resolute*'s designer to have her do so much better than before and to be on one of his yachts that was successfully defending the cup for the sixth time.

This long, drawn-out series of races had lasted twelve days of very tiring weather and both sides and the spectator fleet were relieved when it was all over. I was lucky to see this last race from the deck of one of our destroyers that was detailed to take New York Yacht Club members and their friends to see the races, and was privileged to stand beside E. D. Morgan part of the time. Mr. Morgan had been part owner or in the afterguard of three or four of our previous defenders, and while he was not much of a talker, his remarks were very instructive; he certainly did not think it an interesting race as compared to some of the previous races where there were small handicaps and the finishes very close.

As for the comparison of the two yachts—they were so

Fig. 143. SHAMROCK IV

Fig. 144. VANITIE and RESOLUTE together

different it is hard to make an intelligent criticism, but if *Resolute* had not had her rating increased by increasing her sail area she definitely would have done better. As for *Shamrock IV,* her designer evidently thought he could beat the measurement rule by producing a freak, but the Universal Rule proved that it measured her speed-giving qualities very fairly and not harshly for, although *Shamrock IV* did very well, Mr. Nicholson, her designer, never used any of her peculiarities in the next three cup challengers he designed. Figure 207 shows *Shamrock IV* and Figure 144 shows *Vanitie* and *Resolute* racing together.

This brings this writing up to 1920, a time when many much more qualified than myself could carry it on if it is thought desirable and I would like to recommend Sherman Hoyt's book as a source book for anyone writing about the later history of yachting for I think Mr. Hoyt is accurate and fair, particularly in his criticisms of the yachts concerned. Mr. Hoyt also lived at the New York Yacht Club for many years and, as far as I know, has held some office in the club for more years than anyone else. Another book which is an accurate chronological account of modern European yachting is the one written by Hans Dulk as a biography of the late Henry Rasmussen, called *Henry Rasmussen, Yachten-Segler und Eine Werft,* published in 1956. Although I am not an adept at translating German, this is an account of European and American yachting partially taken from a diary kept by Rasmussen, and it is likely the dates and dimensions are quite correct.

Glossary

BALLOONER, BALLOON JIB   A very full cut jib used for reaching

BEAM   A boat's width

BEAT, BEATING   Sailing into the wind

BOWSPRIT   A spar projecting horizontally from the bow

CATAMARAN   A boat with two hulls placed side by side

CAT BOAT   A boat with one mast and one sail

CENTERBOARD   A plate, usually of metal, that is hinged inside a trunk set on the center line of a boat. It can be raised or lowered to control side slip (lee way)

CLIPPER BOW   A nearly vertical bow that is concave in profile

CLUB   A boom for a jib, staysail, or a gaff topsail

CROSS CUT SAILS   Sails made of cloths that run at right angles to the after edge (leach)

DEADWOOD   Timbers between the hull and the ballast keel

DISPLACEMENT   A boat's weight, measured in either pounds or in the number of cubic feet of water the boat displaces

DOLPHIN STRIKER   See Martingale

DRAFT   The depth of a boat below the water line

DROP KEEL   See centerboard

FIN KEEL   A keel that is built up externally of the hull. It can be of either metal or of wood with a ballast keel attached to its underside

FORESAIL   The sail attached to the after side of the foremast

FRIGATE   A class of sailing warships roughly equivalent in duties to our modern cruisers. The modern Frigate is a type of warship somewhat smaller than a destroyer and used against submarines and for patrol work

GALLEY   1) A ship's kitchen
2) A long, narrow, vessel propelled by oars

GUNPORT   An aperture in the side of a ship through which a gun can be fired

JAGHT   Archaic spelling of YACHT

JIBE, GYBE   Turning away from the wind so that it crosses the stern. The opposite of tacking

KEEL   Either an appendage on the bottom of the hull or the main longitudinal structural member

KNOT   The measure of a boat's speed. Equivalent to a nautical mile per hour

LEG OF MUTTON   A phrase sometimes used to describe a marconi or jib headed sail

L.O.A.   Length over all

LUGGER   A lug rigged boat, technically, but more often used in describing any of the many smaller, coastal vessels used for privateering, smuggling, outright piracy, or in the prevention of these activities

L.W.L.   Length on the water line

MAINSAIL   The sail attached to the after edge of the mainmast

MARTINGALE   A vertical spar (or spreader) underneath the bowsprit to help support it

METAL SHEATHING Metal, usually copper, in thin sheets attached to the hull underwater to prevent marine growth

NOBLE Used in marine context to describe the tendency of a boat to turn into the wind. Two similar words are ardent and proud

OVERHANG Either the forward or after end of a hull that is not in the water

PACKET SHIP A sailing vessel making regular voyages. They were the forerunners of the Clipper Ship

PADDLE WHEEL A wheel fitted to a ship's side and fitted with blades shaped so that as the wheel rotates, the blades force the ship forward

PRIVATEER A private warship commissioned by a government under a "Letter-of-Marque" to attack shipping. It has been called legalized piracy. The War of 1812 saw our last privateer and they were outlawed completely by the Pact of Paris in 1864

PROPELLER (screw) A rotating device used to propel a ship. It is reputed to be the most efficient machine ever designed

RATING RULE Any of the many attempts to make a formula that would represent a boat's potential speed. Starting from the simple measure of the length, they have become progressively more complicated as designers have found ways of taking advantage of any loophole that there may be in any given rule

REACHING Sailing across the wind

REEFING Reducing the area of a sail by bunching a portion of it on the boom

REVENUE CUTTER A vessel used to collect duties and repress smuggling. The equivalent of our Coast Guard Cutter

RUNNING Sailing before the wind

SANDBAGGER A type of very high-speed sailboat. Their name derives from the fact that each of the crew carried a heavy sandbag which he transferred from side to side as the boat was tacked to increase the stability

SCHOONER A boat having two or more masts, all fore-and-aft rigged. In the case of the two-masted schooner the after mast must be at least as high as the forward one otherwise it would be a ketch or a yawl depending on the location of the after, or mizzen mast

SLIP, PROPELLER The difference between the actual distance a propeller moves forward with each revolution and the distance it would go if it were 100 percent efficient

SLOOP A single-masted boat with one sail aft of the mast and one or more jibs forward

SPINNAKER A large balloon-shaped sail used before the wind

SPOON BOW An overhanging, convex bow

TIME ALLOWANCE The amount of time a boat must allow another. In theory, if the allowance is correct, all the competing boats will be exactly equal. The allowance is calculated from the Rating Rule and is expressed in seconds per mile

TONNAGE A method used to determine the size of a boat for customs purposes. Gross Tonnage is the volume of the entire inside of the hull while Net Tonnage excludes machinery and other spaces. These volumes are converted to tons by multiplying the cubic feet by the weight of water

TOPMAST An additional spar attached to the top of a mast

TRUCK The top of a mast. The bottom is the heel

TRUNNEL Wooden dowels, usually of locust, used to fasten two pieces of wood together

WAVE LINE THEORY The idea, advanced some time ago, that the distribution of the displacement should conform to certain curves, or wave lines

YACHT Technically, a boat used for pleasure but more commonly restricted to larger boats and ships

Index